Families in Recovery

Families in Recovery

Coming Full Circle

by

Carolyn Seval Brooks, R.N.

and

Kathleen Fitzgerald Rice, Ms.Ed.

·P·A·U·L·H·
BROKES
PUBLISHING Cº

Baltimore • London • Toronto • Sydney

Paul H. Brookes Publishing Co.
Post Office Box 10624
Baltimore, Maryland 21285-0624

Typeset by A.W. Bennett, Inc., Hartland, Vermont.
Manufactured in the United States of America by
Thomson-Shore, Dexter, Michigan.

Permission to reprint the following materials is gratefully acknowledged:

Cover photo: From Rathe, J. (1990, July 1). Crack babies. *The Boston Globe*; reprinted by permission.

All quotations from Carol, DeDe, Gino, Ida, Lorna, and Patty: From Vida Health Communications (Producer). (1992). *Straight from the heart: Stories of mothers recovering from addiction* [Videotape]. Cambridge, MA: Producer; reprinted by permission.

Children's illustrations: From Philip A. Genatossio, M.Ed., former teacher of health education and substance abuse awareness and prevention for Massachusetts public elementary school students; reprinted by permission.

Extracts, pages 65, 66, and 82: From Fraiberg, S. (1959). *The magic years: Understanding and handling the problems of early childhood.* New York: Charles Scribner and Sons; copyright 1959 by Selma Fraiberg, Renewed; reprinted by permission of Simon & Schuster.

Library of Congress Cataloging-in-Publication Data

Brooks, Carolyn Seval.
    Families in recovery : coming full circle / by Carolyn Seval Brooks and Kathleen Fitzgerald Rice.
        p.   cm.
    Includes bibliographical references and index.
    ISBN 1-55766-264-9
    1. Recovering alcoholics—United States—Family relationships.   2. Recovering addicts—United States—Family relationships.   3. Alcoholics—Rehabilitation—United States.   4. Narcotic addicts—Rehabilitation—United States.
    5. Children of alcoholics—United States.   6. Children of narcotic addicts—United States.   I. Rice, Kathleen Fitzgerald.   II. Title.
    HV132.B74   1997
    362.29′13′0973—dc20   96-19846
                                                                                     CIP

British Library Cataloguing-in-Publication data are available from the British Library.

Contents

About the Authors

Carolyn Seval Brooks, R.N., is Manager of the Maternal Child Health Program of Columbia Homecare at MetroWest Medical Center in Framingham, Massachusetts, which provides comprehensive in-home health care services to children and families from diverse socioeconomic backgrounds. Prior to this, she worked in the Departments of Pediatrics and Substance Abuse Services at Boston Medical Center providing a variety of clinical, training, and supervisory services. She also co-founded two Boston Medical Center programs: the Women and Infants Clinic and the Pediatric Pathways Program.

Throughout her career, Ms. Seval Brooks has worked in various settings including pediatrics, psychiatry, and substance abuse treatment to support children and families and to develop services that are truly family focused. She believes that the family serves as the primary foundation for both individuals and society as a whole. She has lectured throughout the United States about issues that affect the health and well-being of children and families, including substance abuse, abuse and neglect, child development, and family-focused treatment models, and has also co-authored several papers on similar topics.

Kathleen Fitzgerald Rice, Ms.Ed., is an early childhood specialist at Boston Medical Center and a member of the faculty at Boston University School of Medicine. She holds a master's degree in special education from Wheelock College in Boston and has more than 15 years of experience working with families and children living in poverty. Ms. Fitzgerald Rice has worked for 5 years as a clinician in the Women and Infants Clinic, a substance abuse treatment program at Boston Medical Center. In addition, she has 10 years of experience supervising and training professionals in the fields of early childhood education and substance abuse. Ms. Fitzgerald Rice is continuing her commitment to working with families at risk in her role as Co-Director of the Reach and Read Program, a nationally recognized pediatric early literacy program founded at Boston Medical Center.

Foreword

*Too many women in too many countries speak the same language of silence . . .
I seek only to forget the sorrows of my grandmother's silence.*

Anasuya Sengupta
Lady Shri Ram College, New Delhi

The many "silences" surrounding women and substance abuse have been with us for a very long time. Until the 1980s, alcoholism and drug abuse were seen as men's diseases and the term "hidden female alcoholic" was common. Yet much of the denial and stigma surrounding women and addiction continues and indeed has become more punitive, especially in the case of pregnant and parenting women. Images of immoral, promiscuous, negligent, and abusive mothers are all too common.

In addition to societal condemnation, substance abuse treatment systems have traditionally not listened to or responded to "women's voices." When women talk about concerns for their children, they are often told to "put themselves first" and "stop using children as an excuse to avoid treatment." The relational contexts of women's lives, including relationships with partners, children, parents, friends, extended family, community, churches, schools, and so on, are too often ignored or considered outside the scope of recovery services.

There have, however, been dramatic changes in the attitudes about and services provided to substance-abusing women and their families since I first entered the field of addictions treatment in 1972. Some of the major changes have been the incorporation of the relational model and a family focus on treatment and recovery as well as a broader and integrated perspective on the full range of issues affecting women and their families, including violence, sexual abuse, HIV infection, care for children, and co-existing mental health issues.

Carolyn Seval Brooks and Kathleen Fitzgerald Rice, through their work at the Women and Infants Clinic at Boston Medical Center, have been pioneers in changing the existing paradigm within substance abuse treatment for pregnant and parenting women. The Women and Infants Clinic is a national model of integrated comprehensive care for women and children *together*. Its unique placement within a pediatric hospital service provides a nonstigmatizing, family-focused environment that offers women treatment for substance abuse, while it treats their concerns for their children respectfully and provides excellent pediatric and early intervention care for the children. Instead of traditional "turf" battles between child welfare and substance abuse treatment, Carol and Kathleen and others at the Women and Infants Clinic significantly impacted the ability of different systems to coordinate care for the entire family.

The authors are widely known for their commitment to the resiliency and strength of women and families and for their emphasis on empowerment through recovery. In *Families in Recovery*, they speak of silence as the enemy of recovery. This book continues their work and reflects their dedication to "giving voice to" women and families as they heal and grow stronger. It should serve as an affirmation and celebration of family recovery and motivate others to create and sustain more programs that look at the "full circle" of substance abuse prevention and treatment for women and their families.

Norma Finkelstein, Ph.D.
Director
Coalition on Addiction,
Pregnancy & Parenting
Cambridge, Massachusetts

Foreword

I have been a pediatrician for close to 20 years. I have to admit, I seem to have spent much of that time perplexed by the seemingly inexplicable behaviors of some of the families I have served. Only in the last 10 years have I learned why.

I remember well a very bright and verbal young mother of two. We had an excellent relationship, but I was somehow always off guard with her. During one visit she would be exuberantly happy and during the next visit she would be very quiet and seemingly pensive. I never really knew what to expect. Her children always appeared to be neat, well cared for, and exceedingly polite. But they were also frequently brought to my office for trivial concerns, and they always seemed to be on edge, overreacting to any perceived stress during the visit. For her part, the mother never seemed quite satisfied when I explained that her child was fine. She always seemed to be looking for something more definitive, for an answer I was not providing. I sensed she was not happy with my care at those times, although just why I could not tell.

She was unpredictable and something of an enigma to me, but she was also from the middle class and smart. Although I had a vague feeling that there was something going on about which I should discreetly inquire, I never seemed to comprehend what it was and never really got around to asking.

One day I was shocked when her husband informed me that she had been admitted to an inpatient facility for drug detoxification. He explained that she had had a problem for years. "I'm sure you suspected," he said. (Mercifully, he didn't ask me directly.) I nodded noncommittally.

I now know that all the signs of substance abuse had been there, but at the time I lacked the information, sensitivity, and courage to look for them. On some level, I probably just didn't want to know about it anyway. I often wonder how many of my enigmatic families were also struggling with maternal substance abuse.

Fortunately, I now know better. Much of what I have learned has come from the authors of *Families in Recovery*. Kathleen Fitzgerald Rice and Carolyn Seval Brooks are sensitive clinicians and wise teachers. They have alerted a whole cohort of clinicians to the realities of substance abuse in women and, in so doing, have changed the way we do business.

As they have taught me and others, the problems that accompany women and addiction are similar to those of men but unique, requiring us to both sharpen our old skills and learn some new ones. To help us to accomplish this, they present heartbreaking stories of family travail, cautionary tales of missed opportunities by the medical and mental health establishments, and inspiring stories of heroic victory over addiction by courageous women and their families.

All clinicians who care for women and their families need to become educated about this issue so that they do not look back with regret, as I sometimes do, at the missed opportunities to help women and families in desperate need. *Families in Recovery* makes a wonderful contribution to that goal.

Steven Parker, M.D.
Director, Division of
Developmental and Behavioral Pediatrics
Department of Pediatrics
Boston Medical Center

Preface

The truths of relationships return in the rediscovery of connection, in the realization that self and other are interdependent and that life, however valuable in itself, can only be sustained by care in relationships.
Carol Gilligan, 1982

In 1989, we were afforded the opportunity to create a model intervention program at Boston Medical Center for pregnant and parenting women struggling with cocaine addiction. The Women and Infants Clinic, like so many other new programs, was born out of need. Appalling numbers of infants were being born at Boston Medical Center, and elsewhere, having been prenatally exposed to cocaine, alcohol, and other drugs. While these infants needed close monitoring and care, their mothers were in desperate need of intensive treatment. The paucity of treatment programs available for women with children left most of these women with few alternatives. Many of them wanted help but were unwilling to leave their infants. Similarly, child protective services involved with these families were reluctant to send infants home with their mothers but were willing to consider sending the infant to a treatment program with the mother.

Armed with some experience, bounding enthusiasm, and lots of ideas, we formed a multidisciplinary team of doctors, educators, and a substance abuse specialist and set to work designing interventions for families affected by substance abuse. With more than 35 collective years of experience in the fields of pediatric nursing, psychiatric nursing, substance abuse treatment, early childhood education, and child development, we had each experienced the frustration and hopelessness that often accompany the struggle to support families within more traditional medical and educational settings. Coming together with different perspectives from different disciplines gave us the opportunity to learn from and teach one another, just as we learn from and teach the families in our care.

From this knowledge, we developed a comprehensive treatment model of care for addicted mothers, their children, and other family members, which offered key services and was co-located within a pediatric primary care clinic. Drug treatment, which included urine screenings, individual and group counseling, pediatric primary care, family planning, parenting guidance, child development services, and case management, were also offered to participating families. Each package of services was individually designed to meet the unique needs of each family.

Families in Recovery originated from our experiences in the Women and Infants Clinic and is largely based upon the relationships made there and sustained throughout the years with families and colleagues. These relationships have been vehicles for learning; vehicles for connection and affection; and, at times, vehicles of pain and grief. This book is possible because of the relationships formed with the women, men, and children in recovery—powerful relationships that have informed our work and enabled the mobilization of growth and healing in the face of trauma, disease, and loss. We have come to realize that it is the power and quality of, as well as the commitment to, relationships that is most essential to our work.

This book offers lessons learned from the Women and Infants Clinic, in the hope that we can pass on some of what we have learned. In this book, as in the clinic, we have merged traditional models of child development theory, family systems theory, and substance abuse treatment, reworking them to create new models for understanding and supporting families affected by substance abuse. We use the voices of family members in recovery to convey information as often as possible because we passionately believe in their right to be heard and in their great ability to teach us. Many times, we have said, "There but for the grace of God go I." We know the debilitating power of the disease, yet we remain unwavering in our belief in the strength of the human spirit. We believe that recovery is always possible and that supportive relationships play a primary role in a family's journey through recovery.

We have been privileged and feel honored to have stood witness to the remarkable growth and healing of individuals and families and feel that there is no work more honorable than joining a family on their journey in recovery. We feel the utmost respect and gratitude for all those families who are so much at the heart of this book. We hope that *Families in Recovery* will sow some fruitful seeds that will grow into better ways for us all to help families who struggle with addiction.

~ Reference ~

Gilligan, C. (1982). *In a different voice: Psychological theory and women's development*. Cambridge, MA: Harvard University Press.

For the Reader

There is much variability in the terminology used in the field of substance abuse treatment. The media, professional disciplines, areas of treatment, and geographic locations influence the terms people use. Yet, clarification of terminology is important, particularly in helping readers understand content without getting stuck on a word or phrase. The terms used in this book are chosen because they are widespread, widely known, and comfortable to the authors. The authors ask that readers look beyond differences in terminology to view this book in the context of its larger picture. Throughout the book, specific terms are clarified and defined as they are used. Some of the more general terminology is defined here.

The terms *drug/drugs* and *substances* are used interchangeably and include all drugs, licit or illicit, prescription and nonprescription, as well as alcohol.

The term *addict* is used to describe a person who is physically or psychologically dependent upon a substance or process and does not apply to those who use or abuse drugs but are not dependent upon them.

The authors have purposely chosen to describe *addiction as a disease* despite their knowledge that there are many factors that contribute to addiction and many ways to understand addiction. Defining addiction as a disease helps to decrease the stigma and highlight the predictable nature and consequences of the process. Comparing addiction to a disease such as diabetes or heart disease often makes it easier to understand and accept and also helps to dispel the myth of "willpower."

The term *addicted family* is used to highlight the fact that when one person in a family is an addict, the entire family is affected by the process of addiction.

A final note about the terminology in *Families in Recovery:* For ease of reading, the authors alternate between "he" and "she" in the text. This is not meant to stereotype or be exclusionary of either gender.

Acknowledgments

We would like to take this opportunity to thank several of our colleagues, many of whom worked closely with us from the beginning. Dr. Barry Zuckerman made this experience possible through his own concern for families affected by substance abuse and through his guidance and support. His creative ideas, dedication, and persistence in the face of many barriers paved our way. A special thank you to Bill Harris for his faith and trust that we would do the right thing with his support to start the Women and Infants Clinic and to Dr. Margot Kaplan-Sanoff who was an integral part of the development and the day-to-day functioning of the Women and Infants Clinic. This project would not have been possible without her experience, wisdom, and vast knowledge of child development. Two pediatricians, Dr. Karen Bresnahan and Dr. Marilyn Augustyn, worked long hours and were amazingly committed to the families. They taught everyone much about health, safety, and child development and were integral members of our team. Thank you to the many students and volunteers, especially Susan Monnoson and Sophia Padnos, who provided support and child care for the clinic over the years.

There are many others who have contributed to *Families in Recovery* in many different ways. Thank you especially goes to Maxine Weinreb, Steven Parker, Remetrious Pena, Amy Bamforth, and Betsy McAllister Groves for their guidance and wisdom in creating this book and to Jeanne McCarthy for her help in preparing the manuscript. To all of you who have nurtured us, taught us, mentored us, supported us, loved us, and offered advice and criticism, we thank you most sincerely.

We would especially like to acknowledge the contributions of the following people and thank them for allowing us to use their materials: Thanks to Lisa McElaney, President of Vida Health Communications, for giving us permission to quote from the video "Straight from the Heart," which has so richly added to this book. A heartfelt thank you, also, to the women who participated in "Straight from the Heart," whose voices add heart and soul to the material in this book. Thanks to Philip Genatossio, M.Ed., formerly the teacher of health education and substance abuse awareness and prevention for kindergarten through sixth-grade students in public elementary schools in Massachusetts, and currently Director of Health Education at Thayer Academy in Braintree, Massachusetts. The hand-drawn children's drawings that appear throughout the book depicting images related to substance use and abuse come from a project he initiated with children entering the second grade. Thanks to the countless others who have generously lent their images and pictures to the pages of this book. A special thanks goes to Evelyn, Angelica, and Ashley and to Angela and Dexter.

Carolyn extends a special and love-filled thank you to her two wonderful boys, Alex and Evan, who were so patient and supportive. From the first few weeks when each would ask, "Are you done writing your book yet?" it became clear that this project would require sacrifice of both time and attention. Sacrifices of both were indeed made, acts of love and generosity for which she will remain forever grateful. Appreciation is sent to Ed Khantzian, Howard Schaefer, and Janice Kaufman for their invaluable training, and a very special thank you goes to Mary Ann Pingalore.

Kathleen sends her love and gratitude to her family and friends, Mary Ann Pingalore, and especially to Chris, for his friendship, love, and laughter.

To all the families who tell their stories in this book and to all of the families struggling with addictive disease, thank you for sharing your stories. You have taught us much. And finally, to those of you who do this important work, we send our appreciation and our encouragement to continue the journey with the families in your care.

To the families in the
Women and Infants Clinic
and
to Vicki, in her memory

Our thoughts and prayers are with you all.

$\sim$ | $\sim$

ONE IN EIGHT

Nicki was an athlete in high school. She was bright and outgoing and showed skill as a saleswoman working in her father's business. Nicki loved animals and could never resist bringing home stray cats and dogs that needed someone's love and care.

Nicki grew up, married, and had five children of her own. Her home was filled with animals and children. She also took in others who needed her. It was Nicki's way. People were drawn to her, and she responded to them with care.

Nicki was also an alcoholic and heroin addict. She struggled every day of her adult life with a disease that had her in a stranglehold. When she drank or used heroin, she felt numb—numb to the memories of her abusive childhood and numb to the abuse she currently suffered from a violent and addicted husband.

Nicki joined a substance abuse treatment program when her son Darren was born. For 3 years, Nicki stayed in the program and brought her children in with her for treatment. Program staff were drawn to Nicki and her children, as was everyone who came into contact with her family. Nicki, her children, and the program staff struggled together toward healing and recovery.

But Nicki did not make it. She died of a massive heart attack brought on by her drug use in the arms of her young son on New Year's Eve of 1992. Nicki was 36 years old. She left behind a legacy of trauma and pain, and she left behind five children.

L ike an estimated one in eight Americans, Nicki was an alcoholic. Her family is representative of the many families who struggle with substance abuse and addiction. Their story is real, as are many of the stories told throughout this book. Others are composites from the histories of several families. Voices of real children, families, and addicts speak out in this book—voices filled with pain but speaking out with courage. *Families in Recovery* tells Nicki's story, her mother's story, and her children's story—stories of the cycles of addiction, abuse, neglect, and trauma. It is a family's story and a country's story. It is the story of millions of children—it may be one's own story.

～ Prevalence ～

Alcohol and other drugs invade communities through crime, unemployment, and community dysfunction. They creep into one's life through television and advertising and may even intrude into one's home.

It is likely that everyone has been affected by alcohol or another drug in some way, at some point in his or her life. The National Clearing House for Alcohol and Drug Information (1993) reports that, out of an estimated 250 million Americans, as many as 10.5 million show signs of alcoholism (Alcohol Alert, 1990). Another 7.2 million show persistent heavy drinking patterns that are associated with adverse physical and emotional functioning. Another source reported that nearly 9% of adults surveyed in 1988 met the criteria for alcohol abuse and dependence (Grant et al., 1991).

Approximately 11.4 million Americans use illicit (illegal) drugs, 3.1% of Americans over the age of 18 have been formally diagnosed as having a drug disorder, and 7.4% have been diagnosed as alcohol dependent (Substance Abuse and Mental Health Services Administration [SAMHSA], 1994). One in every four families in America is affected by alcohol-related problems, and it is estimated that one in eight American children has alcoholic parents (MacDonald, 1991; Woodside, 1988). It is also estimated that alcohol plays a role in one out of three failed marriages (Institute for Health Policy, 1993).

Addiction crosses all boundaries: socioeconomic, religious, ethnic, and cultural. Both sexes are at risk and the age at which addiction begins to rear its ugly head is becoming increasingly younger. Since 1975, the National Institute on Drug Abuse has been conducting a continuous study of the lifestyles and values of American youth, concentrating on seniors in high school, as well as eighth and tenth graders. This study reported that the use of illicit drugs rose sharply in 1993 in all three grade levels, with increasing usage of marijuana, inhalants, stimulants, cocaine, and hallucinogens (Johnston, O'Malley, & Bachman, 1994a). By eighth grade, 67% of these children reported having tried alcohol, and 26% said they had already been drunk at least once. By the end of eighth grade, 32% of these students had tried an illicit drug. A large number of these young children who are experimenting with "gateway" drugs—tobacco, alcohol, inhalants, and marijuana—are at a significant risk for proceeding along a path of increasing use and abuse. The numbers are more frightening for older children: Almost 40% of tenth graders, and nearly 50% of all twelfth graders, in the United States had tried an illicit drug. By their late 20s, 75%–80% of Americans have tried an illicit drug.

By the time I was 12 years old, I had picked up. The first thing was a drink.
Lorna, in recovery from cocaine addiction

Much has been written in the 1990s about an alarming trend found among college students—binge drinking. *Binge drinking* is consuming five or more alcoholic drinks in a row with the intention of getting drunk (Johnston et al., 1994b). A 1992 survey reported that one in three college students drinks to get drunk (Wechsler & Isaac, 1992). College students in general have a higher prevalence of alcohol use as compared to their noncollege peers, a discrepancy that greatly increases with binge drinking (Johnston et al., 1994b). The Office of Substance Abuse Prevention (1991) cites that between 240,000 and 360,000 of the 12 million students (2%–3%) will die of alcohol-related causes, which is equivalent to the number of students who will receive advanced degrees (Eigen & Quinlan, 1991).

∼ The Toll ∼

Health Risks

Each year, more deaths and disabilities result from substance abuse than from any other preventable cause: 100,000 people die as a result of alcohol, and at least 19,000 deaths are attributed to illicit drug abuse and to drug-related behavior (Institute for Health Policy, 1993). Health-related problems such as liver disease, heart disease, lung disease, and infections are common among people who abuse alcohol and other drugs. In 1993, medical care for alcohol-related injuries and illnesses cost at least $25 billion (Substance Abuse and Mental Health Services Administration, 1994). A significant number of problems requiring emergency room visits and hospitalizations involve alcohol and other drug use. Between 1991 and 1992, heroin-related hospital emergency room visits increased by 34% across the nation, while cocaine-related visits increased by 18% (Substance Abuse and Mental Health Services Administration, 1994). One study reported that between 25% and 64% of admissions to medical or surgical units in acute care hospitals can be related to alcohol abuse or dependence (Garris & Jewell, 1995).

Car Crashes and Other "Accidents"

Traffic accidents are the leading cause of death for every age population from 6 to 32, and nearly one half of these fatal crashes involve alcohol. From 1980 to 1993, 266,000 Americans were killed in alcohol-related traffic crashes (Institute for Health Policy, 1993; National Highway Transportation and Safety Administration, 1994). Statistics show that 17.5% of all 16- to 20-year-olds involved in fatal car crashes have blood-alcohol concentrations (BAC) exceeding 0.1%, the level at which most states consider a person legally drunk (National Highway Transportation and Safety Administration, 1994). SAMHSA also reports that 30% of *all* "accidental" deaths are associated with alcohol abuse. Evidence links alcohol to deaths from falls and fires. Studies estimate that between 17% and 53% of falls are alcohol related and report that half of those who have died as a result of fire had BACs indicating intoxication (Institute for Health Policy, 1993).

Criminal Activity

Between one half and two thirds of all violent crimes involve the use of alcohol, including murder, rape, sexual assault, and domestic violence (Institute for Health Policy, 1993; Substance Abuse and Mental Health Services Administration, 1994). Results from urine samples taken from both men and women arrested for serious crimes from 14 urban areas showed that during a 4-month period in 1988, approximately 75% tested positive for drug use (Wish, Klumpp, Moorer, Brady, & Williams, 1989). In addition, 95% of college-campus–related violent crime involve alcohol (Center on Addiction and Substance Abuse, 1994).

Loss of Productivity

Substance abuse has a major impact upon the workplace as an estimated 59% of adults who report using an illicit drug in the previous month are employed (Substance Abuse and Mental Health Services Administration, 1994). Approximately 27% of full-time workers who use illicit drugs report missed work due to illness or injury, and 18% report that they simply skip work (Institute for Health Policy, 1993). A small percentage of these users report that they have gone to work under the influence of alcohol or other drugs. Health insurance costs for employees with alcohol problems are about twice those of other employees because of alcohol- and other drug-related injuries and illnesses, in addition to the added cost burden of loss of product and high turnover rates.

Children

Each year in the United States, 30,000 infants are born with alcohol-related birth defects ranging from subtle behavior alterations to fetal alcohol syndrome (FAS) (Little & Wendt, 1991). Studies have estimated that from 350,000 to 739,200 infants born in the United States each year are exposed to one or more illicit drugs, not including alcohol and tobacco (Chasnoff, 1991). In one study, an estimated 6.72% of pregnant women used alcohol and 3.49% used an illicit drug in the hours and days preceding delivery (Substance Abuse and Mental Health Services Administration, 1994). In another, 18% of women seeking prenatal care were found to have used cocaine during their pregnancy (Zuckerman et al., 1989). The cost of caring for drug-exposed infants is $1,100–$4,100 higher than the cost of care for non–drug-exposed infants (Chasnoff, 1991).

It is estimated that approximately 30 million American children live in homes where at least one parent is chronically addicted to alcohol (Woodside, 1988) and that in a single classroom, one of five children is being raised in an addicted family system (Robinson, 1990). All children of alcoholics are at risk for a range of cognitive, emotional, and behavior problems (Office of Substance Abuse Prevention, 1991). It was once thought that young children of alcoholics were the least affected by parental alcoholism because of their immaturity, but research has indicated that this assumption is untrue (Nylander & Rydelius, 1982). In the 1980s and 1990s, research has illuminated the impact of parental alcoholism on even very young children (Alcohol Alert, 1990). Most likely, every American has played with, lived with, worked with, or loved someone affected by substance abuse.

The Cost of Addiction

Each year, $34 billion are spent on health care related to alcohol and other drug abuse, while $67 billion are spent on non–health-related costs related to illicit drug use alone (Institute for Health Policy, 1993). In 1990, the United States spent $99 billion on alcohol-related costs such as health care, loss of work, and criminal justice activities (Substance Abuse and Mental Health Services Administration, 1994), meaning each person in the country—children included— pays nearly $1,000 per year to cover the costs associated with substance abuse.

～ The Big Picture ～

Statistics offer only a snapshot of the alcohol and other drug problems that the people in the United States face. Due to the nature of the disease, with its inherently high levels of denial and deception, one must assume that the actual cases of addiction are even higher than the numbers show. Numbers are cold and statistics impersonal. In black and white, numbers are easy to scan and are quickly forgotten. In the three-dimensional world of flesh and blood, however, each statistic represents an immeasurable toll of human loss and suffering.

Attitudes

Although much progress has been made since the 1920s in both the understanding and treatment of addiction, addiction treatment in recovery is still a relatively new discipline and the beliefs and models associated with it vary widely. Models have been based upon viewing addiction as a moral problem, a social problem, a medical problem, a psychiatric problem, a criminal justice problem, and a spiritual problem. Blame has alternately been placed upon society, the individual, and the family. Some believe that certain illicit drugs should be legalized, while others are vehemently opposed. Interventions based upon a variety of attitudes and beliefs, including institutionalization, prohibition, and interdiction, have been also met with mixed success.

Historically, most treatment programs have been developed to treat men and have been based upon an understanding of addiction from a male perspective. Men have also been the focus of the majority of research projects. In fact, until the "crack" epidemic of the 1980s, female addicts were not generally recognized in large numbers and most people were unaware of the large number of women who were addicted to substances and giving birth to infants exposed to drugs in utero.

Attitudes about addiction and toward addicts continue to be quite disparate, ranging from punitive to compassionate, from contemptuous to empathetic. Some believe that all addicts should be locked up, while others believe that more money should be spent on developing better treatment programs. Some think that the government should automatically remove children from addicted mothers, while others advocate for extensive family treatment centers.

Each individual forms opinions and attitudes from his or her accumulated life experiences (early childhood experiences have a great impact on lifelong feelings and attitudes), gender, ethnicity, culture, and religion. Community movements and organizations throughout the years have also helped to shape beliefs. In the 1970s, the Adult Children of Alcoholics (ACoA) movement provided first-hand accounts of the experience of growing up in an alcoholic home (Wegscheider, 1976). In the 1980s, Mothers Against Drunk Driving (MADD) brought us face to face with the tragic results of drunk driving.

From the movements of earlier eras, such as the temperance movement and prohibition, to modern-day epidemics, such as heroin and "crack," alcohol and other drugs shape the personality of the United States. This is a culture that glorifies substance use as it shuns addicts, demonizing them as inhuman and immoral, undeserving of attention and compassion. People rage at the pregnant addict and turn away from the stumbling drunk. Perhaps fear drives American society's loathing of addiction. If one really looks at an addict, he may see a reflection of someone else. Perhaps if one looks too closely, he will see himself. Perhaps ignorance and lack of information make it too difficult for people to see the addict as a human being with hopes, dreams, and desires, not so different from their own.

To recognize the addict's humanity challenges everyone to recognize the universal need for empathy, compassion, understanding, and help as well as to recognize the universal problem—a society and a culture that is struggling with compulsive behavior and addiction.

⌣ Families in Recovery ⌣

This book is about recognizing and accepting that, in society, substance abuse and addiction have become political, social, health, educational, and spiritual crises. Addiction permeates every aspect of society, affecting the health and well-being of individuals, families, and communities.

Families in Recovery is about acknowledging society's need to address the problem of substance abuse in order to ameliorate any of the accompanying poverty, unemployment, violence, crime, and child abuse. *Families in Recovery* attempts to break through the denial that has slowed the progress of prevention. It presents substance abuse as a public health crisis that requires an angry public and a divided electorate to find the compassion to make a commitment to greater change.

Families in Recovery is about forming a community of professionals to share knowledge and strategies about how to work together for the best interests of families. It assembles knowledge from the areas of child development, medicine, psychology, and substance abuse treatment to create a comprehensive resource for understanding the family affected by substance abuse. *Families in Recovery* is about creating programs that work for the child and the family.

Families in Recovery offers principles and practices for successfully serving families and children. It offers insights about how to guide the family through the process of recovery and proposes a model for treating the recovering parent. *Families in Recovery* acknowledges the challenges of this difficult work and offers strategies for supporting professionals who are committed to helping families and children heal.

Families in Recovery is about real human beings. It is about the daily struggle millions face to survive hardship and find hope for a better day and a new tomorrow. It is about the countless individuals who are in recovery or who have been transformed by recovery.

Families in Recovery is about hope and healing. It is about believing that every child and every addict have the potential to survive, to heal, and to be transformed. It is about believing that there is always a chance for recovery and a brighter tomorrow for every child and every family who suffer. It promises that Nicki's children can take a different life path and their lives can tell a different story, one of hope and healing. Nicki's legacy is carried within her children, but it does not have to be perpetuated: They can come *full circle.*

～ References ～

Alcohol Alert. (1990). *Children of alcoholics: Are they different?* [9, Ph228]. Rockville, MD: National Clearing House for Drug and Alcohol Information.

Center on Addiction and Substance Abuse. (1994). *Rethinking rites of passage: Substance abuse on America's campuses.* New York: Columbia University.

Chasnoff, I.J. (1991). Drugs, alcohol, pregnancy, and the neonate: Pay now or pay later. *Journal of the American Medical Association, 266,* 1567.

Eigen, L.D., & Quinlan, J.W. (1991). OSAP college drinking campaign—"Put on the brakes: Take a look at college drinking!" *Alcohol Health and Research World: Special Focus: Alcohol and Youth, 15*(1), 87–89.

Garris, R., & Jewell, D. (1995). Comparison of outcomes between acute care general hospital transfers and direct admissions to a detoxification unit. *Perspectives on Addiction Nursing, 5*(4), 3–5.

Grant, B.F., Harford, T.C., Chou, P., Pickering, R., Dawson, D.A., Stinsin, F.S., & Noble, J. (1991). Epidemiologic Bulletin No. 27, Prevalence of DSM-III-R alcohol abuse and dependence: United States, 1988. *Alcohol Health and Research World: Special Focus: Alcohol and Youth, 15*(1), 91–96.

Institute for Health Policy. (1993). *Substance abuse: The nation's number one health problem—Key indicators for policy.* Waltham, MA: Brandeis University for The Robert Wood Johnson Foundation, Heller Graduate School.

Johnston, L.D., O'Malley, P.M., & Bachman, J.G. (1994a). Overview of key findings [Monograph]. *National survey results on drug use from the Monitoring the Future Study, 1975–1993, Vol. II,* 5–25.

Johnston, L.D., O'Malley, P.M., & Bachman, J.G. (1994b). *National survey results on drug use from the Monitoring the Future Study, 1975–1993, Vol. II* (NIH Publication No. 94-3810). Washington, DC: U.S. Government Printing Office.

Little, R., & Wendt, J. (1991). The effects of maternal drinking in the reproductive period: An epidemiologic review. *Journal of Substance Abuse, 3,* 187–204.

MacDonald, D. (1991). Parental alcoholism—A neglected pediatric responsibility. *American Journal of Diseases in Children, 145,* 609–610.

National Highway Transportation and Safety Administration. (1994). *Fatal accident reporting system.* Rockville, MD: Author.

Nylander, I., & Rydelius, P.A. (1982). A comparison between children of alcoholic fathers from excellent versus poor social conditions. *Acta Pediatrica Scandinavica, 71*(5), 809–813.

Office of Substance Abuse Prevention (OSAP). (1991). *Children of alcoholics: Alcoholism tends to run in families* (NCDAI Publication MS417). Rockville, MD: Author.

Robinson, B.E. (1990). The teacher's role in working with children of alcoholic parents. *Young Children, 45*(4), 68–73.

Substance Abuse and Mental Health Services Administration (SAMHSA). (1994). *Cost of addictive and mental disorders and effectiveness of treatment* (DHHS Publication SMA 2095-94). Rockville, MD: Author.

Wechsler, H., & Isaac, N. (1992). "Binge" drinkers at Massachusetts colleges: Prevalence, drinking style, time trends and associated problems. *Journal of the American Medical Association, 267*(21), 2929–2931.

Wegscheider, S. (1976). *The family trap: No one escapes from a chemically dependent family.* North Crystal, MN: Nurturing Networks.

Wish, E.D., Klumpp, K.A., Moorer, A.H., Brady, E., & Williams, K.M. (1989). *Analysis of drugs and crime among arrestees in the District of Columbia—Final report.* Washington, DC: U.S. Department of Justice.

Woodside, M. (1988). Research on children of alcoholics: Past and future. *British Journal of Addiction, 83,* 785–792.

Zuckerman, B., Frank, D.A., Hingson, R., Amaro, H., Levenson, S., Kayne, H., Parker, S., Vinci, R., Aboagye, K., Fried, L., Cabral, H., Timperi, R., & Baucher, H. (1989). Effects of maternal marijuana and cocaine use on fetal growth. *New England Journal of Medicine, 320,* 762–768.

~ 1 ~

Addiction

A Cunning and Baffling Disease

No other statement more aptly captures the nature of addiction than the Alcoholics Anonymous (AA) description of addiction as a "cunning and baffling and powerful disease" (Alcoholics Anonymous, 1976, pp. 58–59). For centuries, humanity has been struggling with this mysterious human vulnerability. Addiction is "an equal opportunity destroyer," knowing no boundaries. Everyone is vulnerable to either the direct or indirect effects of addiction (Ackerman, 1987, p. 10). Addiction is a disease of the individual, the family, and the community. Some argue that it is a disease of society, born from and nurtured by a patriarchal system in which power and control have more value than compassion and empathy (Kasl, 1992; Schaef, 1987).

Regardless of how one chooses to view addiction, the common experience is one of loss and suffering, but it is not without hope. Anyone affected by addiction has an opportunity, through recovery, to stop the addictive behavior and turn her life journey in a positive direction.

~ A Brief History ~

Accounts of alcohol abuse and addiction can be found dating back to the Bible, as Paul said, "Let us conduct ourselves becomingly as in the day, not in reveling and drunkenness, not in debauchery and licentiousness, not in quarreling and jealousy" (The Holy Bible, Romans, 13:13). Paul's admonishment to the Romans could easily be a sermon topic of today. Roman mythology gives descriptions of festivals in honor of Bacchus who was the god of wine. Characteristic of these celebrations was wild and drunken revelry (Evans, 1981). There is an old French saying that aptly captures the scope of the problem then and now, which translates to "the ale-house has overwhelmed more men than the sea" (Evans, 1981, p. 68).

Opiates have also been used since ancient times, for medicinal purposes as well as for pleasure (Arif & Westermeyer, 1988). For instance, Asia's infamous "opium dens" bear a striking resemblance to the "crack houses" of the 1980s and 1990s. During the 1700s, England began to manufacture gin, a liquor that was cheap to make and easy to sell. The Gin Act of 1776, which placed heavy fines on the makers and sellers of gin, did little to slow the precipitous rise in rates of alcoholism and public drunkenness. Through a series of taxes and rigid control, England was finally able to stem the tide of alcoholism for that period (*The Academic American Encyclopedia*, 1993).

In the 1800s in the United States, there were no controls whatsoever on drugs. Cocaine, morphine, and opium were common ingredients both in over-the-counter medications and household goods (Institute for Health Policy, 1993, p. 11). In fact, Coca-Cola was originally named for coca, the plant from which cocaine is extracted, which was once an ingredient in the original formula. Many people who used these products became addicted, and the statistics for that era reveal startling high rates of narcotic addictions.

The use of narcotics dropped in the United States after the Harrison Act of 1914, which made it illegal to dispense or use narcotics without a prescription. However, alcohol abuse still ran rampant.

During the 1920s and 1930s, attempts were made to eliminate the "evils" of alcohol by making it illegal in the United States. The Volstead Act ushered in the era of prohibition, making it illegal to manufacture, transport, or sell alcohol (Arif & Westermeyer, 1988). This law met with much resistance and the notorious era of "bootlegging" was born. The popularity of "bathtub gin" (illegally distilled gin) and the "speakeasies" (illegal saloons) during this time bear witness to the dimension of this problem. In fact, this "industry" was quite profitable and many millions of dollars were made on the illegal sale and distribution of alcohol (Institute For Health Policy, 1993). In 1933, prohibition was repealed and with this came an end to one of the more colorful and disturbing periods in the recent history of the United States.

The population of narcotics addicts remained stable from the 1910s to the 1960s when the United States experienced a precipitous rise in the use and abuse of drugs (Institute for Health Policy, 1993).

The 1960s brought a tremendous increase in all kinds of drug use and abuse, particularly among young people. The philosophy of the time, "turn on, tune in, and drop out," supported drug experimentation to alter consciousness and "get high." And, more specifically, the philosophy among the youth counterculture—largely composed of white, middle-class children who mounted a social revolution with both a cultural and political philosophy—encouraged peace, love, and tolerance for difference. The open and frequent use of drugs was accepted and encouraged as part of this new lifestyle.

New drugs called hallucinogens, such as LSD, were developed and rapidly gained popularity among this youth counterculture. Marijuana and hashish also found an enthusiastic market among these young people who were experimenting with new ways to think, feel, and live. Other drugs, such as heroin and cocaine, increased in popularity in the 1960s as well.

Because of their widespread drug use and abuse and alternative lifestyle, society began to shun these youth. This backlash, however, only served to fuel their zealousness for a more radical and nontraditional lifestyle, which included an active drug subculture that openly marketed to other youth. In order to join the movement, young people were expected to use drugs, making peer pressure a powerful and widespread proponent of drug use.

As the decade of "peace and love" came to a close, attention to drugs and drug use steadily declined, although the actual use of drugs did not. Drug use and abuse persisted, almost silently, throughout the 1970s until the 1980s, when the escalating problem of drug use and abuse, particularly that of cocaine and crack, exploded onto front-page headlines.

Cocaine and crack (a derivative of cocaine) have monopolized the attention of Americans throughout the 1980s and into the 1990s (Committee on the Judiciary United States Senate, 1990), when television newscasts and exposés suddenly focused on the desperate crack addict as well as the numbers of pregnant women who were using crack and exposing their unborn children to the effects of this drug. For a time, there existed an atmosphere of near hysteria as children exposed in utero to crack were described as a "new breed" of children, hopelessly damaged by their mothers' drug use (Zuckerman & Frank, 1992).

The 1990s have seen a rise in popularity of the so-called "designer drugs," synthetic products such as "ecstasy" (MDMA) and "love drug" (MDA). A *designer drug* is an analogue, or a compound, that is similar in structure and effect to another drug but is manufactured synthetically (National Institute on Drug Abuse, 1995). These drugs are manufactured in illegal laboratories and sold as illicit substances. "Ice," "crank," and "wire," smokeable and injectable forms of methamphetamine (speed), considered to be highly addictive and quite dangerous, are receiving increased recognition (National Institute on Drug Abuse, 1995). The Midwest and West Coast, in particular, are experiencing increasing problems related to the use of these drugs.

In the 1990s, the distribution and sale of illicit substances reap billions of dollars annually. A report in *The New York Times* stated that the marijuana industry in the United States is a $32 billion per year industry, a larger profit than that earned from corn and soybean crops combined. In addition, the manufacture, advertising, and sale of alcohol are each legal billion dollar industries. Like it or not, the use and abuse of alcohol and other drugs in U.S. culture is as embedded as the passion for sports—unlike various other cultures that forbid or discourage drinking (Arif & Westermeyer, 1988). For example, India's constitution requires every state to move toward eliminating the use of alcohol except for medical reasons (*The Academic American Encyclopedia*, 1993). Several Christian religions (e.g., Christian Scientists, Mormons, Seventh Day Adventists, some Baptists and Methodists) also discourage or forbid the use of alcohol. Although, until the early part of the 20th century, alcoholics were considered crazy or immoral and were institutionalized or shunned by society, substance abuse and addiction have been intrinsically tied to the culture of the United States since its inception.

～ Habit or Addiction ～

A distinction can be made about what constitutes habit (i.e., "social use"), compulsive use, and addiction (Arif & Westermeyer, 1988; Kasl, 1992). A *habit* is a behavior that a person regularly engages in by choice but can stop with some effort and few ill effects. Many people have several habits in which they regularly engage: having a beer while watching "the game," going shopping once a month, having a glass of wine with dinner, having sex on a regular basis, exercising several times a week, or buying a lottery ticket. When the behavior becomes more difficult to control, and the person begins to have a nagging feeling that he should try to modify his behavior, the line between habit and compulsion has been crossed.

With *compulsive use,* the behavior becomes more repetitive and excessive, losing its original meaning. The person "forgets" the motivation behind the behavior and fails to get the original effect—relaxation, enjoyment, or relief. The person who started out just drinking beer while enjoying the game, now drinks beer throughout the day and sometimes thinks that he should cut back. The person who goes shopping once a month as a way to have fun, now shops several times a week and worries about the amount of money she is spending. Compulsive behavior can include just about anything, and often feelings of conflict and ambivalence accompany the behavior. "I shouldn't," "I should," "Just one more time," "I'll quit next week," and "I can stop when I want to," are common laments of a person engaged in compulsive use. Compulsive use limits a person but usually does not destroy him. In terms of substance use, compulsive use is recognized as abuse. Those engaged in compulsive use can usually recognize that they feel uncomfortable and are more likely to attempt to stop, control, or modify the behavior. If repeated attempts to do so fail and the person continues the compulsive use, the door from compulsive use into addiction opens.

The progression from compulsive use to *addiction* is often ill defined, as the behavior subtly escalates until it is out of control. Behavior that once limited a person's life now controls it, taking center stage. With addiction, though, usually comes tolerance and dependence. The need to increase the amount of the substance to achieve the same effects previously experienced at lower doses is called *tolerance* (Arif & Westermeyer, 1988). A person who previously used four bags of heroin a day finds that she must use eight bags a day to get the same "high." The need for continued use of the substance to avoid withdrawal symptoms is called *dependence* (Arif & Westermeyer, 1988). If the person stops using heroin, within a short period of time she will begin to feel sick and will need to use more heroin in order to feel better. Both tolerance and dependence are characteristics of a progressive addiction.

Although one can predict quite a bit about the progression of addiction and much is known about its common characteristics, there is no one way to identify the specific path that leads from habit, to compulsive use, to addiction.

⌒ What Is Addiction? ⌒

The man takes a drink, the drink takes a drink, the drink takes the man.
Chinese proverb on a fortune cookie (Kasl, 1992, p. 128)

I never knew he was drunk until I saw him sober.
Often heard among relatives of alcoholics

There are several general defining features of addiction, which can help one to understand addiction as a disease. Combining this information with one's personal knowledge of an individual can foster understanding of each individual's struggle.

People out there look at us, drug addicts and alcoholics, and they think we are all alike, that we will go out and rob the guy down the street.

Lorna, in recovery

In my culture to be an alcoholic is to be a person that has to be thrown in the streets. A bum, you know?

Gina

There is general agreement that addiction is the compulsive use of a psychoactive substance or substances with loss of control over the use and continued use despite negative consequences (e.g., physical illness, failed relationships). It is a chronic and progressive process that, left untreated, can be destructive and potentially fatal. Car crashes, fights, falls, exposure to human immunodeficiency virus (HIV), and rape are just a few of the dangers to which addicts expose themselves.

I put myself in life-threatening situations; guns were pointed at my head. A lot of times I could have died.

Lorna, in recovery

There can be physical symptoms such as headaches; stomachaches; shaking; high blood pressure; and heart, pancreas, and liver disease. The person can experience withdrawal symptoms upon quitting. "Have a hair of the dog that bit you" is a phrase that refers to having a drink the morning after heavy drinking, to help ease the hangover.

Gina: I knew back then that I was having some problems. That I was getting sick, you know, especially when I used to wake up in the morning. Everybody was having breakfast and I was having a beer. I didn't want to feel sick, you know, I was shaking and the whole 9 yards. The men always said when they used to drink, they used to have a beer in the morning for the hangover, to make them feel better.

As the process progresses, the person's life becomes unmanageable, and there is an increase in harmful consequences as the addictive behavior escalates.

Didi: I just wanted to get high and it was getting rougher, believe me. We sat in a room for almost 48 hours and we smoked [crack cocaine]. I had no idea where my kids were. I had three children. I don't even think I cared where they were. I don't even remember coming out to go to the bathroom. I don't remember eating.

Addiction can influence a person psychologically, physically, and spiritually. Usually one becomes increasingly isolated as the addiction becomes the focus of his or her life. Addicts can experience intense despair and a sense of aloneness that reaches to the very depths of their soul. The addict may experience depression, anxiety, or a general numbing of emotions. Emotional and psychological symptoms can progress to include suicidal thoughts or psychosis. The AA slogan, "sick and tired of feeling sick and tired," illustrates the despair and desperation that an addict can experience.

I was ready by then because I was so tired. I didn't want to live no more, you know? I felt like a body with no soul, so sick I was.

Gina

Denial of a problem becomes firmly established as the person continues to believe that he or she can control use because, with addiction, one must experience higher and higher levels of denial and distortion in order to maintain the status quo. Patterns of deception develop as the person struggles to maintain the delusion of control. This illusion—and the denial used to maintain it—is at the heart of addiction.

Gina: Here I am using cocaine and alcohol. I have a boyfriend who is an addict using heroin, but I didn't consider myself an addict just because I didn't shoot drugs. I didn't want to feel pain, you know? So that was my world. I felt like I was powerful, that I could talk, you know, I could express my feelings. And what the heck, you know, I don't remember the next day. My sister used to tell me, you said so many bad things yesterday, you hurt my feelings. I used to say, "What, me? I'm not like that." I used to think that they were exaggerating. They weren't telling the truth. They were making a little story bigger.

Patty: When I was pregnant, my father-in-law mentioned to me, when I was drinking in front of him, he said, they are doing studies now that alcohol affects kids when they're in your stomach. And I told him, that's bullshit, they don't know what they're talking about. And I had switched from black russians (vodka and Kahlua) to white russians (vodka, Kahlua, and milk). I put in the milk and I really thought the baby was going to get the milk and that I was going to get the alcohol. It didn't dawn on me that he was getting the alcohol too. It was like total denial that it could happen.

For people to stop addictive behavior, they must recognize and admit that they are powerless over their addictions.

Jack: For a long time I used to think that I was in control because I didn't drink every day. I would say, I don't have to drink, I can go a day or 2 without beer and be fine. But I wasn't fine. Booze had taken over my life and I spent more and more mental time arguing with myself about controlling my drinking. The fall from the roof brought me to my knees. I completed detox and started going to AA meetings. It was an incredible relief for me to accept that first step, even though it was very hard to admit it, that I was powerless over my drinking. It's strange, but in a way I felt free; I felt that I could do something about me and my life.

～ Process Addictions ～

In the 1990s, more attention has been focused on process addictions in addition to the usual substance addictions (e.g., alcohol, heroin, cocaine). *Process addictions* are about an activity. Addicts simply cannot stop what they are doing (Finkelstein, Duncan, Derman, & Smeltz, 1990; Kasl, 1992; O'Shea, 1995), and their behavior escalates out of control until they face the same situations and consequences of a substance addict.

One well-known process addiction is out-of-control gambling. Men and women who gamble away their last dime or their rent and food money, or who steal and cheat to continue gambling, are addicted. Some of these people place their lives at risk as they borrow money from illegal sources, which they are unable to pay back.

My mother is addicted to Bingo and the lottery. She spends all of the grocery money, and last week our electricity was turned off because she did not pay the bill.

Sherry

Eating disorders are also thought of as process addictions. The process of under- or overeating is comparable to a substance addiction when a person starves himself or binges and purges (the act of eating large quantities of food at one time and then forcing oneself to vomit) and focuses her entire mental attention on eating. Eating disorders can permanently damage one's health and, in some cases, can lead to death (Fornari, Kent, Kabo, & Goodman, 1994). The well-publicized death of the singer Karen Carpenter brought national attention to this condition.

Judy: I never liked the way my body looked. I thought that I was fat. I was pretty skinny, but all I saw was a fat person. I became obsessed with my weight and began dieting when I was 15. I would try all kinds of stupid diets and eventually I began to lose weight. The more weight I lost the more I would diet. At first everyone complimented me. When I was around 17, I had lost so much weight that my family started telling me to stop dieting. I became more and more sneaky about my food and eating. I would eat with the family and then run into the bathroom and force myself to vomit. By the time I finally got help, I weighed 85 pounds and my teeth were all messed up from the vomiting. I am 5'3" and before all of this I weighed 118.

Addiction to sexual activity is another area that has received much attention in the 1990s. With this addiction, a person's mental energy and attention are focused on sex and sexual activity (Carnes, 1983). Individuals with sexual addictions use sexual activity in similar ways as substance-addicted people use substances. People who have sexual addictions put themselves at risk for sexually transmitted diseases, HIV or acquired immunodeficiency syndrome (AIDS), rape, loss of partners, and, in some cases, death by assault. Some sexually addicted individuals victimize others: children, women, and men.

Jerry: I used to go into bars, you know, looking for someone to have sex with. I didn't really care about who they were. It wasn't about having a relationship, I just needed sex. I craved it. If I didn't get it, I would get agitated and angry. There was a time that I was going out 4 or 5 times a week to different bars, always picking up a different person. I wasn't even thinking about infections or HIV.

Many people are familiar with the term *workaholic*, in which a person works compulsively to the exclusion of caring for his personal health and family. Work becomes the focus despite consequences that can include losing partners, family, friends, or even jobs. In many ways, society condones and even rewards compulsive working. Colleagues brag to each other about how many hours they have put in on the job. Some companies set up systems that are overtly competitive, rewarding those who work longer and harder with trips to exotic places. Professions such as law, medicine, and banking are notorious for the long hours of work that are required. Many doctors look back in awe at their internship and residency training as they remember being "on call" 2 or 3 days in a row, meaning they did not sleep for 24 or more hours and made life-and-death decisions in a state of sleep deprivation. Many law firms have unwritten codes about having to "put in the long hours" in order to advance in the firm. Long-distance truck drivers are required to drive long hours with no sleep and little rest in order to meet delivery deadlines. Many truckers have turned to the use of amphetamines [speed] as a way of staying awake.

David: My father was a lawyer. He would leave in the morning before we were even up for school. He would come home late, more often than not, usually around 8 or 9 P.M. I hardly ever remember him having dinner with us. He never helped me with my homework. When he got home, if we were still awake, Mom would usher us out of the room or off to bed because Dad was tired and needed peace and quiet. He worked many weekends preparing briefs and missed a lot of my basketball games. I don't think my father ever really knew who I was, and all I knew about him was that he was a lawyer.

Other activities considered process addictions are shopping and spending money in an out-of-control fashion.

Anna: When I felt bad I would go to the mall and shop. I would buy expensive jewelry and clothes, all kinds of stuff. At one point, I had about 20 pairs of jeans in my closet, most of them still had the tags on. I had a huge bill from the jewelry store that I could not pay. I wasn't even working. I would use my father's credit cards or my own. I knew I couldn't afford any of the stuff and I felt really guilty, but I did it anyway. Sometimes I would return things and turn around and buy something else. It was really crazy.

There are several common emotional and psychological issues that accompany substance and process addictions. In fact, many people often have multiple addictions. For example, some are addicted to alcohol and gambling; or cocaine, sex, and alcohol; or food and "pills," the variations are endless. Addicts also frequently trade addictions (Arif & Westermeyer, 1988). A person may stop using alcohol but begin to gamble compulsively or abuse prescription drugs. Substances can be traded for other substances, substances can be traded for behaviors, and behaviors can be traded for substances. People often attempt to control and deny their "addictive tendencies" by trading addictions. One study reports that dependence or abuse of one substance (including alcohol) increases the risk of becoming dependent on or abusing another substance by 7 times (Regier et al., 1990).

Carol: At that point I was only drinking and smoking reefer [marijuana]. My boyfriend was dealing heroin. I asked him what it was, and he told me and I wanted to try it, you know? I had skin popped it [shooting with a needle under the skin but not in a vein]. I tried it again, but this time I mainlined [shooting into a vein]. And I loved it.

~ Addicted to Relationships—Codependency ~

Another issue that has received increasing attention since the 1970s is the concept of *codependency,* which originated from the notion of "a co-alcoholic" or an "enabler," terms first used to describe common traits in partners of alcoholics (Greenleaf, 1981). These traits include unhealthy caregiving, denying the problem, covering and coping, and an obsession with the drinking partner. Co-alcoholics ignore their own needs in the service of "keeping the family together." The term *enabling* simply refers to any behavior, intentional or not, that permits or even helps an addict to continue her pattern of use. Typical examples of enabling include the spouse who calls in sick for the partner who is too hungover to go to work or the spouse who tries to control the partner's drinking by watering down or hiding bottles of liquor. The enabler is someone whose behavior keeps the addicted system going at any cost.

People who are considered *codependent* consistently put others' needs before their own. They become obsessed with a relationship or a person and believe that they can, or should be able to, change or control the other person's behavior. They ignore their own needs sometimes to the point of serious physical or emotional damage (Beatie, 1980). They often feel unduly committed to a harmful relationship and feel that they can fix things or make things better. The person is preoccupied with the relationship and dependent upon it, often harboring the fear that she could not survive outside of it. Behavior within such a relationship is often passive and compliant, and the person is often incapable of self-motivation, instead motivated by the need to take care of another.

Patty: By the time I was 2 years old I had not really bonded with anyone. I grew up. As a little kid I remember fun things, but I was lost in a crowd. I really felt like I didn't belong. If there were any problems in the family, which every family had, I felt like it was my fault. And if I would just disappear, everything would be okay. My mother was in her own pain from losing her other child, you know. And my attitude at that time was—just be good. I went to school and did well. I came back for Christmas break and met a man. New Year's Eve we went out and we decided that night we'd get married. I married this man the following July, and I figured all of a sudden that I had someone who was going to take care of me.

Deidre: It took me 2 agonizing years to decide to end my marriage to an abusive man. I felt that I had tried everything I could to make things better, and realized that if I didn't get out, I could die. Just after I had made my decision, I remember having a very vivid mental image. I saw myself in my wedding dress and I was holding out my arms to the present me, and I was smiling and saying welcome back. It was at that moment that I realized just how much of myself I had lost.

During the course of history, most enablers were thought to be women. When AA was first developed in the 1930s, it was conceived for a group, most of whom were men, who wanted to stop drinking. Alanon was founded by the wives of these alcoholic men to learn how to support their husbands in sobriety, cope with their own feelings, and change their enabling behavior. There was the subtle implication that the wives were somewhat responsible for their partners' drinking and, therefore, for their abstinence (Brown, 1985).

Over time, it was recognized that the enabler as well as the addict could be of either sex. During the 1970s, when the family therapy movement began to gain momentum, the concept of viewing the family as a system led to the belief that alcoholism is a "family disease" (Wegscheider, 1981).

Patty: I remember looking at this little boy's face with all the destruction going on in his life because of alcohol, and I didn't know it was alcohol. I could see that fear and that something was wrong, but I didn't know what it was. Alcohol played the biggest role. And this child was getting more messed up and more messed up and he was angry, you know, and he'd act out on his anger. I really didn't want to hurt him. And I didn't know it was alcohol. He'd come up to me and say, "Mommy, please don't drink so much."

Kasl (1992) sees codependence as being a disease of inequality, embodying predictable behavior that people in subordinate roles typically adopt to survive in a dominant culture. Codependency, she states, is just another name for internalized oppression, which explains why, in American culture, more women are considered to be codependent. Traits of passivity, compliance, lack of initiative, abandonment of self, and fear of showing overt power are common among people who are oppressed or codependent. In fact, 9 of 10 women who

are married to alcoholics and have children under the age of 18 will stay with the alcoholic. However, only 1 of 10 men stay with an alcoholic woman (Ackerman, 1987, p. 9). Perhaps the reason women stay and men leave has something to do with societal expectations, rigid roles, and ingrained gender differences.

Many people believe that girls in American culture are socialized to be caregivers, placaters, peacemakers, and keepers of the hearth and home. Girls have traditionally been taught to be obedient, compliant, and submissive: "Good girls" don't argue and they don't question authority (Gilligan, 1982). Women have carried the responsibility of "keeping the family together" and have traditionally been expected to maintain the social and moral values of the culture. To this day, females are expected to live up to a higher standard of behavior (Finkelstein et al., 1990). The common saying "boys will be boys" is often used to excuse everything from mild mischief to criminal behavior. Yet, comments such as "that is not ladylike" are admonishments about any female behavior that is even mildly unacceptable.

This double standard applies to men and women who are addicted as well. Although, in American culture, there is a stigma attached to all addicts, male addicts are often considered only selfish or lazy while women addicts are viewed as immoral or inherently bad. Societal attitudes and expectations play a large role in how addiction is viewed in individuals and their significant others and are primarily based upon age, role, culture, religion, environment, and, perhaps most important, gender. They also influence how addicts function in the family.

Men: Fathers, Partners, Sons, Brothers, Uncles, and Grandfathers

Men in the addicted system often focus their energy and concerns around money and finances. Denial of the disease is reinforced by familial and societal messages that if you can hold down a job, you don't have a problem. If a man is "functioning" (i.e., able to work and earn a living) then he isn't really addicted. Perhaps he only drinks after work or uses cocaine just on the weekends. Men are praised for being able to hold their liquor, and it is often considered "manly." Many enabling spouses can hinder a man from seeking treatment fearing the realities of loss of income if the man leaves. They may also be afraid of change.

The health risks to men from drug and alcohol abuse and addiction are numerous. Liver disease from cirrhosis or hepatitis, pancreatitis, endocarditis, and circulatory problems are common. Their behavior can put them at high risk for contracting HIV and other sexually transmitted diseases that they can then pass on to their partners.

Men are also more likely to be involved in illegal or criminal activity as a result of their addiction. Selling drugs, theft, and robbery are common ways of supporting a drug addiction. Men addicts are perpetrators of violent crime, often involved in relationships in which they are physically and emotionally abusive.

Women: Mothers, Partners, Daughters, Sisters, Aunts, and Grandmothers

The stigma for female addicts is even greater than it is for males. Women face a double stigma with addiction of societal disapproval and sexual stereotyping. People frown upon a female alcoholic; it is not considered "proper" behavior when a woman falls off of a bar stool, although a man may just be encouraged to go home and "sleep it off." There also exists a stereotypical sexualized image of the female addict as being promiscuous. "Cheap," "easy," "coke whore," and "slut" are derogatory terms for women addicts. There are no equivalent terms for men.

Female addicts often have significant problems with sexual functioning (Finkelstein et al., 1990), due either to the direct effects of alcohol and other drugs, a history of sexual abuse, or both (Wilsnack, 1992). The emotional secondary effects of addiction such as depression, guilt, shame, and low self-esteem, which female addicts have been found to experience more than addicted males (Sandmaier, 1980), also have a negative impact on sexual function. Women who are addicted become acceptable targets for sexual assaults and other kinds of violence (National Institute on Alcohol Abuse and Alcoholism [NIAAA], 1990). This is compounded when female addicts cannot keep themselves safe due to their own histories of trauma and/or impairment from alcohol or other drugs. Also, some women do prostitute or exchange sex for drugs.

Women's central roles in society and the family as mothers and caregivers place them in a harsh and punitive spotlight when it comes to addiction. A woman who cannot produce healthy offspring and care for them appropriately threatens the continuation of the society in which she lives (Finkelstein et al., 1990). Women may also be grieving the previous loss of children caused by removal by child protective services or death or loss of pregnancies by miscarriage or therapeutic abortion. Losing yet another child can be devastating, and the fear may keep women from getting help.

Patty: I was in a detox that wouldn't allow children and when I was there, there was a 14-day program, they wouldn't even allow my son upstairs to visit me. And I didn't know that when I went there. I was allowed to see him for 15 minutes down in the lobby. And I had been a single parent at the time, his father wasn't living with us, and I asked his father to take care of him when I went into detox. And they really tried to convince me not to go to detox, but wanted to give me these pills so I wouldn't drink anymore, because I would get deathly sick if I drank with the pills, well I got deathly sick and I drank and it didn't matter to me. So when I went in detox I had to take a chance that somebody would take this child because I had to set up the appointment and set up going in there.

And I said, somebody has got to take my son. Are you going to take him?

Didi: I was afraid that if they thought I was doing drugs, that they were going to take my babies. So I didn't tell them. I was scared.

Women are more often isolated and alone with little if any support, especially if their family of origin is not available to them. Women who suffered from child abuse at the hands of family members fear that their own children will be victimized if left in the care of the abuser(s).

There was nobody ever around that I could trust enough, not even my father. I felt lonely and scared.

Ida

In many cases, women can be discouraged from seeking treatment by other family members. Partners and other family members may be actively abusing alcohol and/or other drugs, and family members fear the change that will come when the addict enters treatment, even if they want it to happen.

Well, me and my husband broke up, because I wouldn't stop getting high and he didn't like it.

Didi

Women may also be victims of violence in an abusive relationship where partners subvert attempts at treatment. Entering treatment, refusing to use drugs, seeking outside help—these can be dangerous things to attempt when a woman is being terrorized by an abusive family member.

Women are at an economic disadvantage as well. Many women do not work, or they work at low-wage jobs. Often they do not have insurance or the financial resources to afford treatment or child care. Women can also be involved in illegal activities to support their addiction. Approximately 60% of all incarcerated women have problems with substance abuse, and the majority of these women also have at least one child (Criminal Justice Report, 1992).

Patty: There was a time when you either had to go to jail or a mental institution to detox. And I know that one time I did my detox in Framingham (women's prison in Massachusetts), because there was no other place, and I'm talking about the 1970s. But there was plenty, you know, for men. And it's really sad because the growing number of people, especially women with children, are afraid to go into treatment, because they're afraid of losing their kids. They're afraid of what's going to happen while their kids are gone. Are they going to get their kids back once they are through? There are not that many facilities available for women with children. You know, finding one is really difficult.

The health issues for women are also different than for men. The NIAAA (1990) cites research that has demonstrated that women can be more vulnerable to the physiological consequences of alcohol and other drugs. Women have lower body water content and higher fat content, therefore blood-alcohol concentrations (BACs) in women reach higher levels than in men when the same amount of alcohol is consumed, and drugs are stored in the body for a longer time. The metabolism of alcohol in the stomach is also different between women and men. Diminished "first-pass" metabolism in women allows more alcohol to pass through the stomach and into their system. Female alcoholics have a death rate that is 50%–100% higher than that of male alcoholics. Women die more often from suicide, alcohol-related accidents, circulatory problems, and cirrhosis of the liver (Finkelstein et al., 1990; National Institute on Alcohol Abuse and Alcoholism, 1990).

I had gotten into a car accident, and driven in a blackout and almost killed my husband. I wanted to die. I didn't want to live anymore. And I sliced my wrists but it didn't work.

Patty

Women alcoholics are also at high risk for breast cancer and cancers of the mouth and throat. Menstrual irregularities, infertility, miscarriage, and stillbirth are all increased among alcoholic women. Women are also at high risk for contracting HIV and other sexually transmitted diseases.

The harshest stigma of all is reserved for addicted women who are pregnant or who have children. Societal rage is directed at pregnant addicts, and many women—usually poor women—have been arrested, prosecuted, and jailed because of their disease. Prosecutors have demanded automatic removal of children and some urge sterilization (Magar, 1991). Parenting is difficult enough when one is emotionally mature and relatively healthy. It can be impossible for a woman who is still using.

Patty, learning of her son's fetal alcohol syndrome: And I couldn't function. I could no longer be a good mother to him. I couldn't parent him. I couldn't move on with our lives. And I was stuffing my feelings. And finally the tears came for like 3 days straight. I just cried and cried, and I hadn't done that in years. And it was guilt. You know I was running on guilt.

～ The Faces of Addiction ～

Gina, in recovery: I started drinking more after my husband moved out. He used to beat me up. He beat me when I was pregnant. I drank every day—I think it was wine. I had no self-esteem at all, I didn't know who I was; I didn't know what I was. I had two kids, I had my family, but it was not enough. My sister told me that I had a problem, but I used to argue with her: "Don't call me an alcoholic, I am not an alcoholic. Are you crazy?" But I was having blackouts and I got into an accident.

Patty, in recovery: I was the "Kool Aid" mom. I was the mom who made hot dogs for every kid in the neighborhood. My son did not do well in school. I kept wondering, "What is it? What is it?" It was like a little thing inside of me, like having a bug inside your stomach. I never dreamed it was alcohol. One day I was driving the car with my husband, I blacked out and hit a sign and almost killed him. I don't remember what happened, I just remember pulling him out. I started to drink every day at this point. I drank on the way to work, I would drink on the way home. I drank with my son in the car. I just kept drinking and drinking and drinking, and I didn't know what to do. One day my son got sick at school, and the school found me at the bar. They knew. I thought I was hiding all of this. I increased my drinking—it was the only way to stop the pain.

Carol, in recovery: I had built up a lot of resentment toward my family. My parents got divorced and we had to move and go on welfare. I started to do what I wanted and stopped listening to my mother. I got into a very negative group of kids, but that is where I got attention. I remember drinking and hating the taste, but I kept drinking. I got really drunk the first time I drank. I said I would never do it again, but I was still having those feelings of guilt and shame. I'm also an incest survivor. I just wanted to do something to make me escape. As I got older, the drinking progressed. Later on I started smoking reefer, popping pills, and doing acid. I blamed the '60s, the black revolution, the sexual revolution, and the women's revolution for my using. I had a son. His father denied being the father and said he was a "trick baby," and I wasn't sure myself. He was dealing heroin. I started shooting it. In the beginning, there was money, food, and a nice place to live. That all changed, but I kept using.

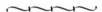

Didi, in recovery: I started using drugs at a real young age. I had a good family background as a young girl. I lived with my grandparents; there was no alcohol, no drugs. My mother came back when I was 8, and she introduced me to marijuana. I think she gave it to me to put me to sleep. She also gave me beer every now and then. My mother was an alcoholic. As the years went by, I continued to smoke marijuana and drink beer. I met a guy and I was living with him and I started taking tabs of mescaline and THC and that kind of stuff. I was off and running—you couldn't stop me. Everywhere I went there was a liquor store or there were guys—it was there. My son's father started dealing again, and I got pregnant again, and that is when I was introduced to free-basing crack cocaine. That was the beginning of my nightmare.

Ida, in recovery: My childhood was abusive, I got beat up, I was ridiculed, I was intimidated. I lived in a foster home with my brother. Almost every day in the foster home we got beat up and were sexually abused. I am a "Johnny come lately" to drugs. I started using when I was 30 years old. I did a little cocaine, I did a little freebase. When I was 32, I got pregnant and my father died. I started free-basing again. But I was getting skinny and I felt lonely and scared, so I dropped the cocaine and the smoking (marijuana). Shortly after this my brother died from AIDS, and I could not go to his funeral because I did not have the money to fly to where he had lived. I couldn't handle this. I hid by starting to use heroin. It slowly progressed. I did like one bag maybe or two bags a month. Then it got to the point where I was doing it every week and then every day. And it went from two or three bags a day up to five and seven bags a day.

David, in recovery: No one in my family ever drank. I always hated the taste of alcohol. When I was in college, I smoked pot and did LSD, but it was part of the lifestyle of the '60s. Some years later, during my divorce, I started having trouble sleeping. I began having a glass of wine or beer to help me fall asleep. I was also very depressed. I felt like a failure, and I was lonely. My drinking progressed, I started having two or three drinks before bed. After a while, I started drinking during the day. In the morning, during lunch—a shot here and there. I was working and doing everything I had to do. I didn't think I was an alcoholic, I just thought my drinking was heavy. This went on for over 3 years: I went to work drunk, missed family events, and would spend time with friends while drunk, all the time thinking that no one knew what was going on. I told myself that I couldn't have a problem because I would bicycle every weekend and work out at the club. I worked and functioned in my life.

Jack, in recovery: My father was an alcoholic. No one ever called him that. We just said that he liked his beers. He was really into sports and wanted me to be a baseball player. I was not particularly good at baseball, I liked football better, but he didn't care. He was always putting me down and calling me names. I was a big disappointment to him. I started drinking when I was 12. I stole beers from the refrigerator to drink with my friends. I drank every weekend through high school and I drank to get drunk. I had my first blackout before I graduated from high school. I started smoking pot and dabbled in other drugs, but I always preferred alcohol. My *father eventually died from liver disease, but no one ever linked it to his drinking. No one in my family ever talked to me about my drinking. I only stayed in college for a couple of years. I always had a dream of becoming a writer, but felt that I was never talented enough. I dropped out and started working at odd jobs—roofing, painting, construction. I began drinking every day. It seemed to be a part of that culture, beer with lunch, beers after work. My drinking progressed to where I would show up for jobs in the morning and already be drunk. One day when I was roofing, I fell off and seriously injured my back. Collecting worker's compensation, I sat around every day drinking and getting drunk.*

There are as many faces of addiction as there are faces of those who are addicted. Each person struggling with addiction brings his own unique set of circumstances to the experience. No two addicts are ever exactly alike; there is no accurate stereotypical picture of an alcoholic or addict, as the previous stories, all true and all quite unique, illustrate. Gina, a Latina, and Jack, a second-generation Irish Catholic, both struggle with the same disease, yet in different ways.

Patterns of addiction vary among users, as do the influential factors of each addict's life, such as age, sex, genetic factors, social class, psychosocial issues, ethnicity, religion, sexual orientation, and geographical location. Carol, an African American, began her life in a middle-class suburban community, but her parents' divorce forced them to move to an impoverished community. David, who is Caucasian and Jewish, grew up in an upper–middle-class intact family in a middle-class community. Didi, an African American, grew up in an inner-city neighborhood where her extended family raised her after her mother left to pursue a singing career. Jack's Caucasian, Irish father was an alcoholic and so was Patty's father, also Caucasian and Irish.

The drug of choice and the availability of that drug also influence addiction. Many people start out using alcohol. Some progress to other drugs and become addicted to them, while others continue to use alcohol, knowing from the first drink that they are "hooked." The progression from habit, to compulsion, to addiction varies for each individual. There are many people who can use alcohol and other drugs without ever losing control, while others become addicted.

For these reasons, it is important to always look at the individuals first, not their addictions. Who are they? What are their life stories? Asking questions can bring understanding about what the addiction means for each individual and help illuminate the human face of addiction.

Ask not what disease the person has, but rather what person the disease has.

Oliver Sacks, M.D., neurologist and author (1995)

～ Models and Theories of Addiction ～

Over time, the common features of addiction have been integrated into several theories about why people become addicted, what addiction really is, and how addiction should be treated. These ideas have come from politicians, religious leaders, and addicts themselves; they have originated from the fields of medicine, psychiatry, and social science. Following are brief descriptions of some of the more widely known theories and models of addiction that have evolved.

Disease Model

The *disease model,* first explained by Jelinek (1960), describes addiction as a biochemically based chronic and progressive disease with specific signs and symptoms to which some people are genetically predisposed. Left untreated, the disease can be potentially fatal. The notion of genetic predisposition gains support from several twin studies demonstrating that a co-twin of an alcoholic is at much higher risk of also developing alcoholism (Kendler, Heath, Neale, Kessler, & Eaves, 1992; Svikis, McGue, & Pickens, 1992). Others report that first-degree relatives of alcoholics are at least four times more likely to develop an addiction than are individuals in the general population (Cotton, 1979). Progression through the stages of the disease eventually leads to dependency and loss of control over the use. Treatment under this model takes a more medical approach, focusing on hospitalization, medication, and the physiological nature of the disease.

Ann: My father is an alcoholic, and his father was also. I have three brothers, and they are all alcoholics. One of my brothers started to drink when he was 11 years old, the other two were a little older before they started. We always felt that alcoholism ran in our family.

～～～～

Traditional Psychiatric Models

Psychiatric models have traditionally considered an underlying psychopathology or major mental illness to be the foundation of addiction. The addict is felt to have a personality disorder that causes him to think, feel, and behave in ways that are significantly different from the cultural norm or have a major mental illness that influences his mood, feelings, and behavior (Wurmser, 1974). Examples of major mental illnesses include bipolar disorder, major depression, anxiety and panic disorders, and schizophrenia (Regier et al., 1990). A person considered to have a personality disorder or major mental illness usually experiences distress and disruption in several areas of his life (American Psychiatric Association, 1994).

There is a significant comorbidity of psychiatric disturbance and drug abuse and dependence (National Institute on Drug Abuse, 1994; Regier et al., 1990). Approximately 22% of the American population are affected by a psychiatric disorder (Regier et al., 1990). Among individuals with a lifetime history of drug abuse or addiction, 53% have a psychiatric disorder; of those who are alcoholic, 37% have a comorbid mental disorder (Regier et al., 1990). According to Regier and colleagues, having a lifetime mental disorder is associated with at least twice the risk of having an alcohol problem and over four times the risk of having a drug problem.

Under the psychiatric model, treatment is focused largely on resolving underlying problems. The addiction is placed in the background with the belief that when the underlying problem is resolved, the addiction will subside. Unfortunately, this is not the case for most addicts. The story of Rowland H., one of AA's earliest members, illustrates the difficulty. Rowland H. was unsuccessfully treated in psychoanalysis by Carl Jung, a world-renowned analyst and colleague of Sigmund Freud. At the time, Jung encouraged this man to seek a "vital spiritual experience," which he felt would produce an "emotional rearrangement" after this man began drinking again following a year of sobriety. Jung further recommended that this man place himself in a religious atmosphere of his choice, recognizing his hopelessness (Alcoholics Anonymous, 1976, pp. 26–28). Jung hoped that Rowland H. would have a spiritually transforming experience that could lead him out of alcoholism, recognizing that psycho-analysis alone was inadequate to treat alcoholism. Chapter 8 discusses this in detail.

Contemporary Psychiatric Models

Contemporary psychiatric models have come to recognize addiction as a primary psychiatric disorder requiring attention and treatment. In agreement with the disease model, contemporary thought places loss of control over a substance at the core of addiction. Although contemporary models still believe that there are important psychological aspects of addiction, the addiction is recognized as needing immediate and primary attention. It is generally agreed that a person who is actively addicted can make little use of psychotherapy in which underlying feelings and dynamics are examined in an attempt to understand or change behavior, thoughts, and feelings.

One such contemporary psychiatric model, the *self-medication hypothesis,* sees drug use and abuse as a way of relieving painful feelings or disordered affect (Khantzian, 1975, 1985; Khantzian, Mack, & Schatzberg, 1974). The person is thought to be unable to self-regulate internal emotional experiences and has difficulty in adapting to external realities, which leads to difficulty in functioning in the areas of feelings, self-esteem, relationships, and self-care. The self-medication hypothesis also recognizes that an addict generally does not choose drugs randomly but rather for the effect each has on the dominant disordered affect. For example, stimulants such as cocaine and amphetamines may be chosen for their ability to relieve feelings of depression, or alcohol may be used to self-medicate attention-deficit/hyperactivity disorder (ADHD) (Pihl & Peterson, 1991). Alcohol also has long been recognized as allowing a person to "loosen up," to be less shy and inhibited. Drinking alcohol is also a socially accepted way of relaxing and relieving tension. Heroin and other opiates may be chosen for the numbing effect they have on powerful feelings of aggression and rage.

Carol: For me, I knew that I never had any self-esteem. I never cared about myself. I never was nurtured. I felt abandoned. I felt shame behind being sexually abused. I felt guilt. For a long time I really felt worthless. And I felt hopeless and helpless.

Trauma Model A refinement of the self-medication hypothesis is the *trauma model.* Many clinicians and theorists have come to recognize the reciprocal influence of trauma and addiction. In fact, the two are inexorably linked in the literature (Herman, 1992; Herman, Russell, & Trocki, 1986; Rohsenow, Corbett, & Devine, 1988; Van der kolk, 1987). It is postulated that early traumatization can seriously disrupt a child's development of a stable sense of self and derail one's sense of inner reliability. The capacity for inner self-soothing and self-regulation are greatly diminished or absent, causing the person to turn to external sources (i.e., substances) for comfort and relief.

History of the Trauma Model Our understanding of the effects of trauma is derived primarily from literature that examined responses and behavior of soldiers returning from war. During World War I, a phenomenon emerged in veterans known as "shell shock," which embodied a number of symptoms, including depression, anxiety, and mood swings. Another syndrome that afflicted World War II combat soldiers was termed "war neurosis." Several important clinical features of this syndrome included physiological responses such as increased startle reaction, increased muscle tension, heart palpitations, and a "sinking feeling" (Everly, 1990).

Behavioral differences in veterans (as described by family members) included a steadfast refusal to talk about anything having to do with their wartime experience, recurrent nightmares, and a sense of ongoing and pervasive distance from those around them. The veterans themselves described having overwhelming anxiety, panic attacks, and difficulty sleeping. Flashbacks were experienced, and the sound of overhead aircraft often sent veterans diving under restaurant tables for cover. Anecdotal familial reports, passed from one generation to the next, depicted an awareness that the veteran had returned a "different man."

He was never the same after the war. He was a completely different person.

May, the sister of a WWII veteran

During the Vietnam War, it became clearer that an emotional syndrome accompanied the war experience. In addition, and unique to the Vietnam experience, American soldiers engaged in open and ongoing substance abuse while in the field—primarily alcohol, marijuana, and heroin. Upon their return, some continued their substance abuse while others spontaneously stopped using. Soldiers returning from this war also displayed an array of serious and disturbing symptoms, including depression, anxiety, and sleep disturbance (e.g., nightmares, flashbacks, hypervigilance, hyperstartle). This was probably the first major glimpse at the association between trauma and substance abuse.

Caroline, sister of a Vietnam veteran: When my brother came back from Vietnam, he stayed in his room and drank daily. We were afraid to go near him because he would get so mad.

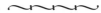

Deidre: I went out on a date with a young man who had just returned from Vietnam. I think he was drunk. As we were driving along a divided highway, he began playing "chicken," driving on the wrong side of the road. He also very proudly boasted about wearing, on his belt, the severed ears of the people he had killed. I was terrified.

Furthermore, many veterans had extreme difficulty adjusting to civilian life, experiencing job and marital or relational problems. The incidence of addiction, joblessness, criminal behavior, and homelessness was striking for this group of soldiers (Hyer, Leach, Boudewyws, & Davis, 1991) and marked the beginning of the recognition and classification of a syndrome known as posttraumatic stress disorder (PTSD).

Posttraumatic Stress Disorder   PTSD refers to a psychological and physiological response to a traumatic event that causes an array of symptoms ranging from mild to severe. *The Diagnostic and Statistical Manual of Mental Disorders,* Fourth Edition (DSM-IV) (American Psychiatric Association, 1994), lists the following criteria as necessary for meeting the diagnosis of PTSD, which can be acute or chronic and have a delay of onset:

1. Exposure to an event that is outside the range of usual human experience, which would be traumatic to almost anyone, and involves actual or threatened death or injury or a threat to the physical integrity of the self or others; also, the person's response involves intense fear, helplessness, or horror.
2. The traumatic event is persistently reexperienced by recurrent and intrusive recollections of the event, including images, thoughts, and perceptions; recurrent distressing dreams of the event; and acting or feeling as if the traumatic

event were recurring with illusions, hallucinations, flashbacks, and dissociative episodes. There can be intense psychological distress and physiological reactivity at exposure
to cues which may symbolize or resemble the trauma.

3. Persistent avoidance of anything associated to the trauma
   and numbing of general responsiveness; there can be feelings of estrangement from others and a foreshortened sense
   of the future.
4. Persistent symptoms of increased arousal including difficulty falling asleep or staying asleep, irritability or outbursts
   of anger, difficulty concentrating, hypervigilance, and an exaggerated startle response.

Since 1980, when PTSD was officially recognized as a legitimate
psychiatric disorder, the understanding about how people develop
this disorder has been broadened. A *traumatic event* is now defined
as any event outside the range of usual human experience that
would be markedly distressing to anyone, including a threat to one's
own life; serious threat or harm to one's children, partner, or others
who are close; sudden/chronic destruction to one's home or community; witnessing serious injury or death of another as a result of
violence or an accident; war experience; physical, emotional, or sexual abuse; and captivity, such as in a kidnapping or being held
hostage. In addition, individuals with histories of trauma are more
vulnerable to developing PTSD in response to a current traumatic
event or re-creating previous traumatic events as a result of an existing PTSD reaction (Herman, 1992).

One single traumatic episode can initiate a PTSD reaction in
any individual. Survivors of repeated and chronic trauma, however,
present somewhat more complicated situations. Often, the presenting picture shows a serious personality disorder or a severe addiction, instead of PTSD. The person may have fragments of memories
that make no sense to him or her, memories without any emotional
feelings, or intense emotional reactions for no particular reason.
When one undergoes prolonged trauma, the accompanying syndrome is often termed "complex posttraumatic stress disorder"
(Herman, 1992, pp. 118–129).

Dissociation, one of the symptoms of PTSD, is a psychological
attempt to adapt to an overwhelming life event. *Dissociation* is
defined in DSM-IV as a disintegration of the functions of consciousness, memory, identity, or perception. The disturbance can be sudden, gradual, or chronic. It can take several forms—ranging from
being unable to recall important information to causing one to travel

away unexpectedly and become confused and amnesiac (American Psychiatric Association, 1994). Unable to escape or resist, a person's usual defenses for handling difficult situations become disorganized and overwhelmed (Herman, 1992), and he or she subsequently loses the ability to integrate and store an event in the usual manner. The traumatic memories are stored out of consciousness along with accompanying emotions, and set apart in a state separate from memory. Often, memories remain unavailable for some time, even forever. In addition, people who are abused can "take themselves away" from the traumatic experience as it is occurring. Trance states, or alterations in consciousness, help one numb or constrict the pain of a situation (Herman, 1992) or cope with sheer terror when no other alternative is available.

Karla, molested repeatedly as a child by her father: I really love my husband, and I know he loves me. But sometimes when we are making love, I get this overwhelming urge to push him away. I feel angry and disgusted, and I don't know why. Sometimes it's the way he moves or the smell, other times I'm not sure.

Emergence of emotions and memories attached to the trauma can occur in isolation from each other or in response to an event that "triggers" recall of the memories or feelings of the trauma. A child who was molested in a park can experience inexplicable terror upon walking in a park as an adult. A young woman who was raped can later experience excruciating pain upon intercourse without any physical cause. These intrusive memories differ from ordinary memories and are stored in vivid sensations and images rather than in words within a context. They often emerge as flashbacks or nightmares. Images can be repetitive, stereotypical, and have a heightened sense of reality.

Karla, molested repeatedly as a child by her father: At first I just remember looking through my crib bars and seeing him walking out of the bathroom naked. Several years later I remember seeing this, and then seeing him walking into my room. After that the memories came back as if I were watching a slide show, slide by slide the memories came until I had the whole experience. And what was so strange is that I was seeing it as if I were floating above the entire scene and watching from above in a very detached state. The memories started coming back after he died.

Those who do not spontaneously dissociate or deal with the trauma and symptoms of PTSD may attempt to numb themselves by self-medicating with alcohol or other drugs (Herman, 1992; Roesler & Dafler, 1993). Alcohol and other drugs are also used to tone down the hyperarousal that often accompanies trauma or to cope with any subsequent anxiety.

Karla, molested as a child by her father: I'm always on the lookout. I expect bad things to happen all the time. When my husband goes out, I imagine he will get into a car crash. I seem to always have my antennae up. If I am sitting in a strange place and someone sits behind me, I feel immediately anxious and have to turn around and see who is behind me. For a long time, I had heart palpitations. I thought it was because I drank too much coffee. But they woke me up at night even after I gave up caffeine. I felt anxious and jumpy.

Brown (1985) makes a compelling argument for seeing alcoholism itself as a primary trauma, hypothesizing that the experience of being alcoholic—the denial, the loss of control, the depression, the anxiety, and the physical consequences—is itself repeatedly traumatizing.

Trauma and Addiction   Data suggest that addicted women have experienced a high rate of trauma. In response to routine inquiry about childhood sexual abuse among women being treated in an inpatient setting for substance abuse, 75% of the women—and 71%–90% of teenage girls—admitted having been abused (Rohsenow et al., 1988). A 1974 study of 118 women in treatment programs for drug abuse across the country found that 52 women (44%) were victims of incest (Benward & Dansen-Gerber, 1975). Anecdotal reports from substance abuse clinicians give even higher rates of abuse, with many clinicians stating that nearly all the women with whom they work have a history of early and often repeated trauma. Another study examining adult sexual abuse survivors found that 66% of the group met criteria for substance abuse or dependence (Roesler & Dafler, 1993).

Patty, in recovery: At 4 years old I was sexually abused by the man who lived upstairs from me. And I knew not to tell anyone. It took me until I was 30 to look at that and to finally admit it to someone.

Ida, in recovery: I was sexually abused, my brother too. We went to school but by 12, I was getting so tired of getting beat up and seeing my brother hurt and bleeding all the time. And we didn't do anything. We were, you know, normal kids trying to play. And everything we did, we just did it wrong. It came out wrong. We always got beat up for it. I got my mouth taped. I got strapped to the bed because I couldn't breathe right. She didn't like it so she used to tape my mouth at nighttime, tape me to the bed so I wouldn't pull the tape off.

Many studies have reported that male perpetrators of incest have a high rate of alcoholism (Coleman, 1987), ranging from 49% to 95%. The reported rate of sex offenders who also have problems with chemical dependency ranged from 30% to 52%, and 56% were sexually abused themselves as children. These statistics indicate that there are unique and interactive dynamics between addiction and sexual abuse, placing those involved at high risk for being molested and becoming perpetrators. However, it is erroneous to think that removing the chemical abuse or dependency will eliminate the sexually deviant behavior, because addiction does not cause sexually deviant or violent behavior.

Social Model

The *social model* of addiction proposes that environmental factors such as poverty, poor job availability, lack of education, lack of housing, racism, sexism, family disintegration, and drug availability all contribute to addiction. In many inner cities and rural communities where poverty is high and jobs are few, people who feel helpless and hopeless are targeted by drug dealers. Once in the drug cycle, their involvement often escalates until they themselves are dealers. Why work at the local fast-food restaurant for minimum wage when you can make hundreds of dollars a day dealing crack?

Traveling through many U.S. inner cities, one is struck by the number and prominence of billboard advertisements for alcohol and cigarettes, which are seldom seen in middle-class or affluent communities. This certainly appears to be an intentional marketing strategy to target those labeled by the social model as at the highest risk. However, inner-city communities are not the only ones vulnerable to the lure of advertising under the social model. As a society, Americans are very vulnerable to advertising tactics that promise that if they use a particular product they, too, can become thinner, richer, smarter, or more popular. Jean Kilbourne (1995) has brought attention to the general trend in the cigarette and alcohol advertising industries of targeting adolescents and women in their advertising campaigns. Picture after picture shows happy, healthy young people doing fun things while smoking or drinking. The boy gets the girl, the girl gets the boy; he is always strong and handsome, and she is always thin and beautiful.

Another tactic aimed at women is "the who needs men" angle. A very popular advertising campaign for cigarettes uses the slogan "You've come a long way, baby," appealing to women who want to be independent. Drinking and smoking are depicted as being sexy, cool, hip, and fun.

Systems Theory Model

The *systems theory model*, derived from work within family therapy (see Chapter 2), considers addiction to be a family disease, in which each person is affected and plays a role in the family drama (Wegscheider, 1981). One of the major principles of systems theory is that whatever affects one person in the family affects all members in the family (Barnes, 1985). An analogy of an elastic band can be used: If one loops an elastic band (the family) around one's fingers and pulls on one end (the addicted member), the shape of the elastic changes, and one can feel the tension from the elastic straining to snap back to its original shape. In the addicted family system, the disease of addiction is the central organizing principle (Brown, 1985). Dysfunctional and addicted family systems can leave their members feeling angry, sad, and abandoned and their children neglected and abused. No one's needs are ever fully met. Many addicts themselves come from just such homes, where one or both parents were addicted and there were early addictive experiences, and so are trapped in their roles created in response to the system (Wegscheider, 1981). This model considers the ways in which each member adapts to the addiction to survive.

Lorna: My parents were alcoholics, mother and father. From a young child, I don't know, 6 on up, I can remember them going out on weekends, leaving my older brother, who is a year older than me, at home with me and my sister. They'd go out, good moods. They'd have been drinking. They'd come home, my father beating up on my mother, you know, just different things like that. And I'd hear her crying, telling him to stop. This went on for years. Then I remember the smell of weed in my house, I was probably about 8 or 9 years old by this time.

Children in addicted family systems often repeat their parents' own mistakes. Although children are inherently driven to master important developmental milestones and move forward to the next challenge, their success depends largely upon the care and guidance they receive along the way. Typical development can be a difficult task when the sum of one's life experiences and caregiving interactions is filled with the pain and confusion of addiction. Still, children move through the developmental process as best they can and often turn to what they know most intimately (i.e., addiction).

Alcoholics Anonymous

An examination of the models of addiction would be incomplete without reviewing the philosophy and program of AA. AA was started in desperation in the 1930s by two men, Bill W. and Bob S., who had struggled in vain with alcoholism but yet had been failed by all interventions. The program is based upon the principles of anonymity and fellowship. One of the central beliefs, and the first of 12 steps, is the need to admit that one has lost control over drinking and life has become unmanageable (see Appendix E for a complete listing of the 12 steps). AA views alcoholism as a disease—a progressive illness that is spiritual, emotional, and physical. All aspects of the person are affected as they become more involved in their addiction (Alcoholics Anonymous, 1976). AA's view of addiction and its program for recovery are interconnected. The 12 steps and 12 traditions address the disease and serve as a guide to recovery as well as a new way of life.

∼ The Best Fit ∼

Each theory or model of addiction is compelling and offers different ways to understand addiction. Addiction, however, is quite complex. Each person struggling with this disease must be understood within the context of his or her unique life experience. Attention must be paid to each person's specific genetic predisposition, family experience, surrounding environment, and psychological development. In addition, a thorough understanding of an individual's psychosocial development is crucial. Encompassing the biological, psychological, and social aspects of a person's life experience is the most thorough way to understand someone's addiction and develop a family-focused model of treatment (see Part II).

∼ References ∼

Ackerman, R.J. (1987). *Children of alcoholics: A guide for parents, educators, and therapists* (2nd ed.). New York: Simon & Schuster.

Alcoholics Anonymous. (1976). *Third edition of the big book, the basic text for Alcoholics Anonymous.* New York: Author.

Alcoholics Anonymous. (1984). *Pass it on: The story of Bill Wilson and how the AA message reached the world.* New York: Author.

American Psychiatric Association. (1994). *Diagnostic and statistical manual of mental disorders* (4th ed.). Washington, DC: Author.

Arif, A., & Westermeyer, J. (Eds.). (1988). *Manual of drug and alcohol abuse: Guidelines of teaching in medical and health institutions.* New York: Plenum Medical Book Company.

Barnes, G.G. (1985). Systems theory and family theory. In M. Rutter & L. Hersov (Eds.), *Child and adolescent psychiatry: Modern approaches* (pp. 216–229). St. Louis: Blackwell Mosby.

Beatie, M. (1980). *Codependent no more.* Center City, MN: Hazelden.

Benward, J., & Danson-Gerber, J.B. (1975). Incest as a causative factor in antisocial behavior: An exploratory study. *Contemporary Drug Problems: A Law Quarterly, 1,* 323–340.

Brown, S. (1985). *Treating the alcoholic: A developmental model of recovery.* New York: John Wiley & Sons.

Carnes, P. (1983). *Out of the shadows: Understanding sexual addictions of every kind.* Minneapolis, MN: ComCare Publishers.

Coleman, E. (1987). Child physical and sexual abuse among chemically dependent individuals. *Journal of Chemical Dependency Treatment, 1,* 27–38.

Committee on the Judiciary United States Senate. (1990). *Hard-core cocaine addicts: Measuring and fighting the epidemic.* Washington, DC: U.S. Government Printing Office.

Cotton, N.S. (1979). The familial incidence of alcoholism: A review. *Journal of Studies on Alcohol, 40,* 89–116.

Criminal Justice Report. (1992). Addicted mothers: Imprisonment and alternatives. In *The decade of the child.* Washington, DC.

Evans, I.H. (Ed.). (1981). *Brewer's dictionary of phrase and fable.* New York: Harper & Row.

Everly, G. (1990). Post-traumatic stress disorder as a disorder of arousal. *Psychology and Health, 4,* 135–145.

Finkelstein, N., Duncan, S.A., Derman, L., & Smeltz, J. (1990). *Getting sober, getting well: A treatment guide for caregivers who work with women.* Cambridge, MA: The Women's Alcoholism Program of CASPAR.

Fornari, V., Kent, J., Kabo, L., & Goodman, B. (1994). Anorexia nervosa: "Thirty something." *Journal of Substance Abuse Treatment, 11*(1), 45–54.

Gawin, F.H., & Kleber, H.D. (1988). Evolving conceptualizations of cocaine dependence. *Yale Journal of Biology and Medicine, 61,* 123–136.

Gilligan, C. (1982). *In a different voice: Psychological theory and women's development.* Cambridge, MA: Harvard University Press.

Greenleaf, J. (1981). *Co-alcoholic/para-alcoholic: Who's who and what's the difference?* Los Angeles: Health Communications, Inc.

Herman, J.L. (1992). *Trauma and recovery: The aftermath of violence: From domestic abuse to political terror.* New York: Basic Books.

Herman, J.L., Russell, D., & Trocki, K. (1986). Long-term effects of incestuous abuse in childhood. *American Journal of Psychiatry, 143*(10), 1293–1296.

Hyer, L., Leach, P., Boudewyws, A., & Davis, H. (1991). Hidden PTSD in substance abuse inpatients among Vietnam vets. *Journal of Substance Abuse Treatment, 8*, 213–219.

Institute for Health Policy. (1993). *Substance abuse: The nation's number one health problem—key indicators for policy.* Waltham, MA: Brandeis University for The Robert Wood Johnson Foundation, Heller Graduate School.

Jelinek, E.M. (1960). *The disease concept of alcoholism.* New Haven, CT: Hillhouse.

Kasl, C.D. (1992). *A new understanding of recovery—many roads, one journey, moving beyond the 12 steps.* New York: HarperCollins.

Kendler, K.S., Heath, A.C., Neale, M.C., Kessler, R.C., & Eaves, L.J. (1992). A population-based twin study of alcoholism in women. *Journal of the American Medical Association, 268*(14), 1877–1882.

Khantzian, E.J. (1975). Self-selection and progression in drug dependence. *Psychiatric Digest, 10,* 19–22.

Khantzian, E.J. (1985). The self-medication hypothesis of addictive disorders: Focus on heroin and cocaine dependence. *American Journal of Psychiatry, 142,* 1259–1264.

Khantzian, E.J., Mack, J.E., & Schatzberg, A.F. (1974). Heroin use as an attempt to cope: Clinical observations. *American Journal of Psychiatry, 131,* 160–164.

Kilbourne, J. (Producer). (1995). *Slim hopes: Advertising in the obsession with thinness* [Video].

Krystal, H.C. (1975). Affect tolerance. *The Annual of Psychoanalysis, 3,* 79–219.

Magar, M. (1991). The sins of the mother. *Student Lawyer, 9,* 30–34.

National Highway Transportation and Traffic Safety Administration. (1994). *Fatal accident reporting system.* Rockville, MD: Author.

National Institute on Alcohol Abuse and Alcoholism (NIAAA). (1990, January). *Seventh special report to the U.S. Congress on alcohol and health.* (From the Secretary of Health and Human Services, U.S. Department of Health and Human Services, DHHS Publication No. [ADM] 90-1656). Washington, DC: U.S. Government Printing Office.

National Institute on Drug Abuse. (1993). *NIDA capsules: Designer drugs* (C-86-5). Rockville, MD: Press Office of the National Institute on Drug Abuse.

National Institute on Drug Abuse. (1994). *Mental health assessment and diagnosis of substance abusers* (Clinical Report Series, NIH Publication No. 94-3846). Bethesda, MD: National Institutes of Health.

National Institute on Drug Abuse. (1995). *NIDA capsules: Methamphetamine abuse* (C-89-06). Rockville, MD: Press Office of the National Institute on Drug Abuse.

O'Shea, M. (1995, February 19). *Parade Magazine: The Boston Globe,* p. 11.

Pihl, R., & Peterson, J.B. (1991). Attention-deficit hyperactivity disorder, childhood conduct disorder, and alcoholism: Is there an association? *Alcohol Health and Research World, 15*(1), 25–31.

Pollin, M. (1995, February). How pot has grown. *The New York Times Magazine, 6,* 30–35, 44, 50, 56, 57.

Regier, D.A., Farmer, M.E., Rae, D.S., Locke, B.Z., Keith, S.J., Judd, L.L., & Goodwin, F.K. (1990). Comorbidity of mental disorders with alcohol and other drug abuse. *Journal of the American Medical Association, 264*(19), 2511–2518.

Rohsenow, D.L., Corbett, R., & Devine, D. (1988). Molested as children: A hidden contribution to substance abuse? *Journal of Substance Abuse Treatment, 5,* 13–18.

Roesler, T., & Dafler, C. (1993). Chemical dissociation in adults sexually victimized as children: Alcohol and drug use in adult survivors. *Journal of Substance Abuse Treatment, 10,* 537–543.

Sacks, O. (1995). *An anthropologist on Mars.* New York: Alfred E. Knopf.

Sandmaier, M. (1980). *The invisible alcoholics: Women and alcohol abuse in America.* New York: McGraw-Hill.

Schaef, A.W. (1987). *When society becomes an addict.* San Francisco: Harper & Row.

Svikis, D.S., McGue, M., & Pickens, R.W. (1992). Sex and age effects on the inheritance of alcohol problems: A twin study. *Journal of Abnormal Psychology, 101*(1), 3–17.

The academic American encyclopedia (Electronic version). (1993). Danbury, CT: Grolier, Inc.

Van der kolk, B.A. (1987). *Psychological trauma.* Washington, DC: American Psychiatric Press.

Wilsnack, S. (1992). *New findings about women and substance abuse: Implications for treatment and prevention.* Presentation, Washington, DC.

Wegscheider, S. (1981). *Another chance: Hope and health for the alcoholic family.* Palo Alto, CA: Science and Behavior Books.

Wurmser, L. (1974). Psychoanalytical considerations of the etiology of compulsive drug use. *Journal of the American Psychoanalytical Association, 22,* 820–843.

Zuckerman, B., & Frank, D.A. (1992). "Crack kids"—Not broken. *Pediatrics, 89,* 337–339.

~ 2 ~

The Family as a System

Expressions such as "blood is thicker than water" or "the ties that bind" are easily recognizable to most people as ways of defining *family*. But what is it that makes the family so special that its members would lie, cheat, steal, and even die for one another? Family members often do for one another what they would never do for an "outsider." Children will go to extraordinary lengths to protect abusive and neglectful parents. Parents frequently say that they would give their own lives to spare those of their children. Women repeatedly return to abusive spouses. A father will work two jobs just to feed his family.

The power of the family unit is great, often greater than each individual's power or any outside influences. For all cultures, the family holds a central place in society, occupying ancient and sacred territory. Each person's sense of identity is greatly influenced by his or her experience of the family.

~ Family Systems Theory ~

There is a fundamental and profound difference between viewing a family as a group of individuals and viewing it as a system. In a system, individual parts come together to create a whole that is qualitatively different from each of its individual parts. The interactions and relationships among the parts constitute the unique characteristics of the entire system (Barnes, 1985).

The concepts of general systems theories that originated in the early 1920s borrowed from principles of biological science (Barnes, 1985). During this time, there was a push to reconceptualize biological principles due to the dissatisfaction of many scientists regarding how systems were broken down into isolated and discrete specialty areas. This made communication across specialty areas quite difficult.

The reorganization of these biological principles was an attempt to organize biological structures into systems by grouping similar characteristics of pattern, structure, and relationship. Instead of breaking things down according to differences, this concept classifies and groups things according to similarities and views them as parts of a larger common system.

Each family systems theorist described here is influenced by his or her gender, ethnicity, socioeconomic experience, cultural practices, and the families with whom he or she worked. Many contemporary therapists borrow and blend theories and techniques from the various schools of thought and use a more generic approach to family work.

Strategic Techniques: The Palo Alto Group

In the 1950s Gregory Bateson and his colleagues from Palo Alto, California, were among the first in human behavior and psychology to look at the family as a system. Their work, borrowing ideas from science and math, looked at the communication patterns in families with a schizophrenic child (Bateson, Jackson, Haley, & Weakland, 1956). They postulated that the patterns and ways of communicating had a primary influence on the child's mental condition—revolutionary thinking in the field of psychology, which, up to this point, had looked only at individual behavior and intrapsychic feelings.

Bateson's group assessed family function by examining and altering the rule systems, communication patterns, and learning patterns in order to decrease conflict and improve family functioning. The goal of this therapy was to change and develop behaviors through learning and problem solving. From this early work there developed a handful of "family system" schools of thinking, each looking at the family in a slightly different way. By the 1970s, several family systems theories had been developed and adopted into practice.

One of the primary strategies of family systems theory, reframing, continues in use in the 1990s. *Reframing* teaches members to look at old experiences in new ways, which can jolt the family system and thus enable members to think and behave in new, often more healthy, ways. Following is an example of the concept and the technique of reframing:

~~~~~

The parents of an adolescent girl who is getting into trouble at school view her as willful and bad. In addition, over the last 6 months, her parents have strongly suspected that she has been drinking. A school guidance counselor urges the parents to seek help for their daughter because the counselor has noticed a clear change in the young girl over the last few months. The parents feel that all their daughter needs is more punishment, but even this has not helped. The parents agree to see a therapist for help.

Over the course of several sessions with the child and her parents, the therapist finds out that part of the child's distress is about her parents' increased fighting, which is especially bad at night. The child is unable to concentrate on homework, is missing sleep, and seems upset and scared. In order to escape this turmoil, she began to sneak out at night and hang out with other kids who introduced her to beer. She realized that when she drank she didn't "feel" as upset about her parents' fighting and was able to go home and go to sleep. In school, she finds it difficult to concentrate and becomes easily irritated. She argues with her old friends, who are concerned about her, and does not complete school assignments.

Her parents have no idea that their daughter is aware of their serious marital problems and believe that they are doing a pretty good job hiding the truth from everyone. They also have no idea that their fighting is having such a negative impact. The therapist talks with the parents about their relationship and learns first-hand about their increased fighting.

In the therapist's assessment, the child's behavior is attributable to the problem within the family and, in particular, between the parents. The therapist reframes the child's behavior for the parents. She tells the parents that their child's behavior is a message about how she feels and how she is reacting to the marital stress. She is sneaking out and drinking to avoid the fighting, and her behavior and school problems seem to be a response to everything that is going on.

In reframing the situation, the therapist helps to shift the focus of attention and blame off of the daughter and helps the parents to have more empathy for their child and to take more responsibility for their difficulties. Attention is redirected to the parents and the marital issues. The couple agrees to meet for couples therapy, and they agree to allow their daughter to see a therapist. The daughter also reluctantly agrees. The therapist reassures the child that the adults will get the help that they need to take care of their situation and that she will have a safe place in which she can talk about her feelings.

Several months later, the daughter has been able to improve her grades and she is getting into less trouble at school. She sees a therapist once a week and thinks that it is helpful to have someone to talk to. The parents continue to see a couples therapist. Although they have not resolved all of their marital conflicts, they have learned how to contain their problems and are working toward improving their communication.

～ᴗ～ᴗ～ᴗ～

Structural Techniques: The Philadelphia Group

Salvatore Minuchin (1974) and his colleagues from the Philadelphia Child Guidance Clinic in Pennsylvania maintain a slightly different view of the family system, in accordance with their clients, who are primarily from poor, urban neighborhoods. Minuchin maintains that a change in the external environment can have a dramatic and positive influence upon an individual and a family system (Minuchin, 1967, 1976).

This model is more structural and less behavioral than that of the Palo Alto group. Instead of looking at rule systems, it looks at the interactions among individual members. Haley, an early colleague of Bateson, worked with Minuchin, particularly studying the boundaries that surround members and the power structures within families. A *boundary* is a concrete or invisible marker that delineates or separates one person from another. The boundary is the threshold across which information passes and exists along a continuum of distance versus closeness, with much variation in between. Each individual and family has its own boundary comfort threshold. Ideally, boundaries should be permeable, allowing movement and communication among members and with the outside world. Optimally, boundaries should be flexible and clear, always present, and allow for adjustments. In this school of thought, boundaries are thought to surround the entire family, each member, and different subgroups within the family, which are formed by members with common roles such as spouses or siblings. Closed, rigid boundaries do not allow family members to enter or exit the family and prevent communication and flexibility within the family. Open, permeable boundaries allow members to move back and forth with ease from the family to the outside world and also allow communication and change within the family. Clear boundaries encourage appropriate rules, role clarity, and hierarchy, while undelineated boundaries cause confusion and a breakdown of roles and functioning. In some cases, however, the boundaries can be too open, making it difficult to tell what the specific rules and roles are. Also, personal privacy can be violated, leaving members feeling vulnerable and unsafe. Relationships in the family become enmeshed, hindering the development of strong separate identities. Boundaries can also be too rigid. In this case, there is distancing from one another and the outside world. Relationships lack closeness and people disengage from one another. Rigid boundaries do not allow for open or spontaneous communication and so people disconnect from one another and from the outside world.

Haley also developed the idea of *coalitions* or special relationships that form between family members and at cross-generational boundaries (Bateson et al., 1956). For example, when a mother and daughter gang up on the husband/father, the mother has pulled the

daughter into the spouse subsystem and enlisted her in a coalition. More pathologically harmful, domestic violence and incest violate boundaries and abuse power to create unhealthy alliances and collusions of secrecy among family members.

The primary goal of the family intervention Haley and colleagues advocate is to relieve maladaptive family functioning by addressing patterns of family interactions and by restructuring the boundaries of relationships (Sargent, 1983). When the external influences on a person—especially relationships that have an impact upon a person's life—are changed, the individual is thought to be able to change (Bateson et al., 1956).

Conflict resolution, another concept of family therapy, was promoted by Ackerman and adopted by Minuchin. Ackerman (1958) believed that one had to recognize hidden conflicts among family members in order to resolve them and to help improve relationships.

Improving Communications: Virginia Satir   Virginia Satir's work with the Philadelphia group led to the development of her own model and style of family therapy. Her strategies were more humanistic, focusing on aspects of increased self-worth and self-esteem, effective communication, and appropriate family rules (Satir, 1972). She emphasized the positive and loving qualities in people and saw people as inherently wanting to do good. Satir believed in developing a collaborative relationship with the family and creating a safe therapeutic environment in which family members can openly communicate with one another. She believed that the therapist should model open communication skills, honesty, and acceptance.

Myth and Paradox: The Milan Group

In another distinctive group, the Milan group, members bridged psychodynamic theory and general systems theory. Their model takes into account the unconscious influences upon family organization as well as its rules and communication systems. In this model, powerful and unconscious rules, myths, and dynamics are believed to have a primary influence upon family members (Selvini Palazzoli, Boscolo, Cecchin, & Prata, 1978).

Therapists identify and interpret these messages and rules while gathering family history. Dramatic revelations can occur by asking parents to relate how they met, how they decided to marry, and if and how they decided to have children. Family stories and myths passed on from one generation to the next can also be examined for the influence they have on current family functioning (Barnes,

1985). This model is especially appropriate when events that occurred in previous generations continue to have a primary influence upon current family functioning.

A mother in a family does not drink at all, under any circumstances. She takes every opportunity to speak about how bad it is to drink, how bad people are who drink, and that no amount of drinking is safe in her eyes. The father, however, enjoys having a beer from time to time. He does not drink every day or even every week and has never had any difficulty not drinking. However, because of his wife's ideas about drinking, he finds himself sneaking the beer. The children are quite aware of their mother's beliefs, but do not know why she thinks this way. They are also aware that their father occasionally drinks a beer but have been asked by him to keep this a secret from Mom. The children are placed in a difficult bind: They do not want to deceive their mother, but they also do not want to get their dad in trouble. The children in this family are developing idiosyncratic notions about drinking behavior and are being forced to keep secrets because of their loyalty to both parents. Over time the children may become confused and angry and begin to manifest these feelings through changes in behavior.

This family's therapist should begin to identify the powerful influences upon the family. After spending some time with this family, the therapist would learn that the mother's father was a severe alcoholic who died in a car crash while drunk. Helping her to relate her strong, negative feelings about alcohol to her father's drinking can begin to free the family from the power of this family story. Next, one can begin to understand and interpret *with* the family how its history has helped to shape relationships. The wife and husband might be encouraged to talk honestly and openly with each other and with the children so that the children can be relieved of their loyalty dilemma.

Triangles: Murray Bowen

Another important theorist, Murray Bowen, developed yet a different model by examining the level of differentiation among family members, or how alike or different each feels in relation to other members. Lack of differentiation in self-development is thought to cause emotional overreactivity among members and lack of individual responses (Liddle, Breunlin, & Schwartz, 1988). In this model, Bowen highlighted the tendency of poorly differentiated families to create "triangles" among themselves, which are similar to coalitions. Two family members having difficulty between themselves may involve a third member to distribute and ease their emotional stress. Conversely, exaggerated differentiation can lead to estrangement and isolation. An individual may become overly differentiated in an attempt to avoid being pulled into what she considers to be an underdifferentiated family system.

Life Cycle Patterns

In the 1980s, theorists discussed the impact of culture, ethnicity, and life cycle changes on the family. Carter and McGoldrick (1980) take a family life cycle perspective that views symptoms and dysfunction in relation to typical function. The family is viewed along a time continuum, current functioning is compared with past functioning, and family tasks and future goals are all considered. This is a multigenerational model that looks at the impact of at least three generations of a family upon current functioning (Carter & McGoldrick, 1980).

This model assumes that certain natural transition points in a family's life cause stress, including the birth of a child, children entering school, young adults leaving home, the joining of families through marriage, the loss of family members through death, and the constellation of the family in later life. Major variations in family cycles include divorce and remarriage. This model highlights the added burden placed upon the family who lives in poverty or who has any other outside negative influences with which to cope. Understanding the impact of these issues upon family functioning is crucial, and helping the family traverse these transitions is a primary goal of therapy.

~ Key Concepts in Family Systems Theory ~

Despite the differences among the various schools of family therapy, there are several key concepts that are generally accepted as ways to understand and evaluate family functioning. The fundamental premise of family systems theory and family therapy is that an individual can best be understood as part of a larger context. People are products of their families and their environments. Family therapists consider it futile to treat an individual in isolation and prefer to work to change familial and environmental interactions as well (Liddle et al., 1988).

Defining the Family

The *family* is defined as a group of people with common ties of affection and responsibility who live in proximity to one another (Sargent, 1983). Individuals can choose to come together through marriage or a commitment of affection and affiliation. There is no ideal, typical, or normal family. Cultural, social, economic, ethnic, and religious factors all shape who a family is and how it functions. In some families, parents are divorced or separated; others have only one parent, because a parent has died or is ill and incapacitated. Some families have stepparents and stepchildren and half brothers and half sisters. Some have adopted children, some have foster children. Some groups of people live together and consider themselves family but are not related.

Nonsummativity *Nonsummativity,* a term borrowed from math and science, describes the idea that the family as a whole system is qualitatively different from the sum of its individual parts. It is a view of family that downplays individual attributes and highlights the family as an interactive and interconnected system.

Circular Causality The idea of *circular causality* is the framework upon which family theory is built. A change in one member of the system produces change in all others; each action within the family elicits a reaction or is in reaction to another member. It is an unbroken chain of events. The image of the mobile (as used by Wegscheider [1979]) illustrates this idea: When you touch a mobile anywhere, the entire structure goes into motion.

Communication *Communication,* both verbal and nonverbal, is how families receive, interpret, and respond to information. Communication within a family and with the outside world occurs by way of feedback loops. Responding to communication can influence a system to change. All systems have communication networks that allow or discourage the passing of information. Behavior is a way of communicating, as those who work with young children know well. A very young child communicates his needs, wishes, and feelings through behavior. One only need witness the temper tantrum of a 2-year-old whose desires are thwarted to learn this point. More often, communication cues are more subtle and harder to read. The way a person holds her body, the tone of her voice, or a particular facial expression are all ways of communicating without using actual words. Words can actually be confusing: A young mother who brought her precocious 3-year-old to a clinic described her as being "bad." The mother was beaming with pride as she said this, and the caregiver was confused. But, to this mother, "bad" meant inquisitive, talkative, and playful—all good things.

Homeostasis   One of the early pioneers in family systems theory, Don Jackson, introduced the concept of homeostasis (Jackson, 1957). *Homeostasis* is a recognized scientific phenomenon that describes how some systems are self-regulating, possessing a primary need to maintain balance. The family system seeks to maintain equilibrium and balance and views anything that may disrupt the status quo with suspicion. Change is difficult for even the healthiest of families and some resistance to change is typical and expected; however, high levels of resistance to change can indicate a serious disturbance in family functioning.

～ Stages of Parenting ～

When a couple comes together to produce a child, each member introduces him- or herself to an entirely new experience. Whether they stay together as a couple, they will forever be connected through their child. If both stay active in parenting, they will share responsibilities and grow and develop in ways made possible only by becoming a parent.

There are several natural stages of development that all parents appear to undergo (Galinsky, 1987). The development of oneself as a parent is dynamic and transactional and dependent upon a variety of external and internal variables, which influence the person and help shape his or her parenting beliefs. Variables such as culture, religion, socioeconomic status, gender, ethnicity, emotional health, maturity, and marital status all affect one's development as a parent, as does having an available support network of family, friends, and community contacts. The parent's ability to provide basic care within the context of a loving and safe environment and level of commitment to care for the child because of the desire for and value of the child also have a tremendous impact. A person's ability to bond with her child has lifelong implications for both, as this is the first attachment an infant makes. An infant's world largely revolves around his or her caregiver. It can be safe, thereby meeting the infant's needs and promoting trust, or scary and unpredictable, which may lead to difficulty with reaching important developmental milestones.

Pre-parenting

Before one actually has a child, there is often a period of thinking about and planning for the birth of a brand-new human being (Galinsky, 1987). This period of preparation provides expectant parents with the opportunity to reconcile themselves to new roles and begin to develop their identities as parents. It is a time when people often review their own childhood experiences and their relationship with their families.

Carol, ACoA and incest survivor, pregnant with her first child: I am stronger now. I am not a victim. Before, I was a victim everywhere I went. I never knew or understood what had happened to me. Looking at my experience and understanding that I was abused and mistreated has really helped me think about how I want to parent my baby. I will not parent like my parents did. I used to be afraid that I would be like my mother. I want my baby to feel loved and safe. I know what it feels like to be scared.

New Parents

The period of adjustment that follows the birth of a baby can be rocky. This is a time when the reality of who this child is can collide with the fantasies and images of the "wished for" child. Many new parents are not prepared for the effort that accompanies parenting a newborn and often find themselves struggling to adjust and meet the multitude of demands placed upon them. This is a crucial time for bonding and attachment and establishing a "goodness of fit" between infant and caregiver.

Mother of two boys: I knew I was in trouble when the nurses brought my screaming and flailing baby to me by announcing, "Here is your wild man." He was nothing like I thought he would be. I thought we would have blissful hours filled with gentle rocking, nursing, and sleeping. Well, did I have it wrong! He screamed for hours at a time for 3 straight months. I was so sleep deprived, I felt physically sick. I often wondered if I was doing something wrong, or if I was just not a good parent. Eventually, he did stop screaming, and we did have many hours of rocking, nursing, and sleeping. He is now an extraordinary child and I am an expert in managing difficult babies. But, while it was happening, it was like a nightmare.

Early Parenting

As the parenting experience continues, most parents feel some relief as the initial dramatic experience ends and they settle into their new roles. Their identities and competence as parents become established, and they begin to develop more sophisticated skills and increased knowledge about the job of parenting. Major adjustments in other relationships have been made, although there remains a need for fine-tuning. The ability to shift boundaries allows the child to move toward a more separate sense of himself while still relying upon the parent(s). Establishment of rules, structure, limits, and methods of discipline all occur as the young child gains mobility and independence. The parent, at this time, also attends to the child's cognitive, social, emotional, and spiritual development by providing opportunities and encouragement in addition to modeling and directly helping the child develop his self-concept. As time goes on, the parent continues to grow and mature in his role as a parent as well as in the journey as a developing person.

Ongoing Parenting

As the child grows, the parent continues to provide age-appropriate experiences and support, including educational opportunities. Events such as the birth of subsequent children or a change in the family configuration through marriage, divorce, or death all require that parents adjust and fine-tune their role and responses.

Mother of two children: My first child was 3 when my second child was born. I felt much more prepared for this baby but anxious about how having another child would affect my relationship with my first child and with my husband. My first child was in love with the world and a handful at that. Having a new baby made it less possible to spend time with him. We figured out creative ways to be together, and other friends and family helped out. He also started in a pre-school program. It was a big adjustment for all of us.

Later Parenting

The tasks of the older parent are focused on launching grown children into the world and adjusting to an empty home. During this time, it is important for a parent to develop interests, hobbies, and activities that are rewarding. Adjusting to the marriage of grown children and welcoming the birth of grandchildren again requires the parents to make adjustments to their identities. Major shifts in the relationship between parent and child often occur at this time as both occupy more common territory as adults. Ongoing tasks in this stage include the continued growth and development of the self and attention to the shifts in relationships with grown children.

Mother of four sending her last child off to college: I have really mixed feelings about seeing my last child move out of our home. I have spent years looking forward to this day when I can have time to myself and do some of the things that I have wanted to do. But I feel sad and a little scared. This is a whole new era for me and it is going to take some getting used to.

Given the variability in families and the numerous cultural, religious, and ethnic influences that exist, determining the common tasks of all families seems daunting, yet it is fairly simple. The health and welfare of all children are dependent upon the family in which they live, and the younger the child the more dependent that child is upon the family.

Abraham Maslow developed a hierarchy of human needs that he believed all people share (Maslow, 1982). This hierarchy moves along a continuum from the most concrete and basic needs to more abstract and esoteric needs. At the top of the list are love, food, and shelter. To exist without love is a human tragedy that can cripple and even kill, and all infants have a primal need for affection, human

contact, and the love of a consistent caregiver. No human can exist without food and many cannot exist without shelter (to do so causes extreme hardship). In order to successfully move on to other levels of development, all children need to have these basic needs met. The other levels have to do with mastery and self-actualization.

Children develop their earliest sense of identity within the context of the family. A sense of identity and belonging, including ethnic, cultural, and religious identities, is influenced by early experiences. Families provide the earliest role models for leadership, communication, and problem solving. A family that is not able to meet the basic needs of all of its members is a family that is not functioning adequately.

～ Family Strengths and Competency ～

It is sometimes much easier to find what is wrong with a family rather than what is right. Every family, regardless of how poorly it is functioning, has areas of relative strength and competency. What follows is one example of finding "the pearl of great price."

A family was presented in which there was domestic violence against the mother and substance abuse by both partners. In addition, the mother of the four young children in this family was depressed, rendering her unavailable to care for her children. As a result, the 8-year-old daughter was getting her siblings up and dressed for school, feeding them meals, and making sure that they had their bookbags and jackets. This child also washed dishes and picked up after her siblings.

The group of seasoned and very experienced clinicians hearing this case listed dozens of negative attributes about the family and, in particular, about the parents. Many were disturbed about how the 8-year-old had become so parentified. Not one positive statement was made about this family until one person spoke up. She made a comment that made everyone pause; in fact, there were audible "mmmm's" as the weight of her statement descended. She agreed that this family was having serious difficulty and, yes, there was cause for the concern about the daughter. However, the daughter seemed to have acquired some very good caregiving skills, which she most likely learned from watching her mother during better times. The mother must have functioned on a more competent level and must have provided care that was good enough for this young girl to imitate.

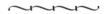

Families may also have strengths about which they are unaware. Like the therapist, they are typically most likely more conscious of what is wrong. But by recognizing positive aspects, families can identify and support strengths to foster resiliency, begin the healing process, and improve their ability to problem-solve.

Sometimes there are barriers, both external and internal, to optimal family functioning. For example, health care problems or housing and job difficulties that families feel unable to negotiate may impede family functioning.

One enormous strength of a family that is easy to identify and commend is their willingness to open their doors to "strangers" and allow them to enter the circle of the private family dance. The magnitude of this leap of faith can never be underestimated for it is extremely difficult for most families to "air their dirty laundry."

Understanding the way in which a family functions is essential in order to understand a child's behavior, and observing and gathering information about the family can be a nice way to begin the therapeutic relationship.

～ References ～

Ackerman, N.W. (1958). *The psychodynamics of family life: Diagnosis and treatment of family relationships.* New York: Basic Books.

Barnes, G.G. (1985). Systems theory and family theory. In M. Rutter and L. Hersov (Eds.), *Child and adolescent psychiatry: Modern approaches* (pp. 216–229). St. Louis: Blackwell Mosby.

Bateson, G., Jackson, D.D., Haley, J., & Weakland, J.H. (1956). Toward a theory of schizophrenia. *Journal of Behavioral Science, 1,* 251–265.

Carter, E., & McGoldrick, M. (Eds.). (1980). *The family life cycle: A framework for family therapy* (2nd ed.). Needham, MA: Allyn & Bacon.

Davidson, M. (1983). *Uncommon sense.* Los Angeles: J.P. Tarcher.

Galinsky, E. (1987). *The six stages of parenthood.* Reading, MA: Addison-Wesley.

Haley, J. (1976). *Problem-solving therapy.* San Francisco: Jossey-Bass.

Jackson, D. (1957). The question of family homeostasis. *Psychiatric Quarterly, 3*(Suppl.), 79–90.

Liddle, H.A., Breunlin, D.C., & Schwartz, R.C. (Eds.). (1988). *Handbook of family therapy training and supervision.* New York: Guilford.

Maslow, A. (1982). *Toward a psychology of being* (2nd ed.). New York: Van-Nostrand Reinhold.

Minuchin, S. (1967). *Families of the slums.* New York: Basic Books.

Minuchin, S. (1974). *Families and family therapy.* London: Tavistock.

Minuchin, S. (1976). *Families and family therapy* (2nd ed.). Cambridge, MA: Harvard University Press.

Sargent, A.J., III. (1983). The family: A pediatric assessment. *The Journal of Pediatrics, 102*(6), 973–987.

Satir, V. (1972). *Peoplemaking.* Palo Alto, CA: Science and Behavior Books, Inc.

Selvini Palazzoli, M., Boscolo, L., Cecchin, G., & Prata, G. (1978). *Paradox and counterparadox.* New York: Jason Aronson.

Wegscheider, S. (1979). *The family trap: No one escapes from a chemically dependent family.* North Crystal, MN: Nurturing Networks.

~ 3 ~

Through a Child's Eyes

A Look at Early Childhood Development

The magic years are the years of early childhood. By magic I do not mean that the child lives in an enchanted world where all the deepest longings are satisfied. These are "magic" years because the child in his early years is a magician—in the psychological sense. His earliest conception of the world is a magical one; he believes that his actions and his thoughts can bring about events. Gradually during these first years the child acquires knowledge of an objective world and is able to free his observations and his conclusions from the distortions of primitive thought. But a magic world is an unstable world, at times a spooky world, and as the child gropes his way towards reason and an objective world, he must wrestle with the dangerous creatures of his imagination and the real and imagined dangers of the outer world.

Selma Fraiberg (1959, p. ix)

The child has a primary need to be regarded and respected as the person he really is at any given time, and as the center—the central actor in his own activity. . . . we are speaking here of a need that is narcissistic, but nevertheless legitimate, and whose fulfillment is essential for the development of a healthy self esteem.

Alice Miller (1981, p. 7)

Selma Fraiberg captures the essence of early childhood when she describes this period as "the magic years" (1959, p. ix). Children are unique beings, different from adults in the way they think, reason, and interact with the world. Jean Piaget, in his theories on cognitive development, described children as "cognitive aliens," not yet able to reason or understand the same way as mature adults (Bradshaw, 1990, p. 22). Alice Miller writes of the child's egocentric nature and the innate healthy narcissistic need to be the central actor in her experience, in order to grow and blossom (Miller, 1981). The phenomena and uniqueness of childhood creates special freedoms and possibilities for children but also places them in a vulnerable position—vulnerable to both the world and the people in it. Freud illuminates this vulnerability when he describes the powerful role parents play in a child's life (Freud, 1908).

Children embarking on their developmental journey remain a source of mystery and wonder. How *do* children develop and grow? How do they understand, respond to, and cope with their world and the people in it? Furthermore, what happens when a child embarks on this journey of development with a family plagued by addiction and trauma? How does the specter of addiction shape and change the child and his journey?

～ Understanding Child Development ～

> Periodically, in his long sleep the newborn baby is aroused by hunger or discomfort and his unfocused milky eyes rest upon an object. In this momentary fixing of his eyes his face takes on a look of concentration and intelligence. "What are you thinking about? Come on, tell us!"
>
> Selma Fraiberg (1959, p. 35)

The intense gaze of the newborn is captivating with its power and purposefulness. One imagines the "wheels turning" in the infant's head as he tries to interpret and interact with the world around him. Although one wants him to divulge the secrets of his inner life, only subtle clues and the interpretations of scientists, theorists, and researchers are available to complete the puzzle.

As a result, there is much debate about the developmental journey of childhood. The disparity between the theoretical perspectives on child development stems largely from conflicting data. Developmental theories emerged primarily from two different sources: 1) by observing the infant and child as he or she grows, and 2) from adults remembering and reflecting on childhood, often through therapeutic experiences. Jean Piaget (1962) developed his theory on cognitive development from observing his young children. Sigmund Freud (1908) drew his theory of personality development from material gleaned from adult patients in psychoanalysis. From these building blocks, theorists created the models for interpreting the workings of the infant's inner world. These theories, when integrated, fit together to create a comprehensive picture of children and childhood.

All of these theories are constructs of the human experience; although they may differ in their organizing principles, they still hold important points in common. The organizing principles of the

psyche, the inner life of the child, use life experiences to create inner formations and memories of how the world and the people in it work. From the beginning of life, the individual forms perceptions, *mental maps*, that shape the way an individual interacts with and perceives the world throughout the life span. In other words, what the individual experiences, from the moment of birth, is the material with which a blueprint of life is created. Profound perceptions of the world as safe or unsafe, nurturing or alienating, are established quickly, as are characteristics of relationships. Although the blueprints of life can be altered and changed by experiences throughout the life span, theorists agree that early experiences in life are the most critical for personality development. Central to this conceptualization of human development is the notion that difficulties in the formation of the personality—unresolved or negatively resolved issues from childhood—can manifest themselves as disorders of functioning in relationships and in the world.

Development as a Transactional Process

One must move from a static model to a more dynamic theory of developmental transaction where there is a continual and progressive interplay between the organism and the environment. The child and his caretaking environment tend to mutually alter each other.

Arnold Sameroff and Michael Chandler (1975, p. 234)

The transactional model addresses the dynamic interplay between the environment and the child. Characteristics of the child shape his or her responses to the environment. These actions, in turn, shape environmental responsivity.

Steven Parker, Steven Greer,
and Barry Zuckerman (1988, p. 1229)

In a discussion of child development, it is important to examine the process of development as it occurs and to understand the roles of both the child and the environment in this process. Sameroff and Chandler (1975), in describing the outcomes of children facing risks to their development, move away from the notion that development is a static, linear process that occurs independently of environmental influences and instead challenge one to see development as a dynamic, transactional process in which the caregivers, the environment, and the child play active roles in shaping and changing developmental and interactional outcomes. Research on developmental risks and subsequent developmental outcomes supports the efficacy of a transactional model of development (Sameroff & Chandler, 1975).

The challenges of and opportunities for understanding children and predicting developmental outcomes grow quite complicated when viewing development as a transactional process. When any part of the developmental equation changes, the child's outcomes are affected because each aspect of the equation plays a significant role in the child's development. Children with very similar life experiences—and even similar risks—may grow up to be very different people.

～ The Infant's World ～

The infant's first knowledge is dependent on actions and perceptual experience. The newborn is ready to experience most, if not all, of the basic sensations given our species from the moment of birth. The baby can see, hear, and smell and is sensitive to pain, touch, and changes in bodily position—the infant is responsive to information from all of the senses.

Jerome Kagan (1984, p. 31)

The infant arrives in the world with innate needs, abilities, and skills. From the first moments of life, she is actively involved in the process of learning about and adapting to her environment (Piaget,

1963). Freud described the infant as an "active agent," seeking pleasure and getting her basic developmental needs met (Moshman, Glover, & Bruning, 1987).

A number of theories about personality development have grown out of psychoanalytic theories of development first conceptualized by Sigmund Freud (Greenberg & Mitchell, 1983; Moshman et al., 1987). Freud, the "father" of psychoanalytic theory, developed a theory of personality development that remains a powerful influence on interpreting human development and the inner world of the child. As one of the first stage theorists, Freud created the organizing principles of *drive* and *ego* as a way of structuring the inner world of the child. Theorists, including Eric Erikson, Melanie Klein, D.W. Winnicott, Margaret Mahler, Heinz Kohut, and Anna Freud, have drawn from Freud's work, rejecting some of his beliefs, expanding on his theories of development, and at times creating substantially separate theories of personality development (Erikson, 1964; Greenberg & Mitchell, 1983; Mahler, 1968; Tyson & Tyson, 1990).

The Id, the Superego, and the Ego

Freud believed that development occurred as a result of one's internal motivations, or *drives,* to seek pleasure—primarily by satisfying one's *libido,* or sexual energy—and relief from pain or tension (Greenberg & Mitchell, 1983; Moshman et al., 1987). According to Freud, the infant's primary goal was to get his basic needs met. According to Freud's theory, each developmental phase represents a shift in libidinal energy, characterized by a desire to resolve specific internal conflicts related to the focus of the libidinal energy. The personality begins to take shape as the individual moves from one stage to the next by attempting to resolve internal conflict in order to achieve a pleasurable, nonconflictual state. The nature of the personality is formed, according to Freud's theory, based on the success or failure to achieve resolution of these internal conflicts.

According to Freud, as the infant's personality begins to take shape, three components—the id, the superego, and the ego—emerge as organizing principles (Dare, 1985; Greenberg & Mitchell, 1983; Moshman et al., 1987). The *id* comprises the individual's needs and desires. The infant, according to Freud, is pure id. Infants need something and they need it now. If left to its own devices, the id would proceed unchecked, seeking its desires without regard to consequences. Therefore, the *superego* emerges as the moral voice and social regulator of the personality. The superego tells the id how guilty and bad it would feel if it behaved without restraint. Finally, there is the *ego*—the great balancer of the id and superego. The ego operates in reality. It works to satisfy the id based on the realities in life, while modulating the moralist voice of the superego. According to Freud, the id, the superego, and the ego are shaped and formed by the persistent drives of development, as the ego is continuously faced with regulating the impulses of the id while adapting to the environment (Greenberg & Mitchell, 1983).

Object Relations Theory and the Holding Environment

Object relations theories of personality development emerged from psychoanalytic theory as interest in the mother–infant dyad grew and theorists began to place a greater emphasis on direct observation of children (Greenberg & Mitchell, 1983). In object relations theory, the *object* (i.e., significant objects in the child's world that become internally represented by the child) takes center stage and becomes a primary organizing principle in structuring the inner life of the child. The object and resulting internal representations include representations of actual external objects (e.g., the breast) as well as representations of the self, significant others, and relationships (Tyson & Tyson, 1990).

Klein, Mahler, Kohut, and others postulated that the infant begins to form the core of her personality based on the internal representations of her experiences with the objects and caregivers in her life. Mahler wrote that "the infant's inner sensations form the core of the self. They appear to remain the central, crystallization point of the 'feeling of self' around which a sense of identity will become established," and believed that the womb of symbiosis (e.g., different nurturing behaviors) gives "psychological birth" to the individual (Mahler, 1968, pp. 11, 49). The infant is able to create internal representations of love objects based on memories of emotional experiences and perceptions.

Kohut expands on his theory of self-development and the significance of the caregiving environment by postulating that the empathetic environment created by the mother figure allows the child to internalize *self-objects* that represent the mother figure/empathetic experience (Greenberg & Mitchell, 1983; Kohut, 1977). These self-objects are then adopted into the child's maturing sense of self and used as material with which to develop a cohesive, organized, independent self.

D.W. Winnicott, a pediatrician and psychoanalyst, provided profoundly influential interpretations of child behavior and mother–infant interactions with his theory of self-development in a relational context. Winnicott's work centered around the child's struggle with individuation and differentiation of the self while maintaining intimacy and connection (Greenberg & Mitchell, 1983). Winnicott believed that the mother figure provides the experiences a child needs for the development of a core self that is individualized, yet connected. According to Winnicott, the infant begins life "unintegrated," with disconnected, free-floating inner experiences. The infant is able to organize his experiences into an integrated self through the mother's organizing and nurturing care. According to Winnicott, the mother provides a "holding environment," within which the infant is contained and nurtured (Dare, 1985; Greenberg & Mitchell, 1983).

The importance of the mother figure is apparent in Winnicott's work, which says this figure should be acutely attuned to the child and mirror the infant's own experiences and gestures so that the infant can integrate his experiences into a healthy self (Greenberg & Mitchell, 1983; Tyson & Tyson, 1990). When the infant becomes connected—through the mother figure—with a sense of his own needs and body functions, he develops a core sense of self that is secure and powerful (Greenberg & Mitchell, 1983; Pine, 1985).

The newborn, first gazing out in the world and stretching her arms wide, sees herself as the center of the world—and she is! She does not differentiate herself from caregivers, instead believing she is a part of a symbiotic whole system where she seeks care and nurturing. Striving to get her most basic needs met, she cries in hunger and fusses to be changed. On cue, the caregiver appears with a bottle and a clean diaper. Amidst the stroking, cooing, and cuddling that accompanies feeding and diapering, the newborn feels safe and supported in the warm nest of her caregiver's arms. It is within this holding environment that the infant begins to first form a sense of self, based on the positive reflections in the mirror of care she receives. As needs are recognized and met, the infant feels powerful and able and satisfied. When the caregiver allows the infant to "just be," the infant has the opportunity to experience her inner state of calm needlessness. These inner sensations of pleasure, satisfaction, and need that become organized and integrated through the caregiver's consistent care form the beginnings of a healthy, competent sense of "I am-ness" (Bradshaw, 1990).

Trust versus Mistrust

Erik Erikson incorporated the organizing principles of drive and ego into his theories on development (Dare, 1985). Although Erikson agreed that there is energy driving development, he believed this energy is psychosocial, not psychosexual, in nature (Erikson, 1964; Moshman et al., 1987). As a result, his stages of development differ from Freud's and encompass the entire life span. Erikson focused more attention and importance on the relational aspects of the child's world, incorporating the significance of the child's environment and relationships into his theory of development with his belief that each stage is driven by an individual's interactional experiences and resolutions of internal conflict.

Erikson's model of human development begins with the trust versus mistrust conflict in the first year of life. Erikson believed that the infant struggles with the most basic conflict: Can I trust the world and the people in it to take care of me? And furthermore, can I trust myself and my abilities to act on the world and get my needs met? Erikson argued that the infant must experience consistent care and need reduction in order for her to develop trust in her abilities and in the world around her.

Attachment

Through attentive care, the infant begins to form the mental representations of the world as a safe, trusting place. The daily experiences of supportive and nurturing interactions between caregiver and infant also form the basis of the attachment relationship. As Bowlby writes, *attachment* is a primary instinctual need necessary for the infant's very survival (Tyson & Tyson, 1990). As the attachment relationship develops, the infant internalizes representations of that relationship to use as blueprints for understanding the nature of future relationships and their functions. Bowlby (1958) postulated that attachment behavior in infants encompasses instinctual responses for attachment need gratification, resolution of internal conflict through maternal contact, and attempts to control anxiety (Bretherton, 1985; Kagan, 1984). Bowlby wrote of the infant's ability to construct working models of attachment figures and integrate the history of attachment relationships into the personality structure (Bretherton, 1985). The child may then be able to call up these representations to seek comfort and relieve anxiety.

Bowlby believed that the infant's interactions with the caregiver as well as the characteristics of the mother figure contributed to the nature of the attachment relationship. He conceptualized the quality of infant attachment and developed models of secure and insecure attachments (Kagan, 1984). Ainsworth expanded on Bowlby's conceptualizations of the quality of infant attachment and described phases of the development of attachment (Ainsworth, 1974). Ainsworth described attachment as developing through four distinct phases.

1. The initial phase of attachment is marked by an infant's social responsiveness that is relatively undiscriminating.
2. In the second phase, the infant becomes more discriminating in her responsiveness to others.
3. The third phase is significant for the infant's contact-seeking, active initiation in proximity-seeking and contact-maintaining behavior.
4. The final phase is described as goal-directed partnerships. The child becomes more adept at predicting his mother's behavior or goals and actively seeks to alter them to meet his needs and keep her close.

Ainsworth also qualified and quantified the nature of infant attachments through her Strange Situation research design (Ainsworth, 1974; Bretherton, 1985), describing them as secure, anxious, avoidant, or anxious/avoidant. A number of subsequent studies on the nature of attachment relationships were able to show risk and poorer outcomes in a number of developmental areas with infants described as anxious or avoidantly attached (Bretherton, 1985; Honig, 1986).

The Relationship Dance

Daniel Stern, a contemporary theorist on the development of self in relation to others, expands on attachment theory by looking at parent–child interaction and its role in the development of attachment (Stern, 1977). He conceptualizes the development of the parent–child relationship as a dynamic transactional process among caregiver, child, and environmental influences, describing their interactions as the "relationship dance"—a series of steps that can flow fluidly and seamlessly if the parent successfully reads and responds to her infant's cues at the same time the infant is successfully able to give signals and respond to the parent's responsiveness (Stern, 1977).

Imagine a young infant waking from a nap. She stretches and gri-
maces as the light meets her eyes. Gazing about, she begins to
fuss and kick her feet. In response to her signals, the parent arrives at her side and begins to coo and whisper soothing noises.
Sensing that the infant is hungry, the parent begins to feed her.
The parent is met with a loving gaze and a calm baby.

Under optimal circumstances, the infant is able to give clear and
readable cues to the parent. The parent feels secure and comfortable
enough to read and respond to those cues. There exists a "goodness
of fit" between parent and child, where both dance partners' perceptions of the other are positive and supportive. The environment, in
the best of circumstances, is also supportive with minimal stress.
When circumstances are less than optimal, missteps in the dance
can lead to frustration, fear, disappointment, and confusion.

Each partner brings his or her own behaviors, perceptions, and
personality to the dance and influences its nature. Fraiberg (1980)
writes of the "ghosts in the nursery"—the history of the parent and
past relationships—that join the dance when parents unwittingly replay interactions from their own childhood experiences being parented. Children also contribute their own unique characteristics to
the interactional process. Thomas and Chess (1977), through their
revolutionary work on infant temperament, were able to demonstrate what appears to be inborn temperamental traits, which can
enhance parent–child interaction but can also challenge parent
receptiveness and responsiveness. Sameroff and Stern, among others, postulated in their work with children at risk that the environment can also contribute to missteps in the dance, particularly when
the environment is stressful and unsupportive (Sameroff & Chandler, 1975; Stern, 1977).

Emotions and the Social Smile

As the infant develops, his innate capacity to feel and express emotions grows and develops as well, although it appears that children
feel and express emotions from the first moments of life (Bradshaw,
1990; Brazelton, 1983). Researchers have been able to identify what
are considered innate emotions in humans—interest, enjoyment,
surprise, anger, distress, and fear—based upon documentation of fa-

cial expressions observable in newborns across cultures (Bradshaw, 1990). Newborns demonstrate intense interest in the environment, often showing joy, disgust, and distress through facial expressions, fussing, or enthusiastic crying, which gradually become more specified as the infant develops (Moshman et al., 1987).

The egocentric nature of the infant prevents her from fully recognizing and understanding emotions in others; her emotional responses typically reflect her needs and perceptions. Although many parents may argue that a newborn is mad *at them,* it is far more likely that the infant's cries are out of hunger or discomfort and are undirected (Fraiberg, 1959). It is generally believed that the newborn infant is unaware of a parent's emotional states but by no means devoid of emotions (Brazelton, 1973). The infant slowly becomes aware of and sensitive to others' emotions, as demonstrated by the appearance of the "social smile" in the first few months of life (Sroufe, 1979). Infants respond with smiles when smiled at and can even frown in response to a stern expression (Moshman et al., 1987).

As the infant develops and becomes more aware of the world around him, he may begin to express frustration and anger when his needs are not met. Infants are also able to express positive affect with a broader range of behavior as they grow. A growing social awakening finds the infant becoming more active in seeking out pleasurable interactions from caregivers. By about 8 months of age, most babies demonstrate feelings of surprise, anger, fear, and sadness (Kuebli, 1994). By the time they are toddlers, children possess a range of emotions, including the subtle shades of positive and negative affect— joy, pride, contentment, satisfaction, hurt, disappointment, rage, fear, grief, and jealousy (Moshman et al., 1987).

Self-Regulation

As the newborn enters the world, she leaves the warm, dark womb to meet lights, sound, and lots of touching, an overwhelming amount of stimulation. Brazelton (1973) describes several observable states of arousal in the newborn and calls attention to reflexive/behavioral responses newborns use to regulate (modulate and adapt to) stimulation. Newborns move from deep sleep, drowsiness, calm alertness, and fussiness to full-fledged distress, depending on environmental stimulation and the child's innate abilities to regulate behavior. Newborns send signals of delight or distress that sensitive caregivers can respond to in order to help the newborn regulate her states of arousal. Newborns follow face and voice when calmly alert and smile in response to caregiver facial expression. Newborns may also sneeze, change color, squirm, avert their gaze, or fuss to communicate that they are feeling overwhelmed or "unregulated." Newborns have a great capacity to "communicate" through their behavior.

Sensorimotor Development

Piaget further delineates the uniqueness of the infant in his theory of cognitive development, which is based upon his conceptualization of learning as adaptation (Moshman et al., 1987; Phillips, 1975; Piaget, 1962). He postulated that children learn (i.e., adapt) through the processes of assimilation and accommodation. Piaget spent many hours observing his own young children and came to believe that infants were active initiators in the learning process. According to Piaget, the infant is aware of his environment and can modify his behavior in response to environmental demands (Ginsberg & Opper, 1988; Piaget, 1963). He can take in (i.e., assimilate) information and apply it to existing mental structures. The infant can also change existing mental structures to accommodate new information. Piaget described these mental structures or maps as *schemas* (Cowan, 1978; Moshman et al., 1987; Phillips, 1975; Piaget, 1963), which are used to understand and organize the infant's world.

Piaget described the first 2 years of life as the *sensorimotor period* of development. He believed that the infant is multisensory and active in the learning process (Cowan, 1978; Kagan, 1984), which is evident when observing infants. Infants learn by throwing their whole bodies and minds into exploring their world and the people in it. Through touch, taste, sight, sound, and manipulation, the infant learns about her own body and the objects in her world. Piaget believed that through sensorimotor exploration, the infant develops increasingly more sophisticated schemas for understanding and interacting with objects. An infant mouthing a book is learning about the nature of the object. An infant throwing his blocks off of a high chair and watching his father repeatedly retrieve them is learning about objects that bounce and also learning about eliciting parent interaction.

Along with this development of more complex schemas, older infants begin to make connections between actions and consequences. An infant makes the connection between throwing blocks and getting attention. Buttons, levers, videocassette recorders (VCRs), and appliances take on great significance for the infant who has learned that his action (pressing the button) causes an exciting consequence (the television goes on). These mean–ends relationships are the beginnings of problem-solving ability in the sensorimotor period.

Piaget postulated that the child develops his ability to learn, think, and reason through assimilation and accommodation as he progresses through a series of developmental stages, each stage marked by an increased ability to think and reason more logically and in the abstract. Practice and imitation are central tenets of Piaget's theories, thought to be primary tools for learning (Piaget, 1962). Piaget emphasized that development was a gradual process with children taking an active role in moving through fluid developmental stages.

Object Permanence

The concept of *object permanence*, first described by Piaget, is another example of an infant's increasing knowledge about the nature of objects in the first year of life. At approximately 8 months, the infant first grasps the notion of permanency as a characteristic of objects. Before this, what was out of sight did not exist. If a parent wanted her infant to stop playing with her earrings, she would place them in a drawer. Gradually, the infant becomes aware of the fact that the object still exists, even if it is out of her line of vision, and now may go in search of the earrings.

Object permanence represents a beginning shift toward more symbolic, abstract thought in the infant (Cowan, 1978; Phillips, 1975; Piaget, 1963). Toward the end of their first year of life, children begin to show evidence of representational thought in their language and play. Verbal language is one of the most obvious examples of this development in cognition. Words themselves are symbolic representations of things, actions, and ideas. Infants become capable of creating mental symbols as their thinking moves toward the abstract, away from sensorimotor behavioral schemas. They begin to use words as representations. Infants will also use representations in their play, as they substitute play telephones for real telephones or blocks for toy cars.

Imitation

According to Piaget (1962), imitation becomes an important tool of learning for infants. Infants take great pleasure in imitating caregiver movements during nursery games, such as "peek-a-boo" and "so big." The infant watches the caregiver's face intently as she makes faces and blows kisses at her baby. The baby struggles to imitate what he sees and suddenly up go his eyebrows as he purses his lips in a kiss! The caregiver exclaims in delight at her baby's imitation. Imitation is a tool used to imitate motor movements as well as language. As the child assimilates new knowledge and develops new schemas, he is able to use more sophisticated and complex imitation to learn new skills. The availability of caregivers to interact with and model for children becomes critical to young infants as they use imitation as a primary learning tool.

Separation Anxiety

The transition to the infant's second year of life is marked by increasing physical separation from the caregiver as the child learns to walk and assert more control with her mastery of "no." Although this also increases emotional and relational separateness, the attachment relationship remains a powerful force in the infant's world. At this time, the attachment relationship is typically marked by "separation anxiety," as the infant solidifies her preference for the significant caregiver (Bowlby, 1958; Bretherton, 1985) and will grieve and protest when that caregiver is unavailable. The infant now sees herself as separate from her caregivers, knows they still exist outside of her field of vision, and feels loss when they are not there.

～ Toddlerhood ～

During toddlerhood, new challenges and adventures confront the caregiver–child dyad.

> This period [toddlerhood] brings [toddlers] face to face with two powerful yet contradictory impulses: the longing to feel safe in the protective sphere of intimate relationships, and the exhilarating thrust of carefree, unrestricted, uninhibited exploration, where one can soar free without looking back at those who are left behind.
>
> Alicia Lieberman (1993, p. 7)

Attachment and Exploration

The drive to be independent and the desire to be connected compose the push/pull life of the toddler. Lieberman (1993) describes these two types of human motivations, prominent in the toddler years, as *attachment* and *exploration*. Toddlers seek to bring the parent close through approaching, following, searching for, clinging to, cuddling, and asking to be picked up, while exploratory behaviors, such as walking, running, climbing, and inspecting, put distance between parent and child (Lieberman, 1993). At no time in human development, except perhaps in adolescence, does the individual struggle with such strong, often opposing, forces (Lieberman, 1993). The child must pull away from caregivers in order to solidify his sense of self, while reconciling his great need for attachment to those caregivers, a connectedness that makes individuation and self-development possible. No child is able to test his own wings and fly without a secure attachment base.

The toddler grasps life with exuberant joy and curiosity. She races forward in the park with great anticipation of what marvels await her, glancing only briefly back at her caregiver before jumping onto the slide. As she climbs to the top, she suddenly realizes how big the slide is and begins to call out frantically for her father. Dad arrives and gently coaxes her down the slide and up again, and down the slide and up again. Now, with a passionate will to master this task, the toddler goes up and down again and again, crying out in triumph and excitement at her success. Dad retreats to a bench as his daughter continues her exploration and play. But she now only goes so far before glancing back to see where her dad is stationed. He is the secure attachment base from which she can explore and master her world.

Sensorimotor Development

Toddlers, according to Piaget, continue in the sensorimotor period of development for much of their second year of life but are clearly moving forward in their development of thinking and reasoning skills (Ginsberg & Opper, 1988; Phillips, 1975). A child's multisensory exploration of her world demonstrates her need *to do* in order to learn—toddlers are learning about themselves and the world through their bodies. Toddlers use imitation and practice endlessly to incorporate new schemas into their behavioral repertoire and refine old ones. Mastery motivation is a powerful drive for toddlers, who want to do everything themselves and want to do it well. Toddlers may want to slide down slides repeatedly or play the same simple games again and again in order to figure them out and master the tasks. Toddlers often crave routine, predictability, and ritual in their world because it helps them to feel safe and allows them to feel masterful.

Autonomy versus Shame/Doubt

Erikson frames the toddler years as a struggle between autonomy and shame/doubt (Erikson, 1964), because of the toddler's struggle to become a skilled, competent, separate individual despite internal doubts about his competence. Through sensitive caregiving, filled with messages of encouragement and reassurance, the child is able to master his doubts and insecurities and strive for independence. A child who is kept safe from harm but also allowed the freedom to explore can learn that the world is an adventurous but manageable place. A child who is treated with respect and positive guidance develops a competent inner core, as opposed to a shame-based sense of self.

Social Awareness

Toddlers increasingly become more verbal, sociable, and vocal about their needs and feelings. They are better able to think representationally and engage in rich fantasy play (Piaget, 1963), which can provide a fascinating window into the inner life of the toddler. They also have a growing awareness of and interest in their bodies and their functions, especially elimination, at this time (Fraiberg, 1959). Freud described this period of development as the anal stage, when the child's energy is, in part, focused on toileting behaviors.

Toddlers also have a growing awareness of other children in their environment. The beginnings of peer social interaction and interactive play can be observed in the toddler years, although negotiating the complex rules of social interaction often remains a challenge (Damon, 1983). It is within the second year of life that the child may display shame, guilt, embarrassment, pride, and empathy (Damon, 1983; Michalson & Lewis, 1985). These emotional states are much more connected to the socialization of the child and her growing awareness of "right and wrong" and "good and bad."

Emotional Struggles

Toddlers have an intense desire to please parents and will do what they can to comply with increasing demands to behave in socially accepted ways (Lieberman, 1993). Toddlers are asked regularly to change their behaviors (e.g., to stop hitting, to use their words, to use the toilet) and become socialized to the larger world. Toddlers struggle valiantly to modify their behavior in the face of caregiver demands. At the same time, though, they are driven to assert their control and maintain their independence, which often puts them at odds with caregivers. This powerful dynamic challenges both the toddler and caregiver to negotiate the rules for living peacefully together. Sometimes the frustration of their own needs colliding with caregiver demands proves too much for the toddler, and she collapses in tears or explodes in a temper tantrum.

With the frustrations that toddlerhood brings (e.g., wanting to "be big" one minute and a "baby" the next, being told "no" countless times, receiving persistent requests to change behavior), emotions run high. Children are able to feel and express emotions before they are able to understand and reflect upon them (Michalson & Lewis, 1985). With a limited repertoire of socially acceptable ways to express their feelings, language ability becomes a critical component in the expression and understanding of emotions. Children typically begin to use words to express their emotions in the second year of life, and can progress rapidly toward verbalizing emotions in others and identifying causes and consequences of emotions.

Anxiety

Feelings of anxiety surface in toddlers primarily around separation and loss of caregivers (Bowlby, 1958; Lieberman, 1993). Separation anxiety is probably one of the most prominent expressions of anxiety in the first years of life. As the toddler grows more independent, he desires his freedom but at the same time is anxious about losing the caregiver entirely (Fraiberg, 1959; Mahler, 1972). Older toddlers, with increasing awareness of right and wrong behaviors through socialization, can become anxious about their desire to please their caregivers. When faced with an angry parent or his own anger, the toddler cannot imagine that the parent still loves him; after all, *he* doesn't feel love for the parent when he is angry (Lieberman, 1993). A parent's anger can cause great anxiety in the push/pull world of the toddler.

Toddlers experience body anxieties as well (Fraiberg, 1959; Lieberman, 1993), especially concerning elimination. Children often feel anxious about the discomfort they feel or the body sensations they cannot control (Lieberman, 1993). Toilet training can be anxiety provoking if children are pressured to be trained before they are ready (Fraiberg, 1959; Lieberman, 1993).

Toddlers, like many adults, fear the unknown (Lieberman, 1993). What is confusing and inconsistent can cause anxiety for a toddler who craves ritual, routine, and predictability. Toddlers, in attempts to master anxiety, play out fears and look to adults for guidance. What they do not understand, they try to interpret with an unsophisticated cognitive system, which often results in illogical conclusions. Therefore, the caregiver must interpret the world for the child and help her to conquer and manage the anxiety she experiences in the typical course of development, because the nature of this resolution will shape the way she experiences and copes with anxiety throughout the life span.

～ The Preschool Years ～

Why dwell on this one-sided view of the two and three year old as a magician? It would be just as fair to call him a scientist, an experimenter, and these things are just what a magician is not! He is a scientist, but he is still a magician. . . even at this stage of development when he seeks causes for phenomena which cannot be accounted for in his limited practical experience, he resorts to magical thinking. Moreover, he tends to explain all unfamiliar or otherwise unexplainable events in his world as caused by human activity, his own or someone else's.

Selma Fraiberg (1959, p. 126)

Magical Thinkers

The preschool years, ages 3–6, are significant for increasing socialization, growing independence, and evolving thinking and reasoning ability. The young child, growing out of toddlerhood, remains a magical thinker, still immersed in egocentric thought and an unrefined sense of logic. Preschoolers lack a clear sense of the boundary between reality and fantasy, believing that monsters *can* live under their beds or that wishing for something *will* make it so. With the belief that they are the centers of their worlds and the cause of events around them, children *are* magicians in their world.

Preoperational Stage

Piaget believed that children, beginning at approximately 2 years of age, make the transition from the sensorimotor stage of cognitive development to the *preoperational stage* of development (Ginsberg & Opper, 1988), therefore ushering in a new era in children's thinking and reasoning skills, marked by the onset of symbolic function (i.e., children's use of mental symbols). The child continues to develop and refine sensorimotor schemas, but he now begins to use mental symbols in both language and play. Thinking and reasoning moves from the concrete to mental schemas and representations. Children begin to solve problems mentally, rather than through trial and error. They can imitate movement and action that is no longer visible to them (Moshman et al., 1987) and use objects in their play to symbolize other objects. They are moving rapidly toward more sophisticated, logical thinking and reasoning. Despite their signifi-

cant leap into the world of mental representations, children still possess a very rudimentary understanding of concepts such as time,
space, causality, and the properties of objects.

Piaget described three different kinds of primitive but methodological reasoning in the preoperational child, which distort reality
and result in what appears to adults to be very illogical conclusions.

1. First, Piaget observed the child's tendency to use *concrete
   reasoning* about a situation based on experience that occurred in the past (Cowan, 1978; Ginsberg & Opper, 1988).
   For example, a child who accompanies his mother to a particular store believes they are buying grapes because that is
   what happened the last time they went to the store.

2. In another type of reasoning, the child's *desires distort his
   thinking,* as he attempts to reason in order to achieve some
   goal. For example, when Piaget's daughter was refused an
   orange because it was green and instead was given chamomile tea, she cried, "Chamomile isn't green, it's yellow already, give me some oranges!" (Ginsberg & Opper, 1988,
   p. 83)—valiantly attempting to reason as best she could why
   she should have the orange.

3. The third type of reasoning is termed *transductive reasoning* (Ginsberg & Opper, 1988), which lies between inductive
   and deductive reasoning. Transductive reasoning goes from
   the particular to the particular, seeing a relationship between two things when there is none. In a classic example
   of transductive reasoning, a 4-year-old boy in a health clinic
   explained to us that his pregnant mother (in acupressure
   treatment for her cocaine addiction) went to the hospital to
   get "dots in her ears so she could have a baby."

A child's thinking skills in the preoperational stage are also in
the here and now, limited to observed realities (Moshman et al.,
1987). The preoperational thinker centers only on a single dimension
of a situation or object, disregarding transformation or processes of
change and, thus, believing it to be irreversible (Moshman et al., 1987).
A more advanced thinker understands that actions can be reversed
and considers that dimension when looking at the situation or object.

The preoperational child, though scientist and investigator, is
still a magical thinker. She remains egocentric in thought, as her
self-development continues to evolve. She thinks in rather black-
and-white terms, unable to see subtle nuances of an event or concept. As a result, she makes inferences and conclusions that are

often illogical and inaccurate. Caregivers remain important inter-preters of the preoperational child's world.

True Self/False Self

Winnicott conceptualized the development of true self/false self as an outcome of the care environment. According to Winnicott, if a child is not allowed the freedom to be solitary, be herself, and dis-cover that she can be in charge of her need satisfaction and is instead expected to be compliant to others' desires, she develops a false self (Greenberg & Mitchell, 1983; Miller, 1981). This *false self* is based on caregiver expectations and perceptions of the child, making the child "the mother's image of her" (Greenberg & Mitchell, 1983, p. 194). The *true self* is the source of spontaneous needs, desires, images, and thoughts and "hides" to protect itself from a threatening envi-ronment. Winnicott postulated that "the false self draws on cogni-tive functions in its anticipation of and reactions to environmental impingement, resulting in an overactivity of mind and a separation of cognitive processes from any affective or somatic grounding" (Greenberg & Mitchell, 1983, pp. 194–195), usually occurring when the self (consisting of desires, needs, emotions, and experiences) re-mains unintegrated and fragmented.

Initiative versus Guilt

As the young child ventures forth, he begins to take a broader view of his environment, actively taking on the world in an attempt to find his place. Erikson describes this stage in the life span as initia-tive versus guilt (Erikson, 1964). The child takes the initiative to master the environment, find his role in the family and community, and feel good about his actions. Positive conflict resolution would mean the child feels greater confidence, independence, and a sense of self in relation to others without feeling guilty or bad that his ini-tiative has done harm. Guilty feelings (e.g., "I've done something bad") can manifest themselves when a child receives negative or ambivalent messages from caregivers about his active initiative (e.g., "You've done something bad").

Young children look to adults as models for the social world. Children identify with caregivers, often along gender lines, and "try on" adult roles in their play. A look into an early childhood class-room will find children playing teacher, doctor, or maybe Mommy and Daddy. Children watch caregivers very carefully, imitating actions and behaviors in an attempt to be just like the important adults in their lives. Young children begin to notice how people talk to each other, treat each other, and cope with life situations. At no time is it more clear that young children imitate what they see than in the preschool years.

Sigmund Freud first described defense mechanisms as tools of adaptation (Dare, 1985), postulating that children who are abused or otherwise victimized by significant caregivers often identify with them and take on some of their personality characteristics as a way to save their own sense of self. If one "becomes" the aggressor, Freud conceptualized, one cannot be a victim. Anna Freud developed the concept of *identification with the aggressor* as a defense mechanism employed by victimized children (Greenberg & Mitchell, 1983), believing that defenses can be motivated by external threat (Greenberg & Mitchell, 1983). Victimized children identify with—and try to emulate—the abuser to defend themselves against external threats to the self (Greenberg & Mitchell, 1983).

Anger

Children in the preschool years begin to expand their repertoire for expressing emotions but continue to feel emotions somatically and struggle to verbalize what they are experiencing. Emotions cause a physiological response in humans (Fraiberg, 1959; Moshman et al., 1987), and children have less ability than most adults to identify and express what they are feeling. They often resort to more primitive means of expression, especially when in distress.

Infants and toddlers certainly feel anger, typically expressing this emotion through crying, hitting, and throwing tantrums. As children enter their preschool years, their anger becomes much more focused and sometimes oriented to revenge. Children direct their anger at objects and people (and sometimes themselves). A preschooler will shout "I hate you" or break something that is valued by the target of his anger to get revenge for whatever sparked the anger.

Feelings of anger can be overwhelming and scary for young children, and they often react impulsively, lacking any inner controls for these intense feelings. Young children feel angry but do not always have a means of expression that is acceptable or tolerated by adults. Patience, tolerance, and guidance can support a child's healthy expression of anger. Young children live in a frustrating world where they want to be big but cannot always do adult things. Their bodies aren't always ready to do what their minds want to do. Anger is a typical response to frustrating situations, and expressing that anger in safe, nondestructive ways is an important task of early childhood.

Empathy

Empathy is defined in the *Merriam-Webster's Dictionary* as "the capacity for participating in the feelings or ideas of another" (Woolf, 1974, p. 237). It can also be understood as a person's capacity to share and connect with another person's situation and emotional experience. Empathy helps to regulate social behavior in humans: to be empathetic is to be compassionate; to empathize is to connect. Fraiberg (1980) writes of troubled parents who are able, through connection with their own childhood feelings, to empathize with their children and nurture them. The parent who is disconnected from his or her own feelings and troubled past and unable to empathize with her fussy baby is at risk for striking out. Research conducted by Letourneau found that more empathetic mothers, even when under stress, are far less likely to physically harm their child than nonempathetic mothers (Honig, 1986).

The capacity for empathy becomes an important component in the development of prosocial behavior (Damon, 1983). Empathy has its genesis in early childhood and is believed to grow over the life span. As children become more social beings, making connections

and relationships outside of their immediate family circles, they begin to develop a sense of right and wrong, what Fraiberg (1959) describes as the "dawn of conscience" (p. 242). Moral development advances with socialization as the child evolves a sense of self in relation to another person. Children begin to notice how another feels and the consequences of negative actions.

Hoffman postulates that the development of empathy is intimately related to a child's evolving sense of self and self in relationship to another person (Moshman et al., 1987). Infants may respond with distress to another infant's crying, but they cannot make the leap to understanding the separateness of the other infant's experience. In the second year of life, according to Hoffman, a child has a better distinction between himself and the individual in distress but still lacks the refined ability to take the other's perspective. By the preschool years, Hoffman believes that a child can understand that people have their own emotions and needs and can respond in kind (Moshman et al., 1987).

Feshbach (1977) postulated that the capacity for empathy develops out of a child's increased cognitive, affective, and social abilities. The affective component regards the child's emotional responsiveness to another's joy or distress. The cognitive aspect involves role taking. Can the child take the other person's perspective or walk in another's shoes? Both of these components are within the capacity of only the preoperational child, requiring more sophisticated thinking than the younger, more egocentric child possesses. The development of empathetic ability is thought to be affected by social and contextual influences in the environment and supported through modeling, reinforcement, and opportunities to practice empathy for others (Damon, 1983).

Grief

Part of being human is experiencing loss and the grief and sadness that follow. Individuals grieve with great intensity when a loved one dies but also grieve to a different extent upon the loss of dreams, possessions, lifestyles, and abilities. Children grieve with as much intensity as adults and in many of the same ways, although it often is quite painful to accept this knowledge.

Bowlby (1958) described grief reactions in infants experiencing separation anxiety, giving rise to the notion that even very young children have some capacity to grieve. Many would argue that true grief requires a certain level of cognitive ability (Moshman et al., 1987), but it is clear that even very young children experience loss deeply and react intensely, particularly to loss of a caregiver (Furman, 1986), which can occur through death, divorce, separation, and family disruption.

According to Pynoos and Nader (1990), "children respond similarly to adults in the nature, frequency, and duration of grief reactions" (p. 341). Children will deny reality, fantasize and dream about being reunited with the loved one, and experience rage, separation anxiety, depression, sadness, and hopelessness (Honig, 1986; Pynoos & Nader, 1990). Children may regress in their behavior, have toileting accidents, sleep disturbances, and other behavioral disruptions. Children experiencing loss, whether it is the loss of a caregiver or the loss of a home or the loss of a pet, respond with a range of feelings that is often hard and confusing for the children. Just like the grieving process for adults, children perceive and experience the loss in a way that is unique to them and their own histories. Regardless of the nature of the loss, grief can accompany the experience even for the youngest of children.

Experiencing the death of a loved one is particularly confusing for a young child because of limited cognitive abilities to understand death. Young children may not have a concrete understanding that dead means you are not alive, you do not move, and your body does not work anymore (Furman, 1986). Furthermore, young, preoperational children believe death is reversible. They do not grasp the finality of it and believe that loved ones will return. Young children cannot think in the abstract, so more religious or philosophical explanations of death are sometimes distorted by the child into confusing or frightening scenarios. Children in the preoperational stage of cognitive development, who are told death is "like sleeping," take that literally and may fear that they will die in their sleep. Young children who are told that Daddy is in heaven may imagine him floating on a cloud in the sky, ready to jump to earth.

What children experience and learn during the wonderful and magical years of childhood definitively shapes and forms their personalities. Much can be learned about one's self by examining childhood experiences, understanding how these have influenced the developmental journey.

> I know what I really want for Christmas. I want my childhood back. I know it doesn't make sense, but since when is Christmas about sense, anyway? . . . This is about a child of long ago and far away, and it is about the child of now. In you and in me. Waiting behind the door of our hearts for something wonderful to happen.
>
> Robert Fulghum (1988)

～ References ～

Ainsworth, M. (1974). The development of infant–mother attachment. In B. Caldwell & H.N. Riccuti (Eds.), *Review of child development research* (pp. 1–93). Chicago: University of Chicago, Society for Research in Child Development.

Bowlby, J. (1958). The nature of the child's tie to his mother. *International Journal of Psychoanalysis, 39,* 350–373.

Bradshaw, J. (1990). *Homecoming: Reclaiming and championing your inner child.* New York: Bantam.

Brazelton, T.B. (1973). *Neonatal Behavioral Assessment Scale.* Philadelphia: J.B. Lippincott.

Brazelton, T.B. (1983). Precursors for the development of emotions in early infancy. In R. Plutchik & H. Kellerman (Eds.), *Emotions, theory, research & experience* (Vol. 2). New York: Academic Press.

Bretherton, I. (1985). Attachment theory: Retrospect and prospect. In I. Bretherton (Ed.), *Growing points of attachment: Theory and research* (pp. 3–35). Chicago: University of Chicago, Society for Research in Child Development.

Cowan, P.A. (1978). *Piaget with feelings: Cognitive, emotional and social dimensions.* New York: Holt, Rinehart & Winston.

Damon, W. (1983). *Social and personality development.* New York: Norton.

Dare, C. (1985). Psychoanalytic theories of development. In M. Rutter & L. Hersor (Eds.), *Child and adolescent psychiatry: Modern approaches* (2nd ed., pp. 204–215). New York: Blackwell Scientific.

Erikson, E. (1964). *Childhood and society.* New York: Norton.

Feshbach, N.D. (1977). Studies on the empathic behavior in children. In B.A. Maher (Ed.), *Progress in experimental personality research* (Vol. 8). New York: Academic Press.

Fraiberg, S. (1959). *The magic years: Understanding and handling the problems of early childhood.* New York: Charles Scribner & Sons.

Fraiberg, S. (1980). Ghosts in the nursery: A psychoanalytic approach to the problems of impaired infant–mother relationships. In S. Fraiberg (Ed.), *Clinical studies in infant mental health: The first year of life* (pp. 101–136). New York: Basic Books.

Freud, S. (1908). *The sexual enlightenment of children.* New York: Collier Books.

Fulghum, R. (1988). *All I really need to know I learned in kindergarten.* New York: Villard.

Furman, E. (1986). Helping children cope with death. In J.B. McCracken (Ed.), *Reducing stress in young children's lives* (pp. 35–40). Washington, DC: National Association for the Education of Young Children.

Gilligan, C. (1982). *In a different voice: Psychological theory and women's development.* Cambridge, MA: Harvard University Press.

Ginsberg, H., & Opper, S. (1988). *Piaget's theory of intellectual development* (2nd ed.). Englewood Cliffs, NJ: Prentice Hall.

Greenberg, J.R., & Mitchell, S.A. (1983). *Object relations in psychoanalytic theory.* Cambridge, MA: Harvard University Press.

Honig, A.S. (1986). Stress and coping in children. In J.B. McCracken (Ed.), *Reducing stress in young children's lives* (pp. 142–167). Washington, DC: National Association for the Education of Young Children.

Kagan, J. (1984). *The nature of the child.* New York: Basic Books.

Kohut, H. (1977). *The restoration of self.* New York: International University Press.

Kuebli, J. (1994). Young children's understanding of everyday emotions. *Young Children, 49*(3), 36–47.

Lieberman, A.F. (1993). *The emotional life of the toddler.* New York: Free Press.

Mahler, M. (1968). *On human symbiosis and the vicissitudes of individuation.* New York: International University Press.

Mahler, M. (1972). On the first three subphases of the separation-individuation process. *International Journal of Psychoanalysis, 53,* 333–338.

Michalson, L., & Lewis, M. (1985). What do children know about emotions and when do they know it? In M. Lewis & C. Saarni (Eds.), *The socialization of emotions* (pp. 117–139). New York: Plenum.

Miller, A. (1981). *The drama of the gifted child: The search for the true self.* New York: Basic Books.

Moshman, D., Glover, J.A., & Bruning, R.H. (1987). *Developmental psychology.* Lincoln, NE: HarperCollins.

Parker, S., Greer, S., & Zuckerman, B. (1988). Double jeopardy: The impact of poverty on early child development. *Pediatric Clinics of North America, 35*(6), 1227–1240.

Phillips, J.L. (1975). *The origins of intellect: Piaget's theory* (2nd ed.). San Francisco: W.H. Freeman.

Piaget, J. (1962). *Play, dreams and imitation in childhood.* New York: Norton.

Piaget, J. (1963). *The origins of intelligence in children.* New York: Norton.

Pine, F. (1985). *Developmental theory and clinical press.* New Haven, CT: Yale University Press.

Pynoos, R.S., & Nader, K. (1990). Children's exposure to violence and traumatic death. *Psychiatric Annals, 20*(6), 334–344.

Sameroff, A., & Chandler, M.J. (1975). Reproductive risk and the continuum of caretaker casualty. *Review of Child Development Research, 4,* 187–243.

Sroufe, L.A. (1979). Socioemotional development. In J.D. Osofsky (Ed.), *Handbook of infant development.* New York: John Wiley & Sons.

Stern, D. (1977). *The first relationship: Mother and infant.* Cambridge, MA: Harvard University Press.

Stern, D. (1985). *The interpersonal world of the infant: A view from psychoanalysis and developmental psychology.* New York: Basic Books.

Thomas, A., & Chess, S. (1977). *Temperament and development.* New York: Brunner/Mazel.

Tyson, P., & Tyson, R. (1990). *Psychoanalytic theories of development.* New Haven, CT: Yale University Press.

Woolf, H.B. (Ed.). (1974). *Merriam-Webster's dictionary.* New York: Simon & Schuster.

~ 4 ~

The Impact of Addiction on the Family

I reach out and no one reaches back,
I fall but no one helps me up,
I cry but no one wipes my eyes,
I scream but no one hears me,
I wait for that special hug
all I get is "you're nothing but a bug."
But what I really need is to be loved,
but how can I be loved when I can't even find that special hug?
I look for guidance to point me in the right direction,
instead I get total rejection.
"Why does all this happen to me?" I ask. What didn't I do?

Cassandra, an ACoA, in recovery from cocaine addiction

The profound isolation, crippling loneliness, and rejection Cassandra describes in her poem is an eloquent portrayal of how it often feels growing up in an addicted family system. Cassandra's mother and father were both alcoholics. Her father came and went unpredictably from her life, and when he was there, he was often drunk and violent. Cassandra's mother was preoccupied with her own relationship with Cassandra's father and did not seem to even notice Cassandra. At best, Cassandra would gain her mother's angry attention when she misbehaved. Cassandra cannot remember being physically comforted as a child.

Her life reflects the weaving of intergenerational webs of addiction and impaired parenting. Cassandra now struggles courageously with her own addictive disease, while trying to give her children the care and nurturing she never received. In her recovery, Cassandra is healing her emotional wounds from childhood and changing destructive patterns of neglect and abuse. Her recovery is not only helping her but also giving her children an opportunity to break free of the cycle of addiction.

Whether a child is exposed to alcohol or other drugs in utero or in the environment in which she lives, that child is profoundly affected by the experience. But how are children and other family members affected by exposure to alcohol, other drugs, and the disease of addiction? What happens to the children, partners, parents, and siblings of the addict? How do they respond to and cope with the disease? How is the family system shaped and changed by the specter of addiction? And, finally, what happens when children of addicts grow up to parent their own children? This chapter elaborates on each of these questions.

⁓ Addiction as a Family Disease ⁓

Addiction is defined as a disease, not just of the individual but of the entire family. Stephanie Brown (1985) describes addiction as a family disease, "with all family members suffering the consequences of one member's alcoholism and all seen to play a role in maintaining the destructive interactional patterns that result from alcoholism" (p. 235). Each member struggles in his or her own way with the addiction, developing individual ways of coping with the disease.

As a child, I felt lost in the crowd. I felt it was my fault. If I would just disappear everything would be okay. Somewhere along the line I learned "don't talk, don't trust, don't feel."

Patty, an ACoA in recovery

I had been using alcohol to anesthetize myself since I was like 11 years old.

Tina, an ACoA in recovery

Many family members are overwhelmed as painful and confusing feelings begin to surface in response to the addict's disease. Cassandra and other adult children describe a process of closing off, turning inward, and numbing out in response to the painful realities of their lives. Family members struggle to adapt and survive, employing numerous defenses to ward off the pain. These defenses cover up true feelings, causing the family to live in a delusional state in which reality and feelings are denied and distorted. As the disease progresses within the family, each member builds stronger defenses, which serve to further hide the pain and continue the trap of delusion.

The Elephant in the Living Room

As reality becomes more confused and denial escalates in the addicted family system, the disease becomes similar to an elephant in the living room, which no one "sees" or talks about (Hastings & Typpo, 1984). A child would never overlook an elephant in the living room. ("Hey, there is an elephant in the living room. Doesn't anyone else see it?") When adults behave as if there is no elephant, the child experiences a distorted reality. The internal and external realities for all family members, in fact, become quite disparate. Messages from within the family ("What elephant? I don't see any elephant!") are very different from what the child is experiencing emotionally. ("The elephant scares me. I don't like it, but no one else even sees it!") Deceptions and distortions are the rule, and the reality of the disease is denied. ("There is no elephant.") This leaves all family members at odds with their internal experiences and serves to further reinforce their denial. ("Well, if no one else sees the elephant, maybe it is not really there. Maybe there is something wrong with me.") This conflict causes extreme confusion, which can be very disturbing for the youngest members of the family. ("I can't trust my feelings. I guess I was wrong about the elephant. There must be something wrong with *me*.") For example, throughout their childhoods, Cassandra and Andrea had tremendous difficulty sorting out the confusing messages from home, trusting their instincts, and deciphering their emotions.

Cassandra, an ACoA: My father was drunk and yelling, when I asked my mother what was wrong, she said that Dad had a bad day at work and to leave him alone. I knew he was drunk, but Mother said he wasn't.

Andrea, an ACoA: My parents were both alcoholics. When my father was drunk, he would delight in contradicting even the most simple of statements. If I would say the sky was blue, he would say it was purple. One time my mother even forgot my name as I stood by her bed while she was in a drunken stupor.

Action/reaction processes such as those experienced by these young women spiral the addicted family system into continued denial, confusion, and distortion in which the disease of addiction becomes the central organizing principle of the family (Brown, 1985). As members hide behind their defenses in attempts to adapt to the system, they become locked into survival patterns and behaviors (Wegscheider-Cruse, 1981). The dysfunction that these children live with each day shapes and forms their views of themselves, relationships, and the world. Children often become stuck in maladaptive patterns of coping and transfer them to the larger social environment. Children of alcoholics are at risk for a range of cognitive, emotional, and behavior problems and report higher levels of anxiety, depression, and stress (Alcohol Alert, 1990). Steinhausen, Godel, and Nestler (1984) reported increased emotional problems in both female and male children of alcoholics, but sons of alcoholics run at least a four times greater risk of becoming alcoholic than daughters (Goodwin, 1985). Historically, girls had appeared to be less vulnerable to the effects of familial substance abuse than boys, but it is now more widely believed that girls simply display distress differently. In girls, these effects often appear later, causing depression, eating disorders, and a tendency to become involved in destructive relationships (Logue & Rivinus, 1991). Female children of alcoholics have been found to exhibit higher frequencies of physical stress-related symptoms such as headaches, nausea, and vomiting, while male children have been found to exhibit more speech, behavior, and conduct disorders (Nylander & Rydelius, 1982).

Why, in my family, are kids not able to talk or to express their feelings? This causes little people to grow with emptiness, anger, confusion, and loneliness.

Gina, an ACoA in recovery

Intergenerational Cycles of Family Dysfunction

Addictive disease is remarkable for the intergenerational family cycles of dysfunction it perpetuates. Children in addicted family systems do what their own parents did growing up in their addicted family systems. Faced with the confusion, chaos, and distortions of the addicted family system, they work to understand their environment, adapt to it, and survive. Children living with addictive disease and the accompanying trauma, caught in the throes of a vicious circle, often grow up to repeat the cycles of pain and illness (Ackerman, 1983). Table 1 highlights some of what a child can live with growing up in an addicted family. For most adult children from addicted environments, what comes around goes around. Poor models for parenting often leave them ill-equipped to parent. Coupled with the baggage from a history of trauma and substance abuse, the task of parenting can be overwhelming. Because of the family disease and dysfunction, Gina's parents were unable to parent her effectively, lacking the experiences every parent needs in order to become a nurturing caregiver. To further complicate matters for Gina, society's unrealistic expectations about parenting await her as she attempts to parent her own children.

Table 1. What families live with and learn in an addicted family system

- Anger
- Chaos
- Compulsive control
- Depression
- Disordered relationships
- Emotional and physical abuse
- Fear
- Impulsive behavior
- Intergenerational cycles of addiction
- Mistrust
- Neglect
- Shame and guilt
- Unhealthy coping strategies

American culture perpetuates the myth that all people should have the innate ability to parent effectively by expecting adults, in general, and women, in particular, to instinctively know how best to care for their children. This myth places an undue burden on all parents. Adults learn much about parenting from the models available to them, namely their own experiences being parented (Galinsky, 1987). Therefore, it is especially difficult for parents struggling to overcome their own traumatic histories, and the often accompanying addiction and low self-esteem, whose only models for parenting have been seriously flawed. Furthermore, many women derive their sense of identity from their views of themselves as parents. There is a strong urge to be the "perfect parent," and being anything less than perfect can be devastating to someone already feeling inadequate and incompetent.

You know, the first child, the perfect mother, the perfect little family. Well it didn't turn out that way.

Didi, an ACoA in recovery

Fraiberg, Adelson, and Shapiro (1980) poignantly describe this intergenerational cycle: "In every nursery there are ghosts. They are the visitors from the unremembered past of the parents; the uninvited guests at the christening" (p. 101). These ghosts shape the interactions between parent and child, who often find themselves reenacting a moment or scene from the parent's past. These ghostly intrusions, however, are not always harmful and can be banished from the nursery under healthy circumstances (Fraiberg et al., 1980). It is when "they have been present at the christening for two or more generations" that significant problems arise: "While no one has issued an invitation, the ghosts take up residence and conduct the rehearsal of the family from a tattered script" (Fraiberg et al., 1980, p. 101).

～ Issues in the Addicted Family System ～

Trust versus Mistrust—A Lifelong Issue

It seemed like I grew up by myself, always had to depend on me, nobody else. There's nobody ever around that I could trust, even my father.

Ida, an ACoA in recovery from alcohol and heroin addiction

I was a man searcher. I trusted men more than I trusted women.

Patty, an ACoA in recovery

Trust is a major developmental issue in the lives of children and can be a lifelong struggle for those from addicted family systems (Ackerman, 1983; Brown, 1985; Woititz, 1983). In addicted family systems, trust is often impaired early in a child's development. If the caregiver is not consistently available to meet the child's basic needs in the first years of life, that child may not learn that the world is a caring place in which adults are predictably available. When a child is not responded to appropriately or is met with unpredictable responses, the resolution of the trust/mistrust conflict can become quite complicated. The discrepancies between a child's external reality and internal emotions leave her confused about whether she can trust others. She also will ultimately begin to question whether she can trust herself and her feelings. According to Erikson (1964), however, the child must still resolve the conflict between trust and mistrust, forming some notion about the world, the people in it, and her own thoughts and feelings. This internal conflict can remain a confusing issue for children of addicts, leaving them struggling throughout their lives with relationships. They may have a very difficult time trusting their own feelings, their thoughts, and their "gut" intuition and perhaps view the world as a fearful, unsafe place.

Attachments and Relationships

I mean, I would run the streets. I was 13 years old running the streets all times of the night. I looked for a lot of negative attention. I was never secure about things, 'cause I had nobody there, no guidance. It was what Lorna wanted to do, you know.

Lorna, an ACoA in recovery

The Importance of Early Relationships There is general agreement among theorists and researchers that there are "ingredients," including consistency, nurturance, empathy, and bonding, to forming healthy attachments and relationships (Ainsworth, 1974; Bowlby, 1958; Stern, 1985). Early relationship experiences are the building blocks for attachments throughout the life span. From the first year of life, children begin to learn the function of relationships through care and interactions from primary caregivers. Children form internal working models of relationships based on these early interactions. Mental representations of caregivers are created, and interactions with others are internalized. These internal objects, or *introjects* as they are known in object relations theory, are thought to shape and influence the development of self in relation to others

(Greenberg & Mitchell, 1983) and serve as points of reference for understanding and functioning in future relationships.

For example, Cassandra saw relationships as confusing, mistrustful, and potentially dangerous throughout her childhood and young adulthood. As a result, she isolated herself from others and did not seek help for her problems. Most damaging, she was unable to determine whom she could trust and whom she could not and placed herself in dangerous and destructive relationships time and again. Cassandra also acted out her worst fears. She alienated and abused people who tried to get close to her, "pushing them away before they pushed me away."

Relationships and Self-Development   Children want and need to see their caregivers as "good" and eternally loving, as their senses of self-worth come from the messages received from their caregivers. Object relations theorists view the caregiver as the mirror in which the child's sense of self is reflected and believe that the child requires an internalized model of the "good" caregiver to use as material for self-development (Greenberg & Mitchell, 1983). Under healthy circumstances, the child uses this internal representation to develop his own ego and sense of self.

When a parent is abusive or neglectful (i.e., not a "good" caregiver), the child becomes confused and, lacking any positive interactional experiences, has difficulty creating an internal representation of a nurturing caregiver (Herman, 1992). When the child looks in the mirror, a demeaning and abusive parent reflects basic negative images, causing ego development to falter and confused feelings for the caregiver to surface, which are increasingly difficult to resolve.

Children, in trying to resolve their conflicting feelings about addicted or abusive caregivers, often may reject, or "split off," their negative feelings in an attempt to "save" the good caregiver image. These feelings are then projected onto others or, often, upon themselves. Children turn their anger inward, blame themselves for the abusive behavior, and see themselves as deficient and unworthy of respect and care. Children faced with the overwhelming task of managing both negative and positive feelings toward such a significant other begin to think in polarized ways—people become either good or bad, with nothing in between. If the parent is good (the child *must* see him that way), then the child *must* be bad. Children, of course, carry this polarized thinking into adulthood, judging people, programs, and their own children in this primitive way.

As children struggle with the family disease, dysfunctional behavior is witnessed again and again, often by teachers, counselors, and others who work with the children. If children have been mis-used and abused in familial relationships, they can have a very dif-ficult time trusting and connecting with others. They may see relationships as threatening or painful. They may have learned that the function of a relationship is to use someone. Even worse, some children who have never been able to form attachments to care-givers grow up to live in a type of ongoing social and emotional isolation by withdrawing or alienating others with destructive, anti-social behavior (Ackerman, 1983).

Unhealthy Coping Strategies

I went home to my mother and fought and fought and fought and fought. And she drank a lot and I drank with her.

    Donna, an ACoA in recovery from cocaine and alcohol addiction

Children exposed to a family member's alcohol or drug abuse strug-gle to cope with the pain, confusion, and chaos, using any tools available to them. Often, however, their only models of coping—the adults in the family system—exhibit unhealthy and destructive behavior. And children, who from an early age are able to put infor-mation together and form conclusions about what is happening around them, often derive illogical and inaccurate messages (see Chapter 3) from these actions.

In a storytime activity in a Boston child care center, preschool children were asked how adults involved in a conflict should resolve their differences without violence. Three of the children reported that they should "drink" or "smoke" something. When questioned further, they described their own parents' fighting at home. One boy said that when his dad yells, he drinks something to "be quiet." A girl described her parents sitting down to smoke cigarettes after an argument, "Then they felt better."

Although children's thinking and reasoning skills are still devel-oping, the inquisitive minds of the toddler and preschooler notice everything. As children venture into the world, they learn more about people, relationships, actions, and feelings through observa-tion. A visit to a preschool classroom during dress-up time confirms this notion. Children identify with important adults in their lives and "try on" adult roles as they play. They want to be "daddies" and "mommies" and "teachers" and do everything the important adults in their lives do. They are watching adult behavior very carefully.

Just as they assume their parents' roles, children often assume their behaviors and attitudes as well. Adult children of addicts describe confusion about their emotions. They can't put words to how they feel and often don't know what to do with uncomfortable affect (Ackerman, 1983; Woititz, 1983). They often turn to substances, such as alcohol, other drugs, food, or processes, such as criminal behavior, gambling, indiscriminate sex, or violence, to cope with negative feelings—a coping technique learned early from addicted parents.

[When my brother died], that's when the don't talk, don't trust, don't feel was really prevalent in my life. I remember being at the door of his funeral. My insides were dying, you know, I really loved him. And I didn't know how to deal with the feelings.

Patty, a recovering alcoholic

Don't Talk, Don't Trust, Don't Feel In the addicted family system, children often witness inappropriate and destructive behavior. Family members use alcohol or other drugs to deal with painful affect. Other family members deny and distort reality in a vain attempt to cope with the dysfunction. All the while, their children are being indoctrinated into the "don't talk, don't trust, don't feel" world of addiction (Black, 1987).

The "don'ts" are what keep the secret in the family and the disease alive. "Don't trust" and "don't talk" messages tell children they can't go outside the family for help—no one outside the system can be trusted. "Don't trust" also means one can't trust one's own feelings or what one sees. Denial does not allow the disease to be seen within the family, therefore one is not supposed to feel (don't feel) or talk about it. Having feelings, talking about feelings, or talking about what's happening in the family is not allowed.

As a result of the "don't talk, don't trust, don't feel" doctrine, children driven to understand and survive in their world often learn to cope in ways that are unhealthy. Children may have to cope in isolation, trapped in a closed family system where no one is allowed to seek help outside the family. Healthy coping through a network of support is not available to the child, which destroys her opportunities for developing skills in gaining access to help and connecting with others as a way of surviving. Children may consequently develop a false sense that they "don't need anyone."

Impulsive Behavior

Children, especially young children, who are struggling with the impulsive behavior typical of various developmental stages look to the adults in their environment to help manage strong affect and impulses. For example, toddlers, eager to explore their world at every opportunity, break away from their parents at the supermarket or sink their teeth into a playmate's arm. Teenagers experiment with all kinds of behavior as part of separation and individuation from the family. Adults serve as both models and regulators for children overwhelmed by these typical, developmentally driven impulses.

Impulses must be managed in the interest of self and others. Freud used the term *delayed gratification* to describe the developing ego's ability to control the impulsive needs of the id (Greenberg & Mitchell, 1983). As the child matures, he is better able to put his needs "on hold" to be satisfied at a later time. A child learns to wait for a meal from a busy caregiver without becoming distraught. An adult learns to save money before taking a desired vacation. Delaying gratification and controlling impulses is necessary in order for an individual to function and survive as a social being.

Adults and families impaired by addiction, because of the very nature of the disease, serve as poor models for managing impulses. There is a sense of "anything goes" in the addicted family system. The addict behaves impulsively with little restraint and goes to any length to continue drinking and/or abusing drugs. There may be no appropriate containment for the child's behavior within the family and no holding environment to keep the child safe.

Inconsistent or Nonexistent Rules

Children learn rules for functioning in the world from the "map" provided by the family. Families teach children how to eat with others, play with others, and work with others. Children best learn to manage their behavior and affect in families where rules are developmentally appropriate, clear, constant, and for the well-being of all. They internalize the family rule system for use in the larger social world. Children learn to control impulsive behavior through internalizing the external structure and rules that the family provides.

In addicted family systems, rules are often arbitrary, absent, and/or punitive. There may be few, if any, restrictions on the addict's behavior and nonexistent, unpredictable, or suffocatingly strict rules for the child, holding the child back from developing a healthy sense of self. Rules may be inconsistent or illogical and, therefore, fail to teach the child or guide the child's social and moral development. Family members may use shaming behavior to enforce rules and force compliance, or there may be a lack of consequences for breaking rules. Children may witness the addict break rules and behave immorally without apparent remorse. Or, the addict's behavior may be tolerated, covered up, or excused by others in the family so the addict does not experience consequences for this behavior. Emotional, physical, and/or sexual abuse may even be tolerated or promoted.

The Rules of Addictive Disease   The addicted family system typically has a set of *covert* rules that serve to maintain the disease. These rules may not be articulated openly, but everyone in the family knows what they are. Wegscheider-Cruse (1981) describes these rules as the guardians of the family disease and cites the first as the understanding that the addict's use of the drug is the most important thing in the family's life—in other words, the central organizing principle of the system. Second, the addict is not responsible for his behavior and the drug is not the cause of the family's problems. A third hard and fast rule in the addicted family is that the status quo must be maintained at all times, and every member must be an enabler of the disease. Finally, the golden rule of the addicted family is always "don't talk, don't trust, don't feel," which serves to keep the system closed and unchanging so the disease can survive.

My uncle would do anything to support his habit. I got the feeling that there was no end to what he would do. And he was my model for how to act in this world.

John, in recovery from alcohol addiction

Chaos and Compulsive Control

My father went back out and picked up [started drinking again] after that . . . and my attitude at that time was "just be good." And I really tried to be good.

Patty, an ACoA in recovery

Children feel empowered when they feel "in charge" of their behaviors and impulses. When children have a clear sense of their own power and what they can control, they are more able to recognize and tolerate that which is out of their power to control or change. The first step in Alcoholics Anonymous is about the paradox of power and powerlessness. In order to gain power in their lives, addicts must admit powerlessness over the drug. This principle may be the same for children in the addicted family.

It is only when I let go of my parents' behavior, really let go, that I was able to find my true power. Admitting I was powerless over their craziness freed me to find my power to get on with my life.

Cheryl, an ACoA

Living with the chaos in an addicted family system can be frightening and overwhelming to young children. They may have no opportunity to develop and internalize feelings of power or mastery. Instead of feeling "in charge" of themselves and comfortable with their abilities to exist with life's confusion and unpredictable nature, they are left feeling incapable of managing life. In struggling to survive amidst the chaos, children can become focused on controlling themselves and their environments in constricting, unhealthy ways. For example, Patty felt that if she behaved, was quiet, and got good grades, her father would stop drinking. Children become obsessed with controlling the addict's behavior by trying to anticipate events or changing their own behavior in a futile attempt to get the addict to stop using. Children begin to see themselves as the cause of the addict's actions, in part to feel a sense of control. They also employ magical thinking to create a false sense that they are in control. This magical thinking is often reinforced in the dysfunctional family system by the blaming messages caregivers give to children.

My mother used to say that we "drove her to drink."

Cheryl, an ACoA

Children can also act out feelings of powerlessness by letting their own actions and behavior spiral "out of control." They demonstrate their feelings of fear and anger through disruptive, antisocial behavior. Children may also become distracted by events at home and, therefore, become inattentive or unfocused in class. Their behavior becomes a mirror of the chaos they witness externally and feel internally.

Poor Self-Esteem

Carol, an ACoA, a recovering addict, and an incest survivor: In order to keep my men, I would get pregnant by them. I didn't think

they would want me for me. For me, I know that I never really had any self-esteem. I never cared about myself. I was never nurtured.

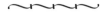

Ida, an ACoA, a recovering addict, and a trauma survivor: Any little thing we tried to do well in the house, it always turned into what we were doing wrong. We got beat up for it. It was like we weren't any good, we didn't do anything right.

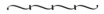

Children from addicted family systems often describe paralyzing feelings of inadequacy and incompetence (Ackerman, 1983; Brown, 1985). They often lack self-esteem and have a very poor sense of self-worth. Their sense of self is confused and sometimes shattered, after years of being devalued through word and deed. The confused internal and external realities experienced by the child further reinforce the belief that she is at fault because of this inherent badness. Carol always felt responsible for the abuse she experienced as a child and blamed herself for the family's inability to keep her safe. Ida recalls being beaten as part of the blame she received as a child.

Many ACoAs, despite their successes in school or careers, admit feeling this internal "badness." They never really feel good enough or deserving of success and happiness or respect and care. So ingrained are their feelings of inadequacy that they fear being "discovered" for the frauds they believe they are. ACoAs may unwittingly place themselves in relationships or situations that further reinforce their feelings of inadequacy and continue to chip away at their self-esteem. They may become codependent and struggle to please others at their own expense in an attempt to win attention and affection. To fill their internal void, they may begin to drink or use drugs or assume the caregiver role in a dysfunctional relationship.

Racism, Classism, and Sexism   Feelings of value and self-worth may be further eroded by racism, classism, and sexism. Children from addicted family systems often hear the taunts of "drunken Irishman," "poor white trash," "crack baby," and "coke whore," which further damage their already fragile self-esteem. One young boy, in therapy because of the abuse he experienced from his addicted mother, was additionally burdened by being biracial in a racist family. His Caucasian grandmother complained about his hair, calling it "nigger nap." When questioned, she seemed completely unaware of the impact her comment had on her confused 7-year-old grandson.

Anger and Fear

I was so angry [at my mother] I thought I would explode. But I was so afraid to express it. I thought she would die or go away forever. So I just pushed the feelings out of my head.

Cheryl, an ACoA

Children growing up in addicted family systems feel the fear and anxieties that all children experience as part of typical development. These children, however, are also experiencing the pathological results of addictive disease. The chaos, neglect, loss, and/or abuse that can accompany the disease and dysfunction leave scars on the hearts of children, who are often unable to express the accompanying feelings of anger and fear.

Children who learn early that anger and fear are unacceptable and "out of control" often act out these feelings in their behavior. These feelings can be manifested in externally projected antisocial behavior, such as violence and delinquency, or in internalized anger and fear in which the child becomes withdrawn or depressed. Children may also begin to associate anger and rage with scary and out-of-control behavior if they watch caregivers use drugs or become violent when angry or scared. In response, the child may split off these vulnerable feelings from himself, hoping to control his own emotions. The child can become consciously disconnected from feelings of fear and anger, although they remain bubbling under the surface in his unconscious.

These feelings of anger and fear continue to exist, regardless of whether the child has learned to "put them away." These feelings may violently explode to the surface when the child becomes overwhelmed or paralyze him with fear when his anxieties are triggered. Because the child may have buried his feelings from conscious awareness, he probably cannot anticipate what may trigger these feelings, identify them when he feels them, or express them in healthy, socially appropriate ways.

Shame and Guilt

I felt shame about being sexually abused. I felt guilt. For a really long time, I felt worthless.

Carol, an ACoA, a recovering addict, and an incest survivor

Shame was the way my parents controlled us. They shamed us in the way they criticized us, punished us, and parented us. We were ashamed for just being us, just being kids.

Cheryl, an ACoA

To escape my father's abuse and drunken behavior, my mother would pack us up in the middle of the night—the whole apartment, all the kids. We would leave in the dark. We couldn't tell anyone. No one was supposed to know.

Jim, an ACoA

Under healthy circumstances, children grow into adults who may feel shamed by certain behavior but not crippled by core feelings of shameful worthlessness. A well-balanced sense of shame is a modulator of social behavior and actions and prevents individuals from behaving destructively. Healthy shame does not smother a child's belief in himself and does not cause him to feel "fundamentally deficient in some vital way as a human being" (Kaufman, 1985, p. 8). Shame is part of human nature, but in unhealthy doses it can be poisonous.

When shame is used to control, manipulate, and destroy, it is toxic. John Bradshaw (1990) says, "Toxic shame feels much worse than guilt. With guilt, you've done something wrong; but you can repair that. With toxic shame there's something wrong with *you* and there's nothing you can do about it; *you* are inadequate and defective" (p. 47).

Feelings of shame and guilt are pervasive in the addicted family system. They are often called the "master emotions" because of the power they wield in the family (Bradshaw, 1990). Shame is entwined around the disease itself and around each member in the family system. Each member, in his or her own way, internalizes this system of shame, making it part of his or her own sense of self and value. To feel shame is to feel exposed, to be seen in a painfully diminished sense, and to feel isolated and alienated (Kaufman, 1985). Shame assaults the very core of one's being.

I come from "shameless" caretakers, abandonment, ridicule, abuse, neglect—
     perfectionist systems
I am empowered by the shocking intensity of a parent's rage
The cruel remarks of siblings
The jeering humiliation of other children
The awkward reflection in the mirrors
The touch that feels icky and frightening

The slap, the pinch, the jerk that ruptures trust
I am intensified by
A racist sexist culture
The righteous condemnation of religious bigots
The fears and pressures of schooling
The hypocrisy of politicians
The multigenerational shame of dysfunctional
   family systems
MY NAME IS TOXIC SHAME

John Bradshaw[1] (1990, pp. 48–49)

Shame in the Form of Racism, Classism, and Sexism   Racism, sexism, classicism, terrorism, and materialism—all are shame based. To shame is to gain control and power over an individual or group. When one shames another, an imbalance of power is created that removes the shamed person's sense of power. Shaming behavior is used in this way to exploit and discriminate against others. When one feels shamed about the very skin he wears or the very faith he believes, he becomes diminished in his own mind just as he is in the eyes of his persecutor. Shame about one's race, class, or belief system is instilled early in children through whatever elitist system is in power as a way for this system to maintain the power structure (Kasl, 1992)—American society has a Caucasian, patriarchal elite. Social shame, when coupled with the family's shame, creates a toxic environment for the child and family.

Grief and Loss

Ida, an ACoA in recovery: I was put in a foster home after a serious accident I had with my father. Then I was put in another foster home. Then, at age 13, I got transferred to another foster home.

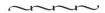

Carol, in recovery: And my parents got divorced when I was 7 years old. And I think it was about that time that I lost a lot of myself.

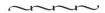

Gina, an ACoA in recovery: My father died before I was born. And I don't remember much about my childhood. I remember I was always real sad. When I was 9, my mother went to New York. . . . And I felt like my mother was, you know, she left, she's not coming back.

Cheryl, an ACoA: Every time my mom left, either in the car or to her room, I lost a little piece of myself until I was sure there was nothing left. I was so scared because I was never sure she was coming back.

Jim, an ACoA: My father, in a drunken rage, threw my cat out the window. We lived several floors up in a tenement building. I think I was about 6.

Two of the most compelling issues related to growing up in an addicted family system are the pervasive losses children experience and the accompanying, often unresolved, grief. Losses are often invisible, difficult for the child to describe. For instance, a primary caregiver may be physically present for a child but preoccupied with an addiction or caring for a spouse with an addiction, to the exclusion of the parent–child relationship. Although subtle, this lack of care and love can perpetuate deep feelings of loss related to important familial relationships as well as a sense of one's self. Internally, the child loses feelings of safety and consistency.

Other losses are immediately apparent, as when an addicted caregiver dies or disappears from the child's life. When a parent is also an addict, inconsistent care and unpredictable separations can be the norm in a child's life, resulting in lost toys, pets, and friends. There are also missed parties, camps, sleepovers, family dinners, and play time—all of those things that constitute childhood. Gina's experience says it all: "I don't remember much of my childhood." Children do not have the opportunity to be children when they are busy caring for the addict or younger siblings. They are not able to truly let go and play when they are worrying about what is happening at home. Adult children grieve the countless missed opportunities to have fun, to play, and to be children.

Cheryl, an ACoA: I would look outside and see the green grass and reds and blues and yellows of summer shirts as the other kids ran and played. They seemed so young and I felt so old, so tall, standing inside in the hallway as I worried about my mother. I was 8.

Loss and Its Impact on Child Development   The impact of loss on a child's development is dependent, in part, upon the child's history and caregiving environment. Freud, Winnicott, and Bowlby, among others, describe the first loss experienced by children as the loss of the mother (primary caregiver) during the typical developmental process of separation and individuation (Bowlby, 1958; Greenberg & Mitchell, 1983), a healthy step in the development of self. According to theory, children fear losing their mother and having to function independently but, in typical development, are able to make healthy separations and tolerate this loss, in part because they have been given the care and nurturing they need in a safe "holding environment."

When early relationships with primary caregivers are impaired because of substance abuse or other traumas, the child's world fails to provide the holding environment the child needs. Feelings of loss, fear, and foreboding can be great. As a result, the typical process of separation and individuation gets derailed, and the accompanying loss felt by the child as he separates from the mother figure is confusing and fearful. The child may never truly be able to separate and resolve issues around that first loss.

To complicate the child's experience further, in the addicted family system, members don't talk to explain why Mom or Dad left. Mom and Dad sometimes will say they will be right back and then disappear for days, leaving children with friends or family members indefinitely and unexpectedly. The holding environment—if it ever existed—may disappear completely, leaving matters confused and unresolved. In this situation, losses build and multiply. Grieving and the healthy resolution of losses are prevented by the family's silence.

Winnicott and others believed that unresolved losses from the earliest experiences of separation and onward shape how individuals experience loss throughout the life span (Greenberg & Mitchell, 1983). If a child never grieved a loss—was not allowed nor helped to grieve—the losses remain unresolved. New losses trigger memories of old losses, which can constrict a person's emotional state, leaving her feeling raw and vulnerable. The fear of loss in relationships can keep one from taking risks in making new connections and relationships. Ultimately, the person will begin to build walls of defenses as protection from the painful feelings.

I would drink and drink and drink, just so I wouldn't feel.

Diane, an ACoA in recovery

Unhealthy, Maladaptive Roles

"Survival patterns," ways of responding to the family system, form the roles taken on by individual family members to maintain the family system and to cope with the dysfunction. These roles are often unhealthy and maladaptive—their boundaries either too rigid or too loose and poorly defined. Yet members adopt them to survive in and maintain the system.

Dear Mommy,
Don't worry. I went out to play. I let you sleep. Harry's book is on the table. Harry will be in the yard and I will be at Joanne's or Mary Ann's. Harry wore a sweatshirt, two pair of pants with a belt, and suspenders with play jacket with just the hood on his ears. I wore my red pants and my shirt and pink sweater with my red and white hat with hood.
From Linda (age 8, a child of an alcoholic parent)

Roles in addicted family systems are often paradoxical: the role that has been adopted for survival can also be the role that will destroy. Some children become caregivers of the addicted parent, making sure the parent eats and keeps appointments. Children learn to cover up and lie to keep the outside world from finding out their situation and maybe breaking up the family. Some children become quiet, passive, "lost children" to keep themselves from being hurt by an abusive parent. Often depressed, they try to attract as little attention as possible. "If I am good enough, quiet enough, maybe this will all get better." Other children act out. They are angry and aggressive, calling attention to their pain and acting out the family drama of anger.

These roles help children survive and help keep the system from changing, but at what cost? What is the impact on the child's sense of self and well-being? Why would members fight frantically to maintain a harmful status quo? Ironically, no matter how much individual members in the addicted family system dislike the pattern they are locked into, the fear of change is often greater than the fear of staying the same. Disrupting the system by "telling the secret" and changing the pattern means risking the unknown, but worse, it means being disloyal. Change for anyone is difficult and unsettling. It is especially difficult for individuals who have been locked in a static system for so long. "The devil you know" takes on profound meaning in an addictive family system. This fear of change and the dilemma of "loyalty" coupled with the most powerful guardian of the addicted system—denial—all work together to perpetuate the status quo.

～ Portrait of an Addicted Family System ～

The Wilsons[2] live with alcohol as an integral member of their family system. As a result, they have developed, both individually and together, ways of being and behaving in response to the disease. As described previously, these "survival patterns" define each member's role in the family. Each member develops a "false self," a self that is formed to please and placate the desires of others or, in the addicted family system, of the disease.

The Wilson family is alcoholic, but they're not talking about it. Ms. Wilson is an active alcoholic, drinking several glasses of wine a night, beginning when she arrives home from her job as an elementary school teacher. On the weekends, she might drink at lunch and dinner, sometimes until she passes out. Ms. Wilson has been divorced from her first husband for 3 years and has little contact with him except during one of his infrequent visits to their children. Ms. Wilson has a fiancé, Mr. Carson, a construction foreman for a local company. He often stays with Ms. Wilson and her five biological children on the weekends. The Wilson family rents an apartment in a suburban, working-class neighborhood down the street from Ms. Wilson's biological parents.

---

[2]This family portrait describes common roles in an addicted family system, the external and internal realities of the members assuming those roles, and the payoff for both the member and the family. The roles named in this system dynamic have been adapted from Wegscheider-Cruse (1981).

The Addict

Ms. Wilson is 35 and has been drinking since her late teens. Her biological father has been alcoholic for much of Ms. Wilson's life. She does not remember much from her childhood except that it "wasn't much fun." She does remember enjoying school and was successful academically. Ms. Wilson drank moderately during the first half of her marriage to a husband who drank "too much." She began drinking more frequently and more heavily during the last half of her 12-year marriage. She has been actively alcoholic for 8 years. Three years ago, Ms. Wilson's grandmother, a close family confidante, died suddenly. Ms. Wilson's drinking increased after her grandmother's death and she began using Valium, given to her by a neighbor, to help her sleep. She experiences bouts of depression and often has trouble sleeping at night.

Ms. Wilson's identifying symptom in her role as addict is her chemical use. The "payoff" of her use is relief from extreme emotional pain. As a child of an alcoholic, she has a lifetime of fear, pain, and grief lying just under the surface of her external self. A destructive relationship with her first husband has left her more wounded and troubled. The strain of single parenthood is taking a toll on a woman who drinks to cope. Ms. Wilson's internal feeling state is dominated by depression as well as shame and guilt for what her alcoholism is doing to her family.

The Enabler

Mark is Ms. Wilson's 16-year-old son. He was attending high school, but recently passed his high school equivalency exam so he could quit school and work full time in a local restaurant. Mark has a few close friends and spends much of his time working or staying home. His other "full-time job" is caring for his mother and younger siblings. Mark wakes his mother for work, gets the younger children out the door to school, and has even been helping his mother grade her students' papers when she gets behind—which is happening more and more these days. Mark argues with his mother about her drinking, will look for and throw out hidden bottles, and threatens to "turn her in," but never does. Mark also argues almost constantly with Mr. Carson, whom Mark sees as a threat to his position in the family. Mark also blames Mr. Carson for his mother's increased drinking.

Mark's identifying symptom of the family disease is his role of enabler. He is powerless to stop his mother from using and unintentionally supports the disease. Mark's internal reality and feeling state is dominated by anger: anger at the addict, anger at himself, and anger at the world and the trap he is in. The payoff for Mark as enabler is that he feels important to the system and righteous in his ability to "do it all." The payoff for the family is that someone is responsible and holding things together. The price Mark pays for being the enabler is great. He loses his childhood in the midst of being a parentified child. He loses his self to the needs of others. The disease of addiction wins because it has a reluctant codependent in Mark. Mark risks involving himself in a lifetime of codependent relationships where he is the caregiver and his needs are deferred for the needs of others.

The Hero

Sheryl is the Wilson's 14-year-old daughter. She is the super-good family overachiever—the hero. A straight-A student, Sheryl is class president and captain of the volleyball team. She is talkative, friendly, and very popular with peers. Her nickname is "Smiles" because it seems as if she is always happy.

Of course, the face Sheryl presents to the world—confident and self-assured—is very different from her internal feeling state. Although her identifying symptom of the family's illness is her overachievement, she hides intense feelings of inadequacy and shame: inadequacy because she can never be good enough (to stop her mother's drinking or win her father's attention) and shame about what is happening in the family. The payoff for the family is the feeling of self-worth generated in having an over-achiever as a member. Having such an accomplished family member reinforces family denial: "How can we possibly have a problem in this family if Sheryl is so successful?" The payoff for the hero is positive attention from others and feelings of accomplishment and competence, but these feelings are squashed by overwhelming feelings of inadequacy. Because of this core feeling of inadequacy, the possible price that Sheryl pays for her role as hero is a compulsive drive to achieve and do battle with her feelings of inadequacy to the exclusion of healthy lifestyles and relationships. She is at risk for becoming a workaholic.

The Scapegoat

At 12, Donna already has a reputation for trouble at school and in the neighborhood. She's hanging out with the wrong crowd and skipping school. Some of her friends have been drinking and smoking, and she's thinking of trying it too. Donna doesn't get along with her older sister Sheryl at all. The teachers at school all want to know why she can't be like her "perfect" sister. Her mother says she's "bad, just like her father." Lately, Donna's been sneaking off to call her dad or taking the bus to the bar where he hangs out. Sometimes he lets her sip his beer.

Donna's identifying symptoms of the family disease are delin-quency, acting out, and experimenting with alcohol and other drugs. Donna is the family's scapegoat. Everything that goes wrong in the family is blamed on her. The message is "If only Donna would straighten up, then Mom would stop drinking and the family would be normal." The payoff for the family in having a scapegoat is that the focus is taken off the disease and the addict's behavior. The scapegoat can be blamed for the dysfunction in the family, thus reinforcing the denial of the disease. The payoff for Donna is the attention she receives, albeit negative. Internally, what Donna is feeling is hurt, fear, and anger. She has an overwhelmingly poor self-image. Underneath the bravado is a scared child who believes the message she receives—she is bad and will always be bad. The price Donna may pay is living a self-fulfilling prophecy. Donna is at serious risk for developing her own chemical dependency.

The Lost Child

Nicole is 8. She disappears for hours in her room with her books. Sometimes she takes her grandmother's dog to the park for a whole morning, until Mark comes looking for her. When Nicole is at home, her family "forgets" she is there. She is very quiet. Her grandmother always asks why she never smiles. Nicole would rather be in her room than at the table with her mom when she's drinking and "being weird." Nicole sits in the back of the classroom at school and rarely raises her hand. Her schoolwork is always done, but she does it half-heartedly. Nicole has few friends and spends lunchtime taking care of the school's pets.

Nicole's symptom of the family illness is her solitary and isolated behavior. She is the lost child, trying to disappear into the woodwork. The family is relieved; they don't have to think about her with everything else going on, which is the payoff for the family. The payoff for Nicole is that she can escape the family craziness by tuning out or literally disappearing. The price Nicole pays is internal—she is lonely and sad. She feels unnoticed and unloved. Nicole may continue to live her life socially isolated, unable to connect or ask for help. She is certainly at risk for depression.

The Mascot

Everybody loves Anthony. He is 5 years old and cute as a button. He's funny and affectionate and entertains everyone at the dinner table with his stories. Anthony can get Mom to laugh when she is crying. Even Donna, who is mean to everyone, loves him. Anthony is the family mascot. In school, Anthony is well liked, but the teachers are beginning to get frustrated with Anthony's fooling around in class. He never seems to sit still and his schoolwork is suffering.

Anthony's identifying symptom of the family disease is his clowning around and acting-out behavior. The payoff for the family is that Anthony is fun and amusing. His antics divert attention from the family problems. The payoff for Anthony is all of the positive attention he receives. Anthony's internal feeling state, however, is predominantly fearful: fear that he will be found out for the bad kid he really is and fear of what is happening in his family. Anthony is also very sad, perhaps laughing on the outside but crying on the inside. And because Anthony always has to be "on" and funny, he can never express those underlying feelings of despair. The possible price Anthony pays for his role as family mascot may be emotional illness as feelings are suppressed or continued out-of-control behavior that results in delinquency or school problems.

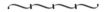

Reading these descriptors, individuals see themselves and familiar others in the roles described. Although one may recognize familiar characters in this family portrait, it is important to remember that each child and each family is very different, and outcomes vary tremendously for children. Outcomes can even vary among children within the same family system. The roles described here are fluid sketches of how family members evolve within the family. Each member can be a combination of roles and can assume new roles if family members leave. For example, the hero can also be the enabler. If the scapegoat leaves the family, the mascot can move into the scapegoat's role. There may not be a lost child in the family, but other family members may feel lost and lonely at times. It is interesting to note how each role has a payoff for the individual and the family but exacts a price for surviving in that role.

～ References ～

Ackerman, R.J. (1983). *Children of alcoholics: A guidebook for educators, therapists and parents* (2nd ed.). Holmes Beach, FL: Learning Publications.

Ainsworth, M. (1974). The development of infant–mother attachment. In B. Caldwell & H.N. Riccuti (Eds.), *Review of child development research* (pp. 1–93). Chicago: University of Chicago, Society for Research in Child Development.

Alcohol Alert. (1990). *Children of alcoholics: Are they different?* (9, Ph228). Rockville, MD: National Clearinghouse on Drug and Alcohol Information.

American Lung Association. (1982). *Roper report: Smoking and pregnancy.* Boston: Author.

Black, C. (1987). *It will never happen to me.* Ballatine, NY: Medical Administration Company.

Bowlby, J. (1958). The nature of the child's tie to his mother. *International Journal of Psychoanalysis, 39,* 350–373.

Bradshaw, J. (1990). *Homecoming: Reclaiming and championing your inner child.* New York: Bantam Books.

Brown, S. (1985). *Treating the alcoholic: A developmental model of recovery.* New York: John Wiley & Sons.

Brown, S. (1988). *Treating adult children of alcoholics: A developmental perspective.* New York: John Wiley & Sons.

Erikson, E. (1964). *Childhood and society.* New York: Norton.

Fraiberg, S. (1959). *The magic years: Understanding and handling the problems of early childhood.* New York: Charles Scribner & Sons.

Fraiberg, S., Adelson, E., & Shapiro, V. (1980). Ghosts in the nursery: A psychoanalytical approach to the problems of impaired infant–mother relationships. In S. Fraiberg (Ed.), *Clinical studies in infant mental health: The first year of life* (pp. 101–136). New York: Basic Books.

Galinsky, E. (1987). *The six stages of parenthood.* Reading, MA: Addison-Wesley.

Goodwin, D. (1985). Alcoholism and genetics. *Archives of General Psychiatry, 42,* 171–174.

Greenberg, J., & Mitchell, S. (1983). *Object relations in psychoanalytic theory.* Cambridge, MA: Harvard University Press.

Hastings, J., & Typpo, M. (1984). *An elephant in the living room.* Minneapolis, MN: Comp Care.

Herman, J. (1992). *Trauma and recovery: The aftermath of violence from domestic abuse to political terror.* New York: Basic Books.

Kasl, C. (1992). *A new understanding of recovery: Many roads, one journey: Moving beyond the 12 steps.* New York: HarperCollins.

Kaufman, G. (1985). *Shame: The power of caring.* Rochester, VT: Schenkman Books.

Logue, L., & Rivinus, T. (1991). Young children of substance abusing parents: Developmental view of risk and resiliency. In T. Rivinus (Ed.), *Children of chemically dependent parents* (pp. 55–73). New York: Brunner/Mazel.

Mathias, R. (1992, January/February). *Developmental effects of prenatal drug exposure may be overcome by postnatal environment.* (NIDA Notes). Rockville, MD: National Clearinghouse for Alcohol and Drug Information.

Nylander, A. (1960). Children of alcoholic fathers. *Acta Pediatrica, 49*(Suppl.), 1–34.

O'Rourke, K. (1992). Young children of alcoholics: Little people with big needs. *Journals of Alcohol and Drug Education, 37*(2), 43–51.

Robinson, B. (1990, May). The teacher's role in working with children of alcoholic parents. *Young Children,* 68–72.

Sameroff, A., & Chandler, M. (1975). Reproductive risk and the continuum of caretaking casualty. In P. Horowitz (Ed.), *Reviews of child development research* (pp. 187–244). Chicago: University of Chicago Press.

Seval Brooks, C., Zuckerman, B., Bamforth, A., Cole, J., & Kaplan-Sanoff, M. (1994). Clinical issues related to substance-involved mothers and their infants. *Infant Mental Health 15*(2), 202–217.

Steinglass, P. (1987). *The alcoholic family.* New York: Basic Books.

Steinhausen, H., Godel, D., & Nestler, V. (1984). Psychopathology in the off-spring of alcoholic parents. *Journal of the American Academy of Child Psychiatry, 23*(4), 465–471.

Stern, D. (1985). *The interpersonal world of the infant: A view from psychoanalysis and developmental psychology.* New York: Basic Books.

Treadway, D. (1991). Breaking the cycle: Treating adult children of alcoholics. In T. Rivinus (Ed.), *Children of chemically dependent parents* (pp. 226–249). New York: Brunner/Mazel.

Wegscheider, S. (1979). *The family trap: No one escapes from a chemically dependent family.* Crystal, MN: Nurturing Networks.

Wegscheider-Cruse, S. (1981). *Another chance: Hope and healing for the alcoholic family.* Palo Alto, CA: Science and Behavior Books.

William Gladden Foundation. *Children from alcoholic families* [pamphlet]. (1989). York, PA: Author.

Woititz, J. (1983). *Adult children of alcoholics.* Hollywood, FL: Health Communications.

Woodside, M. (1988). Research on children of alcoholics: Past and future. *British Journal of Addiction, 83*, 785–792.

~ 5 ~

Special Issues in the Addicted Family System

In Utero Drug Exposure, HIV Infection, and the Effects of Violence and Trauma

To complicate the issue for children growing up in addicted family environments, many face additional risks to their health and development because of exposure to human immunodeficiency virus (HIV) or alcohol and/or other drugs in utero and exposure to violence in the environment. In an already fragile system, with a parent struggling with his or her disease, these can be tremendously difficult experiences. Although the birth of a child exposed to HIV or alcohol or other drugs can precipitate a crisis for families, it can also be a wake-up call to both families and professionals that there is a very serious problem and provide a window of opportunity to all involved. The mother may see, in a moment of fear and clarity, that she needs help. Family members may no longer be able to hide behind the denial of the disease. The mother and family members may mobilize to begin the healing process—or they may not.

I could not believe drugs had brought me this far down, looking at what I had done to my baby.

Donna, a recovering alcoholic

At first I was afraid to hold her, she looked so small. Would she want me as a mom after all that had happened?

Liz, a recovering cocaine addict

When a child is born exposed to HIV or toxic substances such as alcohol, cocaine, or opiates, the mother—and family members—is flooded with very painful feelings, feelings that the addict has often been burying with chemicals. For perhaps the first time, the mother can no longer deny her problem. Yet women delivering in hospital emergency rooms with positive urine screens for cocaine have still reported that they only used because they "had a toothache" or "to help with labor pains." "I'm in control of my use. I can handle it" is their familiar battle cry.

At the sight of their often fragile babies, many mothers are overwhelmed with feelings of guilt and shame and may be tremendously fearful of losing their child—intense and powerful emotions. Of course, these mothers have typically numbed themselves to these intense feelings in the past and have few strategies for dealing with them. When these feelings build up around the birth of a baby, mothers are at significant risk for continued substance abuse—a risk that is greatly exacerbated when something is "wrong" with their child.

This chapter explains what happens to children exposed to HIV and/or substances such as alcohol, cocaine, and opiates by exposing the health and developmental risks and the exposure's impact on the child's behavior, affect, and relationship with the caregiver. This chapter also provides an overview of the effects of violence and trauma on young children.

⌒ In Utero Exposure to Drugs ⌒

Myths and Realities of In Utero Drug Exposure

Although much has been reported about the effects of alcohol and other drugs on the unborn child, a portion of this information has been inaccurate, misinterpreted, and biased (Frank, Bresnahan, & Zuckerman, 1993). The media has deemed children exposed to cocaine as a biological underclass and unsalvageable. Women live in fear that the glass of wine they had before they knew they were pregnant will cause irreparable harm to their unborn babies. What is myth here and what is reality? Sorting through all of the available information on developmental outcomes can be very confusing, as is formulating an accurate picture of what happens to children who are exposed to such substances as cocaine, alcohol, opiates, and tobacco.

Much of this confusion is due to the challenges inherent in the research on the effects of exposure in utero to alcohol and other drugs. The lifestyle and behavior of the addict pose significant challenges to conducting accurate research. Addictive behavior affects the feasibility of conducting research, making it difficult to obtain a large enough sample size to provide accurate and valid findings. Most drugs, for example cocaine and heroin, are illegal, which makes it difficult to get an honest report of use from an addict. Addicts will usually underestimate use by denying and minimizing actual habits or, in some reported cases, will overestimate their use (Frank et al., 1993). Addicts are often polydrug abusers (i.e., use more than one drug), which can confuse studies that examine the effects of a single substance.

Of great frustration to researchers, active addicts are unpredictable and inconsistent in following research protocols. They miss appointments, may have no telephones or permanent addresses, and are very difficult to follow over the long term because of life crises and disruptions. Subjects who do manage to stay involved for the long term may be more resilient than families that drop out, which can skew study results. In addition, clinicians who conduct research are often biased in their sample selection of subjects. It has been found that, at delivery, clinicians are 10 times more likely to identify and report illicit substance use among low-income and African American women than among Caucasian private patients (Chasnoff, Landress, & Barett, 1990; Frank et al., 1993). Another selection bias involves making generalizations about developmental outcomes using a sample of children already identified for medical and developmental problems, which is not representative of the general population of exposed children.

Perhaps the most challenging aspect of research into the effects of exposure to alcohol and other drugs on the unborn child is the confounding variables present in every case of in utero drug exposure. In order to substantiate a main-effects hypothesis—to conclude, for example, that cocaine causes a specific set of outcomes—the research design must control for all of the other factors that may affect developmental outcomes, including a lack of prenatal care, poor maternal nutrition, sexually transmitted diseases (STDs), and other illnesses. For example, if a child is born prematurely, is it the result of the mother's cocaine use or failure to obtain any prenatal care?

Developmental Outcomes of In Utero Cocaine Exposure

Cocaine passes through the placental barrier, creating an opportunity for the fetus to be directly exposed to the substance. Cocaine use in adults alters neurotransmitter levels in the body. Neurotransmitters are found in a part of the brain called the "pleasure center." They help to regulate responses such as sexual excitement, euphoria, and pleasure. When someone uses cocaine, neurotransmitters alter his or her functioning, resulting in a heightened pleasurable response. Norepinephrine, a neurotransmitter chemical, modulates alertness and vigilance in the central nervous system (CNS), affecting heart rate, blood pressure, respiration, and the "fight or flight" behavioral response in the autonomic nervous system, which regulates vascular, respiratory, and other body systems. These physiological changes can be observed in users who report heightened arousal, jitteriness, high energy, and feeling jazzed up or "on."

What does this mean for the baby? Because evidence shows that there are in utero neurotransmitter changes in blood and spinal fluid in exposed newborns, it is certainly possible that cocaine can have an impact on a child's physiological development (Frank et al., 1993; Seval Brooks, Zuckerman, Bamforth, Cole, & Kaplan-Sanoff, 1994). Studies of the effects of these neurotransmitter changes on the developing child are in the preliminary stages (Frank et al., 1993). It is not yet known whether altered levels of neurotransmitters affect brain development. Studies have consistently shown an association between cocaine and symmetrically low-birth-weight babies (Bresnahan, Brooks, & Zuckerman, 1991; Frank et al., 1993), specifically implicating cocaine's effects on maternal vascular systems. Some studies have found, however, a correlation between cocaine and premature birth, while others have not (Bresnahan et al., 1991). Furthermore, there is no reliable evidence that cocaine causes congenital abnormalities and no evidence whatsoever to support a "fetal cocaine syndrome" (Frank et al., 1993). Some studies have found a slightly higher risk of sudden infant death syndrome (SIDS) in children exposed to cocaine, but the results may be confounded because there was no control for cigarette use (Frank et al., 1993).

Maternal lifestyles of pregnant women who actively use cocaine present obvious risks to the developing child. When one is high, one doesn't eat. If an addict is depressed from a drug crash, she may not keep appointments or care for herself and may use other drugs to deal with the crash of the high. She may engage in high-risk behavior, exposing herself to STDs or violence.

In trying to assess developmental outcomes for children exposed to cocaine in utero and exposed to the lifestyles of cocaine addicts after the neonatal period, environmental variables confound research on physiological effects of cocaine exposure. To date, evidence from the newborn period has been too inadequate and inconsistent to allow for any clear predictions of long-term consequences of cocaine exposure (Beeghly & Tronick, 1994; Griffith, 1992; Zuckerman & Frank, 1992). However, if a child comes home to an environment that continues to be contaminated by addictive disease, that child certainly faces further risks.

Chasnoff's Longitudinal Study Chasnoff published preliminary findings from the first vigorous long-term study of children exposed to cocaine in utero, reporting the greatest differences between the polydrug/cocaine-exposed infants and the nonexposed infants during the first few weeks following birth (Griffith, 1992). The infants exposed to cocaine displayed disorganized nervous systems that interfered with their abilities to regulate states of arousal. These infants were easily overstimulated by touch, handling, sights, and sounds. They were jittery, cried easily, and had a hard time calming themselves. Some babies would shut down by going to sleep and were difficult to arouse. These observations are supported anecdotally by hospital staff and early intervention providers but are not consistent over children, not specific to cocaine-exposed children, and do not constitute a withdrawal pattern (Bresnahan et al., 1991; Zuckerman & Bresnahan, 1991). It is unclear what these observed behaviors in the newborn period mean for long-term outcomes.

Researchers in Chasnoff's study followed the infants exposed to cocaine in utero through their preschool years but found no significant difference in the results of developmental assessments between the exposed and nonexposed groups (Chasnoff, Griffith, Freier, & Murray, 1992). Chasnoff did report that about one third of the drug-exposed children displayed delays in typical language acquisition and/or problems in attention and self-regulation (Griffith, 1992).

An important clarification needs to be made in understanding the results of this study: This was an intervention study in which the researchers provided prenatal care and nutritional services to the mothers in order to control for confounding variables. The children also received monitoring and treatment for their health and development, making it inaccurate to generalize these findings to the general population of cocaine-addicted mothers and exposed children (but highly significant for supporting the need for quality intervention services). Clearly, more research needs to be completed before any definitive statements can be made in regard to physiological insults and the origins of puzzling behavior observed in children exposed in utero to cocaine.

Studies since have begun to focus more on qualitative differences in child behavior and development. Rather than only evaluating performance on standardized developmental scales, researchers are now considering the quality of attentional behaviors, play skills, mutual regulation, and components of the parent–child relationship (Beeghly & Tronick, 1994; Frank et al., 1993; Griffith, 1992), which yields a more holistic evaluation of the dynamic parent, child, and family system.

Development as a Transactional Process   To understand the impact of in utero cocaine exposure on children, one must remember the transactional model of development that considers the child, the caregiver, and the environment as integral components of the developmental process (Bresnahan et al., 1991; Frank et al., 1993). Examining the dynamics of caring for a fragile baby within a fragile family system is an important component in researching outcomes and planning interventions. What happens when a mother who is ill-equipped to parent because of early trauma and her addictive disease has a baby who is difficult to calm? How is the infant–caregiver attachment affected by the challenges of caring for a fragile baby—for the biological mother or foster parents who may be caring for the baby?

Developmental Outcomes of In Utero Alcohol Exposure

Alcohol is readily absorbed by the human body and easily passed through the placental barrier. It is not known how alcohol works to adversely affect the fetus nor how much alcohol is detrimental to fetal development (Zuckerman & Bresnahan, 1991). Because the amount of alcohol consumption that is toxic to the unborn child is not known, much emphasis has been placed on total abstinence during pregnancy. This approach confuses the issue and may give the false impression that women who have had a few drinks during pregnancy have permanently damaged their babies. All reported cases of children born with fetal alcohol syndrome (FAS) have been born to women who were drinking heavily during pregnancy (Weiner & Morse, 1992).

Approximately 5–9 women out of 1,000 who drink heavily during their pregnancies will give birth to babies with FAS (Abel & Sokol, 1987). Heavy drinking is defined by some as 14 drinks per day, while others consider it to be 5 or more drinks on some occasions and at least 45 drinks per month (Weiner & Morse, 1992; Zuckerman & Bresnahan, 1991). It is important to note, however, that exposure to low doses of alcohol during pregnancy has not been proven to be either safe or dangerous (Weiner & Morse, 1992). Studies have shown that children born to mothers who drink more moderately—one or two drinks per day and occasionally more—are at increased risk for learning disabilities and cognitive impairments (Burgess & Streissguth, 1992).

The same methodological problems inherent in the research on cocaine exist in studying alcohol effects. Variables such as when and how much the mother drank during pregnancy, maternal nutrition, use of other drugs including cigarettes, and level of prenatal care are all thought to affect outcome in some, as yet undetermined, way (Zuckerman & Bresnahan, 1991).

Fetal Alcohol Syndrome FAS is an identifiable syndrome with a clear pattern of malformations and developmental problems (Jones, Smith, & Vineland, 1973). To receive a diagnosis of FAS, the child must have characteristics in three defined areas:

1. Growth retardation, either pre- or postnatally that continues through childhood
2. CNS dysfunction that is displayed through hyperactivity, motor dysfunction, attention deficits, and/or cognitive disabilities
3. A characteristic pattern of facial dysmorphology (deformity) including at least two of the following signs—microcephaly (small head), poorly developed philtrum (feature over upper lip), thin upper lip, short palpebral fissures (opening between the eyelids), and/or flattening of the maxillary area (lower half of face) (Zuckerman & Bresnahan, 1991)

The term *fetal alcohol effects* (FAE) is sometimes used to describe children who display some but not all of the characteristics associated with FAS. This term, although often used clinically, is not a medical diagnosis (Burgess & Streissguth, 1992).

Although every child's abilities and challenges are unique, the population of children with FAS shares a common developmental and behavioral profile. Children with FAS typically have developmental delays or learning disabilities and require some type of special education services. They are often hyperactive and have attention problems. They also are challenged with motor impairments including poor eye–hand coordination, weak grasp, tremors, and incoordination (Burgess & Streissguth, 1992; Zuckerman & Bresnahan, 1991). It should be kept in mind, however, that behavioral disturbances can also result from living in addicted environments, making it less clear exactly what behavior can be directly attributed to FAS.

Developmental Outcomes of In Utero Opiate Exposure

Morphine, codeine, and heroin are opiates. Methadone, often given to heroin addicts as a medication to temper the effects of heroin withdrawal, is a synthetic opiate, with similar chemical properties. Opiates work in the CNS, producing lowered anxiety, improved mood, drowsiness, and general euphoria. Opiates cross the placenta and directly affect the fetus, causing a decrease in somatic (body) growth and neonatal abstinence syndrome (NAS) (Zuckerman & Bresnahan, 1991).

NAS is triggered when the infant must physiologically adjust to the absence of opiates upon birth; in addicts, this syndrome is referred to as withdrawal. In the womb, the fetus becomes dependent on opiates and makes a biological adaptation to the substance. The infant with NAS often experiences sweating, stuffy nose, diarrhea, and vomiting and requires careful medical monitoring and specialized intervention. Behaviorally, infants with NAS have difficulty with state regulation—they are irritable, difficult to console or arouse, and easily overstimulated. These babies can never seem to make themselves comfortable and often have knee and elbow abrasions from flailing around (Zuckerman & Bresnahan, 1991). Studies of children exposed to opiates have also reported low birth weights, although this is not a universal finding (Zuckerman & Bresnahan, 1991). They tend to have smaller head circumferences as well, although this may be due to maternal lifestyle issues (Zuckerman & Bresnahan, 1991).

As with studies of other drug effects, it is unclear what the long-term outcomes are for children exposed to opiates. Studies document typical scores in cognitive development but higher incidence of behavior or school-related problems (Zuckerman & Bresnahan, 1991). But, again, the impact of growing up in an addicted family system was not controlled for in these studies; therefore, it is difficult to determine root causes of the children's problems.

Developmental Outcomes of In Utero Tobacco Exposure

The American Lung Association (1982) reports that maternal smoking has a clear impact on the health of children, both in utero and postpartum. Numerous studies support findings that newborns exposed to tobacco in utero are symmetrically smaller than nonexposed newborns in all dimensions, including length, head circumference, chest circumference, and shoulder circumference (Persson, Grennert, Gennser, & Kullanders, 1978). The relationship between maternal smoking and reduced birth weight is independent of all other influential factors, including race, maternal size, socioeconomic status, gestational age, and sex of child, and is directly proportional—the more a woman smokes during pregnancy, the greater the reduction in the infant's birth weight (American Lung Association, 1982). Symmetrically low-birth-weight infants are at greater risk for growth and development problems than babies in the typical range of weight and size. In addition, there is some scientific evidence that suggests that maternal smoking is related to problems during pregnancy and delivery that increase the risk of fetal death (American Lung Association, 1982).

Despite these substantiated adverse outcomes to fetal growth and development from tobacco—a highly potent toxin—many women remain unaware of the dangers of cigarette smoking during pregnancy (American Lung Association, 1982). Denial of addiction to tobacco plays some role in this, as does the cultural acceptance of smoking, which is encouraged by the rampant advertising and promotion of cigarettes and the legalization (legitimizing) of this drug.

～ HIV Infection and Substance Abuse ～

There's a child that doesn't know that she will die,
There's a child that will never ever get to see much of life,

There's a child that does not understand why most of her life will be
    spent in and out of the hospital,
Every 2 weeks she will be stuck with needles,
She is small and her immune system is weak
    so she has to take medicine to keep her from getting sick,
Why? because when Mommy was carrying her she needed a fix
    and in order to get it she had to find a trick
that would give the biggest treat of her life—HIV
that would soon destroy her and her baby's life,
That's what wanting and needing to get high did for me,
Destroyed my life and my baby's

Cassandra, alcoholic, cocaine addict,
infected with HIV, and the mother of four

It is difficult to discuss HIV infection without feeling overwhelmed
by the complexity of the issue and the tragic consequences of the resulting disease, acquired immunodeficiency (AIDS). In 1981, women
comprised only 3.8% of all AIDS cases in the United States. By 1990,
11.5% of AIDS cases involved women, and women of childbearing
age accounted for 85% of this group. Nationwide, AIDS is one of the
top five leading causes of death for women of childbearing age, who
are also among the groups documenting the fastest growing rates
of HIV infection (Centers for Disease Control and Prevention, 1993–
1994). In 1995, there were 6,817 documented cases of HIV infection
in children from birth to 13 years old ("First 500,000," 1995). This
includes 5,432 cases in children less than 5 years old. These numbers, however, for both women and children, are likely grossly underestimated.

HIV Infection and Women

The majority of women with HIV infection contracted the virus
through intravenous drug use—of which reports are declining—or
from a sexual partner with HIV infection—a phenomenon that is on
the rise. Of women with HIV infection, 52% are African American,
27% are Caucasian, and 20% are Latino (Act Up, 1990).

There is a large discrepancy in survival statistics between women
and men who have HIV infection. Women die sooner and are more
often misdiagnosed and underserved than men. There are many issues that contribute to this discrepancy, including lack of access to
proper care, lack of information about the disease, denial that women
contract HIV, and lack of funding for research and treatment for

women. Women also may manifest the disease differently from men, with women-specific infections, namely gynecological problems such as pelvic inflammatory disease, chronic yeast infections, chlamydia, and human papillomavirus. Because these diseases are not among those listed as criteria for a diagnosis of AIDS, many women who have AIDS and die from a female-specific opportunistic infection are not included in the AIDS statistics (Act Up, 1990).

Children and the HIV Diagnosis

Children are diagnosed with HIV when they test positive for the virus, not for the *antibodies* produced by the body to fight the virus. All infants born from mothers who have HIV infections during pregnancy receive their mother's antibodies via placental transfer, but this does not mean that the infant has HIV infection. Although HIV antibodies in adults are a positive confirmation of infection, for an infant in the first year of life, the presence of antibodies may mean only that he still carries his mother's antibodies in his system. As most tests identify HIV antibodies, complex and multiple tests are necessary in order to determine a child's HIV status in the absence of symptoms and illness. Some infants born with their mother's HIV antibodies will seroconvert; that is, they will eventually test negative for HIV infection, although they initially tested positive.

The vast majority of children with HIV infection contracted the virus in utero from their mothers (Sison & Sever, 1992). A very small number have been infected through blood transfusions or the breast milk of their mothers with a relatively new HIV infection. One study reported that a mother who is HIV positive but has not given birth to an infant with HIV infection has a 20%–40% risk of giving birth to a baby with HIV infection. If a mother has previously given birth to an infant with HIV infection, the risk of transmission to subsequent infants may be higher (Lambert, 1990). Another transmission study reported a perinatal transmission rate between 15% and 30% (Sison & Sever, 1992).

Developmental Outcomes of HIV Infection

Often children with HIV infection are products of an addicted family system, with drug-addicted mothers, fathers, or both. Drug addiction and its accompanying behavior (e.g., sharing infected drug paraphernalia, having unprotected sex, trading sex for drugs) place the addict and his or her child at serious risk for contracting HIV. Children with HIV infections who live in addicted family systems are at developmental risk from multiple causes, including familial substance abuse, poor prenatal care, low birth weight, prematurity, and trauma, which make it difficult to determine the exact causes of behavioral or developmental disorders.

It has been well documented, however, that the progression of HIV causes degenerative brain damage (Belman, 1988). Most children with HIV infection develop disabilities because of the virus's progressive effect on the CNS (Belman, 1988). Research has also found that prenatal and acquired brain damage, which can result in delays or disorders in cognitive, motor, linguistic, psychosocial, and behavioral functioning, are linked to HIV infection.

The progression of HIV infection to AIDS varies with each child, as does the insult to each child's development. A child with HIV infection can be delayed at birth or may show age-appropriate development for several years. Typically, as the disease progresses, children lose previously gained developmental milestones (Seidel, 1992).

All children with HIV infection and their families require specialized intervention and care. The impact of being born with a chronic disease into a family that may be crippled with addiction can be devastating to a child's well-being. Society's anger, fear, and lack of compassion for the victims of HIV infection and AIDS add to the challenge faced by both families and providers, especially compounding sensitive psychosocial issues. Not so long ago, children with HIV infections were banned from school, taunted, and ridiculed. Families were threatened as the ignorance and fear connected to HIV fueled irrational responses from friends and neighbors. Although this situation has improved somewhat, much of the stigma surrounding HIV and AIDS remains, and families still experience severe hardships. When a family member is diagnosed with HIV, families undergo tremendous stress and often feel as if they have been handed a death sentence. The overwhelming guilt that parents feel upon learning that they may have infected their children is devastating. In addition, children whose parents die from AIDS are often left orphaned and must struggle with their grief and social ostracism alone.

⌒ Violence, Trauma, and Addicted Families ⌒

Angelina is a quiet, reserved woman in her late 20s. She is bright and hard working and devoted to Damon, her only child. Angelina is in recovery from alcohol and cocaine addiction. She struggles with a number of health problems, some of which are exacerbated by her obesity.

Birthdays, holidays, and anniversaries are hard for Angelina. She was celebrating her eighth birthday when her 2-year-old sister was shot and killed in her arms during a neighborhood dispute. Angelina is convinced that her sister would still be alive if Angelina had left when the neighbors started arguing and hadn't stopped to grab a piece of her birthday cake. Angelina's family never celebrated her birthday after that and covertly blamed Angelina for the tragedy.

Angelina became pregnant with Damon after being raped by an acquaintance. She welcomed Damon into her life and carried him almost constantly in a blue snuggly on her chest. She began carrying an old picture of her deceased sister and told everyone that Damon looked just like her. She thought they looked identical.

Angelina was haunted by dreams and memories of the violence she witnessed as a child. She would become anxious and depressed around certain sights, sounds, and smells. Thanksgiving was the worst. Her sister was killed in November and all those smells and sights of the holidays triggered horrible memories. Angelina drank a lot during the holidays. And she never celebrated her birthday.

Sara is 8. She is tall and athletic and loves the color purple. She gets good grades in school and has lots of friends. Sara is also anxious, depressed, and traumatized. Sara's mom is addicted to cocaine and has been actively using since shortly after Sara's birth. Sara has a 5-year-old sister, Celia.

The first time Sara's mom left them alone in their apartment, Sara was 4 years old and Celia was a baby. Her mom didn't come back for a long time. The second time her mom left, Sara was really scared. A man had broken down the door to their apartment a few weeks before and beaten her mother up, while Sara hid under the bed. This time, when her mom left, Sara went to her neighbors' apartment. They called the police. Sara let them in and showed them where Celia was sleeping. When the police officers told her that they were taking her and her sister to the hospital, Sara ran to find Celia's shoes. She found the purple ones under a chair and grabbed the police officer's hand. Sara was 5 years old.

The increased incidence of substance abuse coexisting with violence has been well documented among families in the United States. Studies show that physical, sexual, and emotional abuse are three times more common in alcoholic families than in the general population (William Gladden Foundation, 1989). The National Committee on the Prevention of Child Abuse reports that as much as 80% of all cases of child abuse involve drinking before, during, or after the incident (The Children of Alcoholics Foundation, 1994). The National Clearing House on Domestic Violence states that alcohol is a factor in approximately half of the reported cases of domestic violence.

The violent and antisocial behavior that accompanies illegal drug use exposes more and more children to murder and mayhem in the home and on the streets. The long-standing use and abuse of alcohol and prescription drugs, the surge of crack use during the 1980s, the increase in the use of a powerful form of heroin in the 1990s, and increased drug use among women of childbearing age have all had a significant impact upon children and families. Understanding the interrelated dynamics of substance abuse and violence is crucial in determining what types of interventions are most useful with these families.

Children exposed to violence and substance abuse can experience a range of adverse outcomes, from adjustment disorders, such as school problems, to affective disorders, such as depression or anxiety, to more complex disorders, such as *posttraumatic stress disorder* (PTSD). Since 1980, the reasons individuals develop this disorder have been broadened and now encompass a range of events and include children (see Chapter 1). The trauma can be acute or chronic and includes physical abuse, sexual abuse, emotional abuse, witnessing violence, natural disaster, accidents, murder, and assault.

Since the 1970s, many clinicians and researchers have observed and studied the reactions of children to traumatic events, concluding that children can and do experience PTSD (Eth & Pynoos, 1985; Lyons, 1987). The disorder is similar in children and adults; however, symptomology and outcomes do differ. (PTSD symptomology and diagnosis are discussed in detail in Chapter 1.)

Factors that Influence the Impact of Trauma

Individuals who have been traumatized in childhood can experience lifelong problems as a result of this early insult. A number of factors determine just how damaging the trauma is and causes outcomes for different children to vary tremendously. The particular nature of the event itself contributes to the potential effect of trauma on the individual. Witnessing a stranger being shot on the street and witnessing a family member being shot in the home are both traumatic events, but the shooting of a familiar caregiver inside a child's own home most certainly has a greater impact. In a study of a schoolyard sniper shooting in California, researchers discovered that children's responses to the traumatic event varied depending on their proximity to the shooting (Eth & Pynoos, 1985). Angelina's experience with her young sister was an acute traumatic event—horribly violent and in proximity to Angelina.

To determine the potential impact of trauma on young children, one must also consider individual child characteristics. A child's age, cognitive abilities, verbal abilities, and coping abilities all contribute to the impact the trauma has on that child, both in the short and long term. Young children do not have the verbal skills and cognitive abilities of older children and adults, making it difficult for them to sort out the intense feelings and confusion that surround the trauma.

The support system available to the child also strongly influences the impact of the trauma on the child. Angelina lost her sister and was blamed by family members. She had no family support system to help her deal with the murder of her sister. Sara's mother was unavailable because of her addiction, leaving Sara with no family support system. Important questions to ask when assessing the impact of trauma on children are: Are schools and community supports available to children? Is there a holding environment in place for the child? What kind of individual coping skills does the child possess?

A few years ago, in the Boston area, two very similar family tragedies occurred almost simultaneously in vastly different communities. In both cases, a father abducted and killed his children during the school year. One family lived in an affluent community, the other in an economically deprived, high-crime neighborhood outside of Boston. In the aftermath of the murders, a fleet of psychologists and clinical social workers was brought in to the more affluent school district to counsel children and families. There were days of community debriefings and memorial services that the media covered in detail. In the more deprived community, little, if anything, happened to heal the wounds of the community and help the children process what had happened. This is not because the impoverished community didn't care; it is because it lacked the resources to help. Perhaps they were also psychically depleted from the ongoing cycles of community violence.

Children who experience a single, acute traumatic event (e.g., a car accident) have different outcomes from children who experience more chronic, ongoing trauma (e.g., child abuse) (Terr, 1991), although both types of childhood trauma are associated with re-experiencing the event, repetitive behaviors (observed in play), trauma-specific fears, and changed attitudes about people, life, and the future. Children who are chronically terrorized, as many children from addicted family systems are, face lifelong negative outcomes from their early experiences. A single traumatic event in childhood can trigger the symptoms of PTSD but does not appear to "breed the massive denials, psychic numbings, self-anetheses or personality problems" often seen in children victimized by chronic trauma (Terr, 1991, p. 14).

Judith Herman writes, "Repeated trauma in adult life erodes the structure of the personality already formed, but repeated trauma in childhood forms and deforms the personality" (1992, p. 96). Herman further postulates that traumatized children must decipher how to trust when people are untrustworthy, find power in the helplessness of victimization, gain control in a wildly unpredictable environment, and salvage a sense of safety when everything around them is unsafe, all this while using an immature system of psychological defenses. Consider, for example, Sara: what courage she had to take that police officer's hand, what a heartbreaking effort to gain some power and control over her terrifying experience of abandonment she displayed by going for help and then finding her sister's shoes.

Terr (1991) describes the symptoms of PTSD manifested in chronically traumatized children as the defenses and coping mechanisms they employ to survive—denial, repression, dissociation, identification with the aggressor, and aggression turned against the self. Chronically traumatized children have a range of emotions, from numbing nonresponsiveness to rage, then hopelessness.

Denial and Psychic Numbing Chronically traumatized children exhibit massive denial, do not talk or tell of their experiences, and desperately try to look normal to the outside world. Children who have been chronically traumatized appear as if nothing fazes them, when, in fact, they may be shut down inside. Children who have been chronically traumatized dissociate from their traumatic experiences by entering into a type of trance state in which they separate their feelings from themselves to survive.

I would just go away in my head. It was as if my body were there but my head detached itself. I would go away to some quiet place in my mind.

Cheryl, an ACoA

Rage Rage is a common symptom of children who have undergone chronic trauma. Rage can be wildly uncontrollable and extremely frightening to the child. Children turn their rage outward and become menacing and dangerous. They can pick up weapons and use them without apparent feeling or remorse. "How do you feel," asked one young murderer, "when you're already dead inside?" Children who have been chronically traumatized identify with their aggressors in a desperate attempt to feel power and save their tortured egos, possibly becoming the victimizers. Conversely, children can turn their rage inward and engage in self-destructive behavior or become depressed or involved in abusive relationships (Terr, 1991).

Pessimism and Hopelessness Disheartening, but understandable, children who have been chronically traumatized have a very pessimistic outlook on their lives and futures. Many believe they have no futures at all or that their futures will be filled with pain. When a young mother, chronically traumatized all of her life, was asked about her son—himself a victim of the family's abusive drama—she replied without emotion, "A future for Anthony? There is no future for Anthony." The son she was speaking of was 4 years old.

～ References ～

Abel, E., & Sokol, R. (1987). Incidence of fetal alcohol syndrome and economic impact of FAS-related anomalies. *Drug and Alcohol Dependence, 19*, 51–70.

Act Up. (1990). *Women's treatment agenda.* Paper presented at the First National Conference on Women and HIV Infection, Washington, DC.

American Lung Association. (1982). Roper report: *Smoking and pregnancy.* Boston: Author.

Beeghly, M., & Tronick, E. (1994). Effects of prenatal exposure to cocaine in early infancy: Toxic effects on the process of mutual regulation. *Infant Mental Health, 15*(2), 158–175.

Belman, A. (1988). Pediatric acquired immunodeficiency syndrome: Neurological syndromes. *American Journal of Child Disabilities, 142*, 29–35.

Bresnahan, K., Brooks, C., & Zuckerman, B. (1991). Prenatal cocaine use: Impact on infants and mothers. *Pediatric Nursing, 17*(2), 123–129.

Burgess, D., & Streissguth, A. (1992, September). Fetal alcohol syndrome and fetal alcohol effects: Principles for educators. *Phi Delta Kappan,* 24–30.

Centers for Disease Control and Prevention. (1993–1994, Winter/Spring). *HIV/AIDS Prevention, 4*(4), 3.

Chasnoff, E., Landress, H., & Barett, M. (1990). The prevalence of illicit drug use or alcohol use during pregnancy and discrepancies in mandatory reporting in Pinellas County, Florida. *New England Journal of Medicine, 322*, 1202–1206.

Chasnoff, I., Griffith, D., Freier, C., & Murray, J. (1992). Cocaine/polydrug use in pregnancy: Two-year follow-up. *Pediatrics, 89*(2), 284–289.

Eth, E., & Pynoos, R.S. (1985). *Post traumatic stress disorder in children.* Washington, DC: American Psychiatric Association.

First 500,000 AIDS cases—United States, 1995. (1995, November 24). *Morbidity and Mortality Weekly Report, 44*(46), 849–853.

Frank, D., Bresnahan, K., & Zuckerman, B. (1993). Maternal cocaine use: Impact on child health and development. In Y.B. Barness (Ed.), *Advances in Pediatrics* (Vol. 40, pp. 65–99). St. Louis, MO: Mosby Yearbook.

Goodwin, D. (1985). Alcoholism and genetics. *Archives of General Psychiatry, 42*, 171–174.

Griffith, D. (1992, September). Prenatal exposure to cocaine and other drugs: Developmental and educational prognosis. *Phi Delta Kappan,* 30–34.

Herman, J. (1992). *Trauma and recovery: The aftermath of violence from domestic abuse to political terror.* New York: Basic Books.

Jones, K., Smith, D., & Vineland, C. (1973). Pattern of malformation in offspring of chronic alcoholic women. *Lancet, 1,* 1267–1271.

Lambert, J.S. (1990). Maternal and perinatal issues regarding HIV infection. *Pediatric Annals, 19,* 8.

Lyons, J. (1987). Post traumatic stress disorder in children and adolescents: A review of the literature. In S. Chess & A. Thomas (Eds.), *Annual progress in child psychiatry and development* (pp. 451–467). New York: Brunner/Mazel.

Mathias, R. (1992, January/February). *Developmental effects of prenatal drug exposure may be overcome by postnatal environment.* (NIDA Notes, pp. 14–16). Rockville, MD: National Clearinghouse for Alcohol and Drug Information.

Persson, P.H., Grennert, L., Gennser, G., & Kullanders, S. (1978). A study of smoking and pregnancy with special reference to fetal growth. *Acta Obstetrica et Gynecologica Scandinavia, 78,* 33–39.

Sameroff, A., & Chandler, M. (1975). Reproductive risk and the continuum of caretaking casualty. In P. Horowitz (Ed.), *Reviews of child development research* (pp. 187–244). Chicago: University of Chicago Press.

Seidel, J. (1992, September). Children with HIV-related developmental difficulties. *Phi Delta Kappan, 38–56.*

Schecter, S. (1987). *Guidelines for mental health practitioners in domestic violence cases.* Washington, DC: National Coalition Against Domestic Violence Cases.

Seval Brooks, C., Zuckerman, B., Bamforth, A., Cole, J., & Kaplan-Sanoff, M. (1994). Clinical issues related to substance-involved mothers and their infants. *Infant Mental Health, 15*(2), 202–217.

Sison, A.V., & Sever, J.L. (1992). HIV-1 infections in pregnancy and perinatal transmission of HIV: Current issues. *Pediatric AIDS and HIV Infection: Fetus to Adolescents, 3,* 1.

Stern, D. (1985). *The interpersonal world of the infant: A view from psychoanalysis and developmental psychology.* New York: Basic Books.

Terr, L. (1991). Childhood traumas: An outline and overview. *American Journal of Psychiatry, 148,* 10–20.

The Children of Alcoholics Foundation. (1994). *Twice at risk: A forum on children affected by family violence and parental addiction.* New York: Author.

Weiner, L., & Morse, B. (1992). *Prevention and treatment of fetal alcohol syndrome and fetal drug effects.* Brookline, MA: Fetal Alcohol Education Program [training handout].

William Gladden Foundation. (1989). *Children from alcoholic families.* York, PA: Author.

Zuckerman, B., & Bresnahan, K. (1991). Developmental and behavioral consequences of prenatal drug and alcohol exposure. *Pediatric Clinics of North America, 38*(6), 1387–1406.

Zuckerman, B., & Frank, D. (1992). Crack kids: Not broken. *Pediatrics, 89,* 337–339.

~ 11 ~

PROGRESS, NOT PERFECTION

When Nicki died of complications from her alcoholism and heroin addiction at the age of 36, she left behind five children. She and her children had been involved in the Women and Infants Clinic, a family-focused drug treatment program, for 3 years. The program staff readily agreed to continue their work with the family after Nicki's death, redeveloping a treatment plan that fit the new needs of the family.

Nicki's mother, although debilitated by illness and depression, agreed to assume custody of the children. Each child, traumatized by the sudden loss of Nicki and already fragile from experiencing years of familial substance abuse, needed much love and therapeutic care. The grandmother, struggling with her own needs, did the best she could, but couldn't adequately care for the grieving children. They began to fall apart.

Kara is Nicki's teenage daughter. She is bright and beautiful and full of hopes and dreams of becoming a doctor. She is also plagued by self-doubt and anxieties brought on by years of family trauma and turmoil. Desperate to escape an impossibly hostile grandmother, Kara left home frequently but had nowhere to go. A therapist in the Women and Infants Clinic saw Kara teetering on the edge of delinquency and despair. She began to offer Kara the support and guidance she had offered her mother, Nicki. The older daughter became pregnant and moved in with her boyfriend at this time, but the clinic maintained contact with her, offering assistance as needed.

Charles, Darren, and Robert are Nicki's sons. They each show their grief for their mother in different ways. Charles began failing in school. The two younger boys cried a lot and then grew silent. They all struggled with a grandmother who wouldn't allow them to speak of their mother and kept them at an emotional distance from her. The Women and Infants Clinic extended an offer to the grandmother to support her during this very stressful time. Together the children's grandmother and clinic staff made a plan to guide the children through these very troubling times.

~~~~~~

Nicki's family and their story were introduced at the beginning of *Families in Recovery*. When Nicki began her journey toward recovery, her family's treatment needs were very different from this vignette, where her journey ends. By understanding the intergenerational cycle of family dysfunction and the ravages of addictive disease on the family, one can begin to understand what Nicki's children need to recover and heal. As often stated in Alcoholics Anonymous, the goal is progress, not perfection. Families can heal, but it is a lifelong journey with many obstacles along the way.

In Part I of *Families in Recovery*, the groundwork is laid in preparation for a detailed description of models of successful intervention and treatment strategies for families affected by substance abuse. Part II focuses on key principles and practices of family-focused treatment, including strategies for fostering resilience in children and families. Part II of *Families in Recovery* offers successful intervention strategies for individual and group work with families and children—strategies that can be adapted and integrated into family-focused treatment programs.

Recovery

A Journey of Growth and Change

Patty: Today, I'm most proud of my recovery and the fact that I've been able to put one foot in front of the other and stay clean. I'm proud of my family; without them, I couldn't have done college and the other things, because I'm not lost in it. You know, I'm proud that I'm able to keep my own identity in this family unit—that my being a mom is not my total identity, that it really is a job, and I'm doing a real good job. Yet I'm able to keep Patty in the midst of all this.

Because of my recovery program, I'm able to reach out to help other addicts and alcoholics, to share with them my life and have them share their lives with me. I'm not alone anymore. My proud accomplishments: I graduated from Tufts University. I've allowed people to help me with my son. I have a great guy in my life who helps take care of my son and ease some of the responsibility, and he deals with him well. I plan on starting law school this year. I want to work with kids that have been affected [by alcohol and other drugs] and parents, advocating in the field of addiction.

I don't know whether I am an alcoholic because my father was an alcoholic, because I was brought up in a dysfunctional family, or because I was raped and sexually abused as a child. It doesn't matter where my alcoholism and my addiction came from. It's *what am I going to do about it today. And that is the most important thing I could do.*

What is responsible for this amazing transformation in Patty? Remember her story? She drank daily for years. She endangered her life and the lives of her husband and son while driving drunk. She reached the depths of despair upon learning that her alcohol consumption during her pregnancy tragically affected her son, who was born with FAS. How did she turn her life around in such a dramatic way? It would be simpler in some ways to attribute her metamorphosis to a miracle, to a fluke, or to luck. Her transformation, however, occurred as a result of the active and conscious process of recovery.

Recovery gives all those who experience addiction an opportunity to turn their lives around. Some believe that recovery is a miracle, and perhaps it is to those involved. In reality, however, recovery requires individuals to make a conscious choice to embark upon a journey that will release them from the darkest regions of themselves. It is a choice that requires mustering courage and faith: two attributes with which most addicts struggle. The work of recovery is arduous, often painful, and demanding. Those who have taken the journey of recovery, or who have walked with another through recovery, can attest to the lifesaving, life-altering, and life-affirming experience.

∿ What Is Recovery? ∿

The word *recovery* simply means returning to a former state of health or regaining a previously typical emotional state (Tabor, 1965). At one time, people believed that recovery from addiction meant simply restoring a person to his or her previous state of functioning. The development of Alcoholics Anonymous (AA) brought forth the concept of recovery as a complex and dynamic process of growth and change, rather than merely a reversal of signs and symptoms. AA was one of the first proponents for viewing recovery as a physical, psychological, and spiritual transformation that allows a person to live a positive and meaningful life free of addiction.

∿ Recovery as a Developmental Process ∿

Some theorists have cultivated other models of recovery, all of which are based upon AA's belief system, which stipulates that recovery is a developmental process that is dynamic and fluid and can enhance growth (Brown, 1985; Prochaska, DiClemente, & Norcross, 1992). These models assume that as people mature and learn how to experience and cope with feelings, aspects of their personalities that contributed to their addictions can evolve.

Although recovery sounds great in the abstract, many people don't know how to begin to pursue it. What follows is a detailed description of Brown's (1985) developmental model of recovery, as detailed in her book, *Treating the Alcoholic: A Developmental Model of Recovery.*

Loss of Control

In Brown's (1985) model, the central organizing principle of addiction—loss of control over a substance or process—is also applicable to recovery. Paradoxically, in recovery, admitting a loss of control liberates one to move toward taking control. Admitting defeat in the battle with addiction and surrendering to recovery ultimately enables one to win the battle. The first challenge is to abandon the denial and the delusional thinking that accompany addiction and recognize that the addiction has spun out of control. Next, the addict must completely stop all use—although recovery is not achieved simply by abstaining. Abstinence is an absolute requirement for recovery, but it is only the beginning of the journey.

One goes through a series of stages in recovery, in a gradual process that requires the construction and reconstruction of knowledge, information, and experiences, guided by the individual, not the therapist, partner, or children. The individual gradually creates a way of living that allows her a life free of addiction by re-creating her system of beliefs and values. Recovering addicts select various resources to integrate for use in their personalized and highly individualized itineraries for recovery and choose particular tools from a variety of available options. These plans usually become people's way of life and a part of how they define themselves.

Carol: I fight my disease by trying to do things that are positive. There are tools I use in my recovery. I go to counseling. I belong to a women's group. My sponsor always helps me and the treatment program and the nuns in it helped me.

Patty: You know I go to (12-Step) meetings all the time. The minimum I get to today—and I have $6\frac{1}{2}$ years' sobriety and clean time back to back—is five meetings a week.

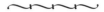

Didi: I'm in a residential treatment program today and what's good about that for me in my recovery is there are 21 recovering addicted and alcoholic women who are there for me every single day, including the counselors. And we have a director and night staff. And whenever there is a problem or I just can't see my way out of anything, I can always turn to someone and say, "You know today, I'm just really having a bad day." There is always someone there for me, and that is better for me because I don't think when I came out of the detox that I could have made it out here right out of detox. I needed some more support.

Parallels Between Recovery and Child Development

Movement through the stages of recovery requires mastery of specific, sequential tasks, comparable to the progression through the developmental stages of childhood in which children resolve specific tasks in order to mature and further their development. Many of the tasks of recovery and child development are, in fact, quite similar: from the narcissistic stages of early infancy, through toddlerhood and a developing sense of autonomy and self, to a healthy self-esteem, and sense of interconnectedness and productivity. The phenomenon of this parallel development makes parenting in recovery a uniquely challenging experience for everyone involved.

Gino: I think that my recovery is about searching, trying to understand not only myself, but my kids as well. Because when I started drinking, my mentality was like a 9-year-old's. When I stopped, I think I was still learning. Now I'm 35, but I feel like I'm 20. With my kids, I tell them I'm growing with them. I don't have all the answers. And I had a little argument with my son and I was so confused. I was mean, and that was awful. I thought the world was going to come down and kill me. But I didn't pick up. All I did was try to listen to him, and I didn't hit him.

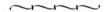

Lorna: My kids have played a big part in my recovery. I think of all the dirt that I did to them back then when I was drugging. I mean I did some terrible things. And I look at them in their face today, and they don't look at me with that look of disgust. I feel better. My last baby I just had, she's great. She wakes me up early in the morning, she gives me something to look forward to for the whole day. And I get my other children on the weekends now. I'm having a hard time dealing with them. But this has taught me a great lesson: where I was and where I am today with these kids. They ask me a lot of questions about my meetings and a lot of things about my recovery.

Didi: A lot of people ask me about having a new baby and being in recovery. They say, "Isn't it hard?" And I say, "Yeah, it's hard, but it's not that hard—I feel that if I can do it, so can other women, and I have a lot of help."

～ Components of the Recovery Model ～

Brown's (1985) model of recovery describes three interrelated axes areas through which the recovering addict moves: the addiction axis, the environmental axis, and the axis of interpretation of self and others. Here, an *axis* is defined as an imaginary straight line around which an area of functioning rotates. It is a focal point, similar to the hub of a wheel or the axle of a car. Brown's three axes are simply arenas of functioning that are always present throughout the stages of recovery, interwoven and multidimensional.

As recovery progresses, there is a shift in emphasis from one arena to another. At first, the arena of the addiction has more significance, and recovery focuses on the source of the addiction. Next, this focus is slowly diminished as the other two arenas gain significance. Issues that were ignored during active use now are addressed, including health, family, friends, and careers.

Addiction Arena

The addiction arena—what Brown refers to as the addiction axis—focuses on the substance or process that has been the primary organizing factor in the individual's life, pushing everything else into the background.

Carol: I gave my son methadone by accident, and he almost died from it. I rushed him to the hospital, but the next thing I knew, I took my son home and I was right back out there. And that couldn't even stop me, because I loved the effects of the high. And nobody was going to take my dope away from me.

The primary relationship with the drug must be abandoned, and abstinence achieved, for recovery to move forward.

Environmental Arena

The environmental arena involves interactions between the individual and various aspects of his personal world. As the focus on the addiction decreases and awareness of other life concerns and interests moves into the foreground, the individual begins to experience a widening of his world experience. The mental haze created by the addiction is beginning to clear and the person can think more clearly. The intense focus on the addiction diminishes, as does the obsession with getting and using the substance and hiding the addiction. No longer tied to an exclusive relationship with the addiction, the individual is free to direct attention to new activities, occupational choices, hobbies, and interests.

Susan: I hadn't worked in 5 years. My life became so involved with the cocaine that I couldn't think about anything else. I was selling, but I was using up most of the profits. Before this, I took dance classes and I used to love to go to the ballet. I had a group of dance friends and we would go to performances together. I've lost touch with them. I didn't do any of those things when I picked up the cocaine. Now that I'm in recovery, I'm getting back into the things I used to like to do, and I'm taking a refresher course so I can get a job.

Arena of Interpretation of Self and Others

With interpretation of self and others, the individual examines and revises her frame of reference in terms of relationships, which also serves as a reflection of herself in relation to others. Before this time, the addict has been isolated, and relationships were primarily associated with the addiction. Now, the person sees herself as part of a larger whole, instead of thinking of herself as the center of the universe. This egocentric, "me first" attitude evolves into a more mature concern for self and others as well as a greater good.

Carol: I was basically a selfish person. I would never do anything for anybody without expecting something in return. And at the treatment program I was in, I had all these plans, after I'd gotten to a certain phase in the program, to go get a job. And they told me I wasn't going to get a job. They said, "We want you to volunteer." And I said, "What? I don't volunteer." And I fought and fought. I had to listen to them because I've always done things my way. So I volunteered, and I started working with the elderly. I started having good feelings that they really cared about me and they really liked me, and I was doing something constructive with them and could make them feel happy and I could make them feel good. And we could identify with each other. They didn't pick up a drink or a drug, but they still felt abandonment, they still felt unwanted, a lot of the feelings that were engrained in me.

∽ Stages of Recovery ∽

I'm the person who used to love to get high.
I'm the person who used to always black out before the end of the night.
I'm the person who sometimes got locked out of her own house.
I'm also the person who would slip into your house by day and out by night.
I'm the person who used to walk up and down your street praying for that ride to pull over or just beep.
I'm the person who always got into jams.
I'm the person who always landed on her ass not her feet nor her hands.
I'm the person everyone called a sneak.
I'm the person who would drink and get loud.
I'm the person that would want to kill all those in the crowd.
I'm the person you would want to be a friend.
I'm also the person you would want to turn on before the night's end.
So, what you see here is not a lost cause, my friend.
What you see here is an addict in remission.

Brown's (1985) model of recovery also includes four stages: 1) the addiction stage, 2) the transition stage, 3) the early recovery stage, and 4) the stage of ongoing recovery, in which the three arenas of recovery are embedded (see Figure 1). Movement is away from the egocentric focus on the addiction toward a healthier sense of self, relationships, and the world in general.

Addiction

In the first stage, the addiction stage, the person is actively engaged in his addiction, still believing that he can control his addiction. The level of denial is very high. As the addiction progresses, the addict's world view narrows, and the addict becomes increasingly isolated.

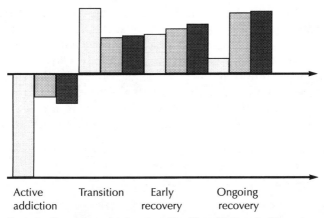

Figure 1.   Four-stage model of recovery. (Key: ▨ = addiction axis; ▨ = environmental axis; ■ = axis of interpretation of self and others.)

In the framework of Piaget's theory (1970), the addict is unable to assimilate and accommodate information about his addiction. People in the addict's life may confront him about the addiction, especially as the addict's behavior escalates out of control; nevertheless, the addict is unable to make use of this information to change his behavior. It is as if the person is stuck in a rut or unable to find the "reset" button.

In this stage, the person in many ways resembles a baby. Like the infant, the addicted individual uses extremely primitive defenses. Addicts can be quite narcissistic and self-focused: The world exists to serve their needs and give them what they want. Impaired abilities to soothe and regulate themselves interfere with their ability to delay gratification of needs and impulses.

From a psychodynamic perspective, the addict has an inflexible and immature ego. His narrow perspective on behavior focuses on getting and using the object of the addiction. The primitive denial used to maintain the addiction prevents addicts from examining and changing their behavior.

Other immature defenses used are rationalization and projection. Addicts often make excuses for why they use. Common rationalizations include "My life is so bad," "My family hates me," or "Nobody understands me." The list is endless. In addition, the addict assumes little if any responsibility for the behavior. Painful feelings, impulses, and ideas are projected onto the outside world (Edward, Ruskin, & Turrini, 1981), and blame is cast onto other people or events. This type of thinking is similar to the "magical thinking" of very early childhood in which children struggle with their ability to control their world, believing that they act on the world to produce the pleasurable effects they desire and that the world acts on them to cause them to think and behave in particular ways (Fraiberg, 1959).

The longer one remains in this stage, the more her world perspective narrows, plunging the individual further into the nightmare of addiction. Some addicts spend their lives in this primitive state of denial, distortion, and disease, until their addiction kills them.

I have lost so many people in my family to drugs and alcohol. Two of my brothers died from AIDS that they got by sharing dirty needles. My mother died from liver disease from her drinking, and my sister died from shooting drugs.

Delores

To be forced out of denial, an addict needs some type of motivating physical, emotional, or spiritual experience, often referred to as "hitting bottom." All recovering addicts tell of their own personal and unique "wake-up call" that signaled the shift in the way they thought about their addiction.

In early childhood development, Piaget (1970) refers to this phenomenon as the "grasp of consciousness." A sudden insight brings a new awareness and allows movement in a different direction. For addicts, the blinding insight of recognizing that they cannot control their addictions and that their lives are unmanageable nudges them toward recovery. This acceptance of failure of control over the addiction and the willingness to consider abstinence moves a person toward the next stage of recovery.

Lorna: Before I knew it, I was spending my welfare check up on cocaine. I was doing nothing for my children in the end. I was taking off on weekends, I remember. I would leave on Friday, I wouldn't come back until Sunday or Monday. I wasn't worried about who my kids were with, what they were doing, if they were eating. Every time I would come back, it would be the same thing. There would be no food in the house. The kids would say, "Ma, I'm hungry. Ma, where have you been?" Cocaine brought me to my knees. It took everything from me: my children, my family, and, most of all, it took me. I was a prostitute by this time, doing everything there was just to get a hit. I was getting real bad feelings there toward the end. I

didn't want to live anymore, but then at the same time, I didn't want to die.

Didi: DSS [Department of Social Services] got involved in my life and they took my kids. When they took my kids, they asked me if I had a problem. I told them I did and I asked them to help. At this point, drugs had brought me down so bad, I had no refrigerator in my house. I had just enough beds for us to sleep in and there was no kitchen table. My kids sat on the floor and they ate. I had a drug dealer coming in and out of my house. And I didn't think anything was wrong with it because they ate every day, their clothes were clean; I washed them in the tub at night, but they were clean. I was pregnant with my youngest daughter. I finally got to the point I didn't want to be a mother anymore. I didn't want my kids. I didn't want to take care of them. I didn't want to live anymore. I just didn't want anything. I just wanted to stop getting high and I didn't know how.

The primary task of the addiction phase is to break down the addict's distorted belief system and denial, which facilitates the shift toward abstinence and sobriety. As addicts strive for abstinence, they must transfer their object attachments from the sources of their addictions to healthier, outside sources, much like a maturing infant learns to suck his thumb to provide self-soothing and replace reliance on outside sources. They may begin to talk with others about their burgeoning awareness of their addiction. They may attend a 12-Step meeting, read a book about addiction, or seek professional help. The addict also must discover inner resources to replace the reliance on the addiction.

Unable to survive in early recovery without much external support, the addict, like the infant, depends heavily on outside sources to meet his most basic needs. Individuals in early recovery need much external structure in this early stage to help them maintain abstinence and begin to make the cognitive and behavior changes necessary for recovery. Change is difficult for everyone, particularly addicts and very young children.

Movement in the addiction stage requires a concrete and carefully titrated cognitive and behavioral approach. During this time, the addict learns about the disease and creates a supportive structure to help maintain abstinence. The primary developmental task for both the infant and the addict is to develop trust. The addicted individual must begin to trust that there can be a life free of addiction and that there are ways to achieve this. They must trust that they are capable of change and growth. They must begin to trust other people and create new environments that will support their sobriety. For many, it requires a leap of faith. Infants must learn to trust that when they cry, someone will attend to them and give them what they need. Addicts must learn to trust that when they reach out for help, someone will take their hands and guide them in a new and healthier direction. AA's 12-Step program addresses this phase of recovery in the first two steps (Alcoholics Anonymous, 1976):

Step 1: We admitted we were powerless over (the addiction) and that our lives had become unmanageable.
Step 2: We came to believe that a Power greater than ourselves could restore us to sanity.

At this point, special mention must be made about the role of grief in recovery. Very few people understand the intense feelings of loss and grief that addicts experience when they give up their addictions. It is difficult to imagine that one could be sad about the loss of a negative and destructive way of life. People assume that because addicts are giving up an unhealthy way of life, they experience less of a loss or no loss at all. They assume that most addicts feel relief, when, in reality, most addicts feel grief. Until now, their addictions have been their best friends—they have depended upon them and they have always been there for them. They have defined their identities to friends and family and established the blueprint of their relationships. The addict, with the loss of the addiction, is losing a familiar role and familiar territory. Often, those involved with the addict experience a sense of loss as well. Therefore, those who guide addicts must remember to validate this grief and take every opportunity to identify and manage these feelings. Working through grief is a valuable learning process that allows us to move ahead in life. Expecting and allowing for grieving in early recovery is crucial in order to put the addiction to rest and move on.

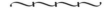

Claire: I was not prepared for how sad I would feel, no one told me I would feel like my friend had just died. I remember when I realized I could never use again. I was frantically pacing around the room and then I locked myself in the bathroom and cried for a long time.

I remember thinking that it felt the way I cried when my father died. I felt confused. I had this big empty feeling in my stomach, I felt empty and sad. This feeling stayed with me for a while, even now I occasionally feel sad about not ever being able to use.

Transition

In the transition stage, there is both a cognitive shift and a behavioral shift. Cognitively, the addict shifts his view from denial to acceptance: "I am not an addict" becomes "I am an addict." Behaviorally, there is a shift from using to not using. An anecdote about one young woman's therapy illustrates these shifts.

Carla spent 2 years of a long-term therapy bouncing back and forth between thinking she was an alcoholic and then denying it. One week, she would come in and emphatically state, "I am definitely an alcoholic," the next week, she would take back her claim and wonder whether she should test herself by drinking. A few times she did drink, each time renouncing alcohol and seemingly accepting that she could not control her drinking. This ambivalence continued until she was able to finally decide that she could not control her drinking and therefore would not drink.

New behaviors and new ways of thinking begin to substitute for old patterns. Once primarily competitive, the person in the transition stage is more cooperative.

Individuals often move back and forth from the transition stage to the addiction stage as they struggle to come to terms with their addictions and the issue of control. Denial and the struggle for control can leave a person teetering between these two stages, sometimes for a long time. Periods of abstinence may be punctuated by active use as the addict questions whether he is really an addict. Resolving this conflict helps addicts come to terms with their denial and move toward the next stage.

In transition, the primary task is maintaining abstinence. This task requires addicts to see themselves differently and to change their identities. This process is reminiscent of the toddler who must begin to develop a separate sense of identity from her mother. The child learns to correctly identify herself in terms of sex, culture, religion, place in the family, and numerous other factors. To shift their distorted self-perceptions, addicts need to correctly identify themselves as addicted. This change in perception assists them in interpreting themselves realistically in relation to others in their lives. Accepting responsibility for one's life and being able to realistically accept shortcomings, as well as strengths, furthers one in the journey of recovery.

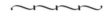

Claire: At this point in my recovery, I knew I had to face up to myself and where I was. I had to take stock of the good stuff and the bad. Before I used to think it was all bad, now I'm beginning to discover good things about me too. I know I have hurt a lot of people, including myself, but I can't beat myself up. I have to say I'm sorry and change so I don't do it again. This is new for me.

The transition phase is a time of rapid learning and mastery of new skills for the addict, and, like toddlers, addicts in this stage need much external structure and support. Language development plays a pivotal role in early recovery as well. The comparison between this phase of recovery and the development of language in the stages of later infancy and toddlerhood is also striking.

Silence Is the Enemy of Recovery: Language Development Piaget (1970) emphasizes the importance of language development in allowing the maturing child to mediate thoughts, emotions, impulses, and behavior. Without an internal language structure, a child cannot identify and label thoughts and feelings and has much difficulty controlling impulses. Language can mediate between internal processes and external behavior. The process of taking in new information, making sense of it, and then applying it to one's experience enables a person to adapt and grow. Piaget (1970) calls this the process of *assimilation and accommodation,* and it is easily applied to the recovering addict.

As in toddlerhood, the recovering individual must learn how to identify and experience thoughts, feelings, and affect. He must be able to cope with and tolerate adversity without his addiction. Construction and reconstruction of information and knowledge (e.g., reinterpreting and gaining new insight) move one toward sobriety.

In the early period of one young woman's therapy, she would frequently come in with a variety of physical complaints. Heart palpitations, stomachaches, headaches, chest pain, back pain, numbness in her hands, poor memory, and fatigue were all part of her daily life experience. At times, she would become convinced that she had brain damage or some disease such as multiple sclerosis or cancer. Despite numerous visits to different doctors who invariably gave her a clean bill of health, she continued to think that there was something physically wrong; however, a balanced diet, routine exercise, and adequate sleep were all foreign notions to her, as was expressing her feelings. "I don't even think I know what a feeling is," she would say.

She began adhering to more positive self-care routines, which did help alleviate some of her physical discomfort, while she and the doctor began having a "dialogue" with her symptoms—asking her "heart" why it was having palpitations and her "stomach" why it hurt. Slowly, her physical symptoms opened the door into her emotional life, which was fraught with feelings she could neither identify nor understand. She learned that her heart palpitations represented anxiety and her stomach hurt when she felt frightened. Headaches and poor memory bothered her when she was feeling overwhelmed and confused. Body aches and pain literally represented psychic aches and pain. When she began recovering memories of early traumatic events, she stopped experiencing numbness in her hands. Identifying her feelings and connecting them to her experience enabled her to live her life in a new way. She could talk about how different things made her feel and she could make decisions about how to respond. She could evaluate her behavior and decide if she needed to make adjustments. In the past, her repertoire of responses was mostly unconscious, usually impulsive, and almost always included drinking and self-destructive behavior.

The use of language allows a delay in gratification of needs and impulses. Silence is the enemy of recovery. As one moves forward into early recovery, he continues to mature and grow, resembling the preschool-age child, who is practicing and mastering new skills to become more self-reliant as his world expands. Preschoolers establish firm senses of identity and self-esteem by mastering language and using it as a cognitive anchor. When a child is feeling upset, sad, or angry, she can use language to convey feelings and needs. She can verbally ask for help or turn to familiar stories, nursery rhymes, books, and songs to help soothe her and give her a sense of familiarity and comfort.

Transitional Objects   Toddlers are famous for their use of "transitional objects" to help ease them through the rugged terrain of separation. Teddy bears, blankets, and dolls are common transitional objects that offer comfort to the distressed toddler. Children can also use diverse objects such as a piece of masking tape planted on the cheek or mother's full-length silk slip as objects of comfort and security. The objects, regardless of what they are, are imbued with the power to bring a sense of safety and security and can help bridge the gap between external and internal reliance.

Recovering addicts also employ this coping mechanism. Many may be familiar with the plethora of AA slogans displayed on car bumpers, T-shirts, and key chains, for example, "Easy does it," "One day at a time," "Let go, let God," "Stinking thinking," "Came to believe," and "Higher Powered." On the surface, these slogans appear as simple, albeit clever, and pithy statements. Some think that they are dumb and meaningless or just plain annoying. But, with attention to the process of recovery, one can recognize these gems for what they are—cognitive anchors. These bumper stickers, T-shirts, and key chains are similar to the toddlers' "transitional object" (Winnicott, 1953).

Most recovery programs rely heavily on the use of written or recorded material in helping with the transition into recovery. If a person is struggling in her recovery, it is reassuring to have familiar words that offer comfort, support, and wisdom. The use of books, pamphlets, and audio- and videotapes is encouraged as adjuncts to treatment.

The use of readings and slogans also resembles how some people rely on prayer, bringing a sense of peace, comfort, and connection. Others may use meditation as a way of finding peace and serenity. A very widely known AA prayer, "Serenity Prayer," opens and closes countless meetings, giving millions of people a sense of peace and serenity each day.

God grant me the serenity
to accept the things I cannot change,
the courage to change the things I can,
and the wisdom to know the difference.

Early Recovery

Addicts in early recovery have accepted that they cannot control their use, which brings them to a deeper level of surrender and prepares them to move forward. The person who used old experiences as an excuse to drink or abuse drugs may now see the merit of examining and understanding these experiences as a way to move forward in recovery. The young woman who experienced multiple early childhood trauma realizes that she drank to numb the pain of those memories and within the context of supportive treatment can come to terms with her history. She may even decide at some point to volunteer at a shelter for battered women or to pursue a career in human services. Newly developing attitudes and values influence individuals in adopting new ways of evaluating themselves and their experiences. Reemerging moral development, which up to this point has been arrested, enables them to create clear values and codes of behavior.

In this stage, the newly recovering individual still resembles a preschooler, who has gained some mastery over his environment and continues to expand his use of language. Preschoolers are learning to delay gratification and to control impulses by redirection and substitution of wants and needs (Fraiberg, 1959), and are able to function autonomously for periods of time. Adults in recovery, too, must learn to delay gratification and control impulses and see themselves as autonomous and able to function without alcohol or other drugs.

Another important cognitive achievement for preschoolers is developing the capacity for empathy. Preschoolers must learn to put themselves in someone else's place and begin to identify what it must be like for the other person. Learning about how another person feels, and being able to empathize with that person, is crucial in a civilized society (Fraiberg, 1959). This capacity for empathy is also important for the addict in early recovery, whose developing sense of self depends on the ability to be empathetic.

Addicts in the early recovery stage must also continue to develop their language skills. Many have only a rudimentary internal language structure for identifying thoughts and feelings. In addition, many addicts have heard negative messages about themselves since early childhood, including "you're lazy," "you're stupid," "you're no good," "you deserve to be abused," and "you're unlovable." Over time, they have come to believe these negative messages. Erasing old messages and rerecording new, positive, and more realistic messages is an important goal in recovery.

Gino: You know when I was active, I didn't know how to describe my feelings—when I was sad, when I was angry, or even when I was happy. Now that I'm in recovery, I'm still a little confused. I have to find out why I'm sad or that I'm really angry. I'll allow myself to be angry with somebody or to have resentments. I used to blame myself for everything, now I know I'm human. It's all right today though, I don't have to drink because I tell people my feelings. It is kind of hard to get used to this. I never learned how to describe my feelings.

Maturing infants and young children begin to learn and use language to identify thoughts and feelings. Whereas the young infant can only scream out or cry when she feels angry or sad, the more mature child can put words to those feelings and say, "It makes me mad when you grab my toys." The addict in the addiction phase or very early transition phase may drink or use other drugs in response to feeling upset, angry, afraid, or depressed. In recovery, he learns how to identify and talk about feelings without using alcohol or other drugs. The mastering of language helps children and recovering addicts manage feelings and behavior, bringing clarity to their understanding of themselves. Maladaptive patterns change and become adaptive while the addict maintains abstinence.

Gino: When I feel frustrated, I try to look for help and I ask people for help. Am I right? Am I wrong? I think it is okay today to feel like this because every day you've got to be struggling. And it is not a matter of staying stuck, but trying to keep on searching. I think this is what my recovery is about.

Learning new language and how to use it while developing a supportive treatment structure creates the scaffolding upon which recovery is built. As the addict actively practices new ways of thinking and acting, she is integrating the new behaviors into a daily routine. The act of doing and redoing provides an opportunity to solidify and incorporate more mature ways of functioning. This process of assimilation and accommodation facilitates growth. AA has a slogan that is particularly apt for this phase of recovery:

Fake it, until you make it.

In the early recovery stage, it is very important for the individual to have external structure and support. Addicts need someone to teach and guide them as well as act as an external source of rules, limits, and conscience. A therapist or counselor, along with a 12-Step sponsor, can provide the structure and guidance that is so crucial. Very often, people choose to combine a 12-Step program with individual and/or group therapy, perhaps beginning with an inpatient detoxification program or a longer term residential treatment program. The individual chooses specific strategies for recovery with the aid of others.

Ongoing Recovery

The process of growth and change continues to flourish in ongoing recovery. Newly mastered language is used to negotiate and navigate in the world with maturity and a sense of purpose. The individual continues to gain insight about feelings and experiences, while reworking the past and creating the present in safe and healthy ways. There is growing self-acceptance, self-reliance, and positive self-regard. Interdependent and sharing relationships, including a cooperative world view, gain priority. The fluid shifts among arenas take the person farther away from the addiction arena. Although the addict is still learning how to care for himself in positive ways, including how to eat, rest, play, and exercise, he is also discovering how to balance the many aspects of his life, such as work, family, relationships, and leisure time.

At this time, people in recovery have more flexible ego functioning and are no longer focused only on themselves. Using inner resources, they have learned how to self-soothe and self-regulate. They have made great progress toward integrating the physical, psychological, and spiritual parts of themselves and are functioning in the world by using mature psychological defenses. They have established a plan for recovery and are following that plan, modifying it as needed. They can ask for and accept help, as well as offer help.

In this stage of recovery, the individual mirrors the growth through the childhood stages of latency, adolescence, and young adulthood. Although achieving ongoing recovery is no guarantee that one will never make mistakes, never feel depressed, or will not regress to an earlier stage, it does mean that a person has acquired many of the tools needed to cope with adversity and crisis in a healthier way. Although relapse is part of the disease and always a possibility, the more time in recovery, the better the odds are for preventing a relapse.

The tasks of ongoing recovery allow addicts to continue to solidify their newly acquired behaviors and skills, using them to continue to grow and mature. One of the important tasks in this phase is connecting with one's sense of identity, accepting that one is indeed an addict while exploring and defining other areas of one's identity. This process is analogous to the child using what she has learned about herself to navigate in the world apart from the family or the adolescent who grapples with her sense of herself as a maturing sexual being and gains increasing independence. In ongoing recovery, relationships are reworked and new relationships form with more altruism, empathy, and interdependence. Addicts are able to set boundaries for themselves and see themselves in the larger context of their life.

Patty: Now I have other people I've learned to trust. I've learned to open up to other women. I need other women in my life. I was a man searcher, I trusted men more than I trusted women. I need other women in my life who share my experiences, my strengths, and my hopes. I have to share and talk to another recovering addict or alcoholic every day. I have a sponsor whom I use every day. I am in a healthy relationship today; he is my friend. It wasn't a relationship like let's go out and get married on the first date. I did that when I was out there. I'm learning about Patty. I have to keep my recovery first, and it's really difficult in today's society, because dealing with my alcoholism is a full-time job. My son is a full-time job. This relationship is a full-time job. I go to school full time. That is another full-time job. You know, my recovery has to come first. This was the hardest turnaround for me. I thought my son came first, but you know I can't have him if I don't have my recovery. If I give up my recovery and go back out there and use, I'm going to lose him, I'm going to lose me. I'm no good to him if I'm using, and today my kid's got a real good mom.

Maturity and equilibrium in the areas of emotions, cognition, behavior, and attachment allow more stability and flexibility and enhance continued growth.

Didi: For me, being clean has been really awesome. I have my bad days, but generally I feel great. My worst day in recovery beats my best day out there using.

Gino: Since I've been in recovery I've been revived. I could say it's the first time that I am living. And it's wonderful. It's wonderful to know that I have two beautiful kids and they tell me, "Mommy, I'm so proud of you." I studied for 2 years and got certified as an alcohol and drug counselor. I have worked with people who are addicted, and it's wonderful. I wouldn't change anything, I wouldn't trade my worst day in recovery for my best day when I was high. I am proud that I am not using and that I am clean and that my higher power gave me another opportunity of being on the road and learning who I am. I'm proud because I still have my kids, and I'm proud because there are so many things I could do and choose and I have a whole lifetime until God takes me.

Lorna: For me, getting clean and staying clean is a lot of hard work. I have to constantly be on guard for my disease. I go to regular meetings, and I go on commitments. I joined a group. I deal with the five basics. I try to keep myself busy. There are a lot of things my disease comes in on and tries to take away from me. I want to be able to go to school and get a good job and own a home. By the grace of God, it will happen.

～ Pitfalls in the Recovery Process ～

Don't quit trying
Is a hard thing to do
Because every time you turn around
Something else tries to stop you.
But you keep on trying
But it is never enough
You keep telling yourself not to let those that care for you down
But as you try to turn the next corner
Someone knocks you down.
You try not to cry
For the pain is so great
So you pick yourself up and say this time I'll wait.

So you try to walk a little slower so you won't get knocked down
But soon as you hit the corner
Someone knocks your ass down.
So you ask yourself, why is this happening to me?
And a little voice says: "Either you're too slow or you just can't see"
Or maybe, it's just plain negativity!

Cassandra, an ACoA in recovery

As Cassandra's poem so poignantly illustrates, recovery is fraught with pitfalls. There are numerous challenges for all addicts in recovery, which, left unmanaged, can lead to relapse. Knowing how to navigate around the pitfalls and anticipate problems is life insurance for the addict. People in recovery quickly gain knowledge about the disease of addiction and work to increase their understanding about what addiction means to them. Because no two addicts are alike, opportunities for relapse greatly vary.

One of the first concrete tasks for all addicts in recovery is identifying their individual triggers (Brown, 1985; Gorski, 1989; Gorski & Miller, 1984). A *trigger* is anything that elicits a craving or desire to use. Early recognition of one's triggers and patterns can alert one to danger and help to prevent relapse. The list of triggers is endless, but there are some common danger zones for all addicts, including specific people, places, and things; certain feeling states; and physical illness and pain.

People, Places, and Things

The ability to recognize the "people, places, and things" that trigger use can prevent a relapse. Being in the presence of drugs, drug users, or places where one used or bought drugs can be very dangerous. For an alcoholic, this can be very difficult because alcohol is legal and so available. For many, this means forming new friendships, avoiding familiar places, and perhaps even moving to a new home. Sometimes people who have been in recovery for a while test themselves by revisiting the scenes of their drug use, which can be very risky. Although gradual and well-planned exposure to triggers can help to neutralize their power, one must proceed with caution and support.

Feeling States

Difficult feelings, such as anger or sadness, can sometimes act as powerful triggers, particularly if one has not established mediating language. Fear and anxiety—feelings that are often difficult to identify—can trigger use, as can guilt and shame or any other feelings that make a person want to disappear. Negative thinking, such as "I will never be able to do this," and negative self-talk, such as "I'm such a loser. I can't do anything right," can also act as triggers.

Although a somewhat insidious dynamic that is often hard to comprehend, feeling good or having something to celebrate can trigger a relapse. Sometimes people believe that, because things are going well, they will not get into trouble if they use "just this once." Feeling successful can also create an inflated or distorted sense of invulnerability—a particularly vulnerable state for the recovering addict who, far removed from the old experiences of depression and failure, may be tempted to take risks. Also, as most addicts have used in the past primarily out of negativity such as failures, hurt, or emotional pain, they may think that using for a "positive" reason is harmless.

Physical Illness and Pain

Physical illness or pain causes stress and discomfort, two feelings that can trigger relapse. Feeling depleted or exhausted can strain coping capabilities and render the recovering addict vulnerable. Careful monitoring of the use of some prescribed medications, particularly pain medication or mood altering medications, which can be addictive, may be necessary. Generally, one should be on the lookout for any significant changes in mood and activity, including irritability, depression, or isolation.

Many people in recovery who are required to take medications for medical reasons are both leery and anxious. They may also hear from others in recovery that they should take no medication at all, including aspirin or other over-the-counter drugs. People who must take medication to stay healthy should have access to a physician who is both sensitive to their recovery issues and willing to monitor them carefully.

Haunted: Cravings and Drug Dreams

Knowing and accepting that relapse is part of the disease can help by preparing a person to cope with cravings and wishes to return to use. Relapse prevention requires that a person actively manage urges and cravings (Gorski, 1989).

Karla: I had a dream last night that I was using. It was so real; I could smell it and taste it. I remember waking up in a panic, thinking, "Oh my God, I've relapsed, now I have to start all over." It took me a few minutes to realize that I was dreaming. I was so scared, because I thought that it meant I was going to use and I felt out of control again. I called my sponsor first thing, and I went to a meeting with her. A lot of people told me that they had drug dreams there, but I never knew about them before.

Shana: My cravings aren't in my head; they are in my body. I get this tight queasy feeling in my stomach and I want to go and use immediately. When it happens, I feel as if I can't control it because it is so strong. In the past when I had this feeling, I did go back out there and use. Now, I know I can manage the feeling, I don't have to use. I get on my knees and I pray, and I call my sister who is in recovery, and I go to meetings and talk about it.

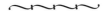

Cravings and drug dreams are parts of addiction and can often plague a person long after he has become abstinent. Cravings can occur with or without being triggered. Drug dreams are often an ongoing occurrence during recovery. The craving can be so strong that it overwhelms the person with the urge to use and the fear of relapse. Determination and willpower are inadequate defenses against cravings. The AA term "white knuckle sobriety" addresses the poor choice of relying on willpower to stay clean, conjuring up an image of a terrified person hanging on for dear life as he tries to "tough out" an urge to use. Expecting cravings to occur and having a plan for managing them can help a person survive these frightening experiences and gain strength. A tight recovery plan that includes a wide support network, an individualized treatment program, a balanced lifestyle, and the acquisition of knowledge and skills are all components of a good prevention strategy. A good relapse prevention plan enables a person to be in control of her disease, not a victim of it (Gorski & Miller, 1984).

Didi: I consider my children my gifts from God. I consider my recovery a gift also, one that I gave to myself and my children. For those of you who are out there and still struggling, don't give up. It may not work the first time, but eventually it will. Just pick up the telephone and ask for help; just don't give up. Someday you will succeed.

～～～～～

Dealing Successfully with a Relapse

If a relapse does occur, it is not the end of the world, although it may feel that way to the addict. Relapse can be reframed as a learning experience. A plan for relapse damage control should be in place and the person should immediately get back on the path of recovery. People often feel that they have failed because they have relapsed and they may as well continue to use. Relapse is an opportunity to re-examine the recovery program and how one is living one's life. It most likely means that a better plan and more support are necessary.

～ With Recovery Comes Change for the Family ～

Recovery is a time of great change, not only for the addict but for the entire family system. Caregiving arrangements change, routines are disrupted, and patterns of functioning are redesigned. Everything that was once controlled and defined by the disease is now up for grabs. Family members and their specific roles within the family system are forever altered by the process of recovery.

Reconfiguring the family in recovery affects all those involved and demands that members alter their roles and responsibilities. Some of the changes are welcomed, while others are dreaded. Examples of transitions to navigate include a parent moving home from an extended stay at a residential program, parents regaining custody of their children and the resultant reunification, active participation in a treatment program, and reconstructing damaged relationships.

Partners are asked to participate in recovery and are expected to make changes to accommodate the family's new lifestyle, often while simultaneously dealing with their own recovery and emotional issues. Parenting responsibilities may be disrupted for them and further compounded by the complicated dynamics of the new family reconfiguration. Children are asked to make adjustments and shifts in their lives that they neither asked for nor understand. Moving from one home to another, leaving friends, changing schools, leaving a foster caregiver to be reunited with a parent, living with a parent with whom they have had a difficult time, becoming accustomed to new routines, and dealing with myriad emotions all require much strength and courage from children.

Brown (1985) conceptualizes recovery as a developmental process, in which each member is given the opportunity to become part of the process of growth and change, beginning his or her own unique journey toward health. The process is different for each member because each incorporates his or her own issues and needs, which alters the tasks, meaning, and outcomes of recovery for each (Brown, 1985).

⁓ Gender-Specific Considerations ⁓

Our experiences are shaped, in part, by our age, our sex, our ethnicity, and our cultural practices. This holds true when examining both the causes and effects of addiction and understanding the process of recovery. Issues affect individuals differently depending on who they are. A general discussion of some of the major areas of difference for various family members in recovery follows.

Women

Comes the Dawn

After a while, you learn the subtle difference
Between holding a hand and chaining a soul.
And you learn that love doesn't mean leaning.
You begin to learn that kisses aren't contracts.
And presents aren't promises.
And you begin to accept all your defeats
With your head up and your eyes ahead,
With the grace of a woman, not the grief of a child.
And you learn to build all your roads on today
Because tomorrow's ground is too uncertain for plans
And futures have a way of falling down in mid-flight.
After a while, you learn that even sunshine burns
If you ask too much.
So you plant your own garden,
And decorate your own soul,
Instead of waiting for someone to bring you flowers.
And you learn that you really can endure.
That you really are strong.
That you really do have worth.

And you learn, and you learn.
With every good-bye,
You learn.

Stephanie E., 1985

Women have a special place in our culture as caregivers and nurturers and often put the needs of their children, partners, and others before their own. Think of Patty, who said that the hardest thing for her in recovery was realizing that she had to put her recovery at the top of the list ahead of her son, her partner, and her education. Putting their own needs first is difficult for women to do and often contributes to much inner conflict. Externally, women may not have the understanding and support to help them make this shift. Creating the time to go to meetings, to check in with sponsors, to think, and to meditate and pray requires persistence and support. And, often, addicted women find themselves very isolated. Family members may accuse the recovering woman addict of being selfish or negligent. In recovery, she must begin to build a support network, while repairing and developing relationships, which can be most difficult. Relationships with children have often been damaged and disrupted, and parenting children who have their own addiction-related pain is difficult for women struggling with recovery and growth. Dealing with parents, partners, and friends may increase the burden even more.

Women also struggle with the general cultural biases toward them in our society and may be even further stigmatized because of their ethnicity. Finances and housing issues also loom large for many women in recovery. The emotional issues that often contributed to the addiction can resurface once a woman is clean. Depression, anxiety, posttraumatic stress disorder (PTSD), and eating disorders are commonly found among women who are addicted and are serious issues that require prompt attention in recovery (Bollerud, 1990; Sutherland, Weaver, McPeake, & Quimby, 1993; Young, 1990).

A woman's personal recovery, her children, her relationships, and her emotional and physical health all vie for priority status. Trying to sort out what is important and how to accomplish multiple tasks at the same time can be confusing and overwhelming.

Men

Men in U.S. culture are often regarded as the "hunters and gatherers," the protectors of their families and communities. The traditional roles and expectations for men revolve around them acting primarily as "breadwinners" for their families. Men are also expected to be both emotionally and physically strong and independent. They are traditionally discouraged from expressing emotions, which is seen as a sign of "weakness." Stoicism, fierce independence, self-reliance, and isolation are the norm for most men. The results of living a life in such a way can be devastating. Men often find themselves extremely isolated and without intimate relationships. This isolation is heightened by their belief that they must "tough things out alone," which makes asking for help an anathema to their life experience.

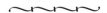

Jim, in recovery from alcoholism: You know, I feel that I have abandoned my whole family and I feel very guilty. When I was drinking, I was gone. I didn't spend time with my kids. My wife and I did not speak. I didn't talk to my brother for months at a time. When I lost my job, I was really humiliated. I still have my drinking buddies, but now I cannot hang out with them because they are still drinking and I am not. I am trying to put the pieces back together. I got into a long-term treatment program through my job. I stayed for 9 months and it was good because I could really focus on myself and my recovery. I started to have family meetings and began to get to know my kids again. My wife and I have meetings also, although I'm not sure what will happen with our relationship. She really stuck by me for a long time, and she took care of the kids and the house the whole time I was drinking. I really messed up. I feel at times that I am a real failure as a man, as a husband and as a father. I didn't do what I was supposed to do, I didn't take care of them, I deserted them. I'm trying to deal with that now.

When a man enters recovery, he is expected to do things that may be completely foreign to him. Asking for help, talking about feelings, and sharing his experiences with others can be threatening to his image of who he is as a man or perceived as a sign of weakness. He may not have any idea about how to talk to another person or how to develop a relationship. If he has lost his job he is likely to suffer much shame and feel that he is a failure as the head of the household. If he is married or in a relationship, he is likely to feel guilty that he has let his family down, perhaps for having left his family while he was actively using.

A high incidence of domestic violence is associated with substance abuse, making it necessary to investigate this possibility with men in recovery. Traditionally in American culture, men are the perpetrators and women are the victims of domestic violence, although violence can be perpetrated by either sex. Any violent or abusive behavior should be addressed immediately and directly with all involved. And any other emotional and psychiatric problems present should be identified and treated. The myth that a person will not be violent once he or she has stopped drinking and/or using other drugs is false. Substance abuse and addiction may have an enhancing and disinhibiting effect, but they do not cause violence.

Everyone involved in domestic violence or other abuse is a victim. Often, both male perpetrators and female victims report early histories wrought with abuse and victimization. However, their outcomes are usually quite different because of gender-related social and cultural norms. Although both sexes usually grow up to repeat the cycle of violence, men do so by becoming violent and women do so by choosing violent partners.

Because men generally do not play such a primary role in caregiving and parenting, they most often are able to enter a treatment program without worrying about who will care for the children while they are gone. The flip side of this, however, is that the man can become even more disconnected from his family if the recovery program is not family focused. It is extremely important when feasible to help men in recovery develop positive relationships with their families. Men have suffered a great disservice as a result of their cultural role. Making men and women more equal in sharing responsibilities both inside and outside of the family helps to balance the power structure, which for so long has found men on the top and women on the bottom and cheated both.

Grandparents

Grandmother: Here I am 52 years old. I've raised my four children. They are all out on their own. I have a job at the registry, and I am really enjoying it. I like my free time. I like the quiet. I like watching what I want to watch on the television. All of a sudden I get a call from my youngest daughter. She tells me she has been reported to DSS [Department of Social Services] for using crack and that they are going to take her two daughters away and put them in a

foster home. She has to go into a residential treatment program. I couldn't even think about letting them put my grandbabies into a stranger's home. I called DSS and told them that I would take them. That was 6 months ago. Boy, has my life changed. I had to take a leave from my job. Even though I get benefits for the girls, it is not enough for everything they need, so money is always tight. I had forgotten what it is like to have little ones around. I have to get up very early to get them both off to school, and there are doctor appointments and dentist appointments and birthday parties to get them to. They are really upset about not being with their mother. The little one gets really wild sometimes and the older one is sad a lot. Recently, the oldest has started to wet in the bed and have bad dreams. The younger one went and cut all of her braids off one morning because she didn't like the way they felt. They keep me running, those two, and I'm pretty tired. But, I am doing it for them and for my daughter, I sure hope she can get over this problem she has with cocaine.

This grandmother faces the very difficult task of caring for young children at a time of her life when she was preparing for retirement. Having finished her own child-rearing responsibilities, she was looking forward to having more time to herself. In addition, she has her problems, which put such a strain on the family's financial situation that, at times, there is not enough money to buy groceries or pay the electric bill.

More and more in American culture, grandparents are caring for their grandchildren. According to the 1991 U.S. Census Report, 12% of all African American children, 6% of Latino children, and 3.6% of Caucasian children are being raised by grandparents (National Institute on Drug Abuse, 1994). When a parent is unable to care for a child because of addiction or addiction-related health problems, or is absent or dead, grandparents often take on the role of primary caregiver.

Taking on the responsibility of caring for grandchildren is an enormous job that requires changing one's lifestyle and postponing the things to which people of that age generally look forward. Often, the situation becomes even more burdensome due to financial strain and lack of resources. Gaining access to needed resources is often difficult because many grandparents do not know where to look for help. In addition, the grandparent may have health or substance abuse problems of her own that limit her capacity to care for her grandchildren. Those who assume care for their grandchildren usually require additional support with their tremendous responsibility.

Most grandparents have been out of the loop of caring for children and are out of touch with the daily routines of schoolchildren or the day-to-day activity levels of preschool children. Chasing after a toddler is hard work when one is in her 20s, and even harder for someone in her 60s. In addition, child-rearing practices that a person may have used while raising her own children may no longer be effective or appropriate with grandchildren. Issues of monitoring, safety, limits, rules, and discipline must be reevaluated.

Grandparents may not be able to effectively parent grandchildren, particularly if their grandchildren have emotional or behavior disorders. Children are often upset, angry, and sad about what has happened to them, which can cause emotional and behavior problems that place an added burden on grandparents. Children may need to attend therapy or require school intervention, both of which necessitate the grandparent's time and energy. As parents, they may be steeped in their own grief over their child's addiction or may be grieving the death of that child. They can be plagued with feelings of guilt and regret and be ambivalent about taking on the care of the grandchildren.

Mrs. P is a 60-year-old woman who had raised six of her own children when her daughter Victoria, who was an alcoholic and a cocaine addict, died of AIDS at the age of 35. She left four children: a 2-year-old, a 3-year-old, an 8-year-old, and a 14-year-old. Victoria's husband, from whom she was estranged, did not offer to assume care for their children. Mrs. P, who had cared for the children on many previous occasions, made the difficult decision to take over the custody and care for her daughter's four children. Mrs. P herself had many health problems and had to give up her job in order to stay healthy and care for her grandchildren. Finances were very tight, compounded by extreme difficulty in getting state assistance for the children. Mrs. P was stricken with grief and shock at finding out for the first time that her daughter had AIDS.

Finally, grandparents are often asked to relinquish the care of their grandchildren after working heroically to provide and care for them once the parent is through recovery. Once the primary caregiver, they must step aside and allow the parent—their child—to take over. If grandparents stay actively involved at this point, old dynamics between them and their children may surface and further complicate the situation.

～ Children's Responses to Recovery ～

There is very little information in the literature specifically addressing children's responses to a parent's recovery. However, much can be conceptualized using Brown's (1985) model of recovery, child development theory, clinical experience, and the accounts of ACoAs. It is strikingly apparent that children entering the recovery process with their families do move through their own unique developmental process, which differs from both that of other family members and from their own experiences in an actively addicted family system. Again, recovery is not merely a reversal of symptoms but rather a re-birthing process for the individual. This is true for children as well. Children who move through the recovery process emerge as new individuals, with new beliefs, attitudes, and perceptions. Particular patterns of responding, adapting, and functioning are observable and common with children in recovery, although each child's journey is quite unique.

All of a sudden, here was this person making rules and telling me what to do. Who was she to tell me what to do? I ran things in the family, not her.

Daryll, age 15, describing his newly sober mother

So what he's in recovery. He'll just be out there again using in no time.

Angel, age 11, responding to her father's recovery

Sometimes I want things to be different, for my mom to get well. Sometimes I wish things would just go back to the way they were, I get so sick of wondering what's happening next.

Terry, age 10, describing feelings about her mother's recovery

Children from addicted families must navigate their developmental journeys on both the well-worn path of human development and the painful path of addiction and recovery, in order to create their own identities. From the beginning, the desire to trust and connect is at odds with the battle to survive the pain of familial addiction. For children, the process of recovery involves resolving issues that are integral to the addiction experience and learning new ways of living in an environment free of the addiction. Children's needs, behaviors, and foci shift as well, and ultimately, health and healing become the final goals.

A child may first be preoccupied or overwhelmed by fears that a newly sober parent may relapse and abandon them. Angel and Terry were both preoccupied with whether their newly sober parents had really stopped using or were going to pick up again. Angel's dismissal of her father's recovery—"He'll just be out there again using in no time"—speaks volumes about her mistrust and fear. Terry spent each day anxiously awaiting her mother's return to drugs.

Later in a parent's recovery, a child may become more rebellious and noncompliant as the parent tries to reestablish his role as the adult authority in the family system. Children may need to test the situation to determine the stability of the parent's authority. As the child's needs, behaviors, and perceptions evolve in concert with the parent's recovery process, there are several issues that can resurface at any time: the struggle for authority and control, resistance to change, disruptions in roles, transformed relationships, upended rules, vacillating emotions, losses that can build and multiply, and shattered trust.

The Struggle for Authority and Control

Particularly compelling in the process of recovery is the struggle for control, which affects children both internally and externally, in relation to the family. Issues of control (i.e., who has power within the family) color every experience and every interaction. The process of recovery shifts control from the disease to family members. Family members who felt control over family functioning in the past, having spent years with the disease and having developed a compulsive need to control people and events, now see the control shifting or slipping away from them as the family landscape is redefined. For example, Terry felt in control when she knew what to expect from her addicted mother and followed established family routines to live with the disease. Now that her mother is sober, she has lost the predictable sameness that helped her feel in control.

Resistance to Change

As with adults, change can be scary and anxiety provoking for children. Toddlers entering child care for the first time, children moving to a new neighborhood, or siblings awaiting the birth of a new family member are events in the everchanging cycle of life; nevertheless, these experiences can be unnerving. Living with the chaos of addiction and uncertainty of recovery can evoke powerful reactions, emotions, and behaviors.

When children are prepared for changes in their lives with support and communication, they are better able to understand, adapt, and accept whatever new experience life brings to them. But families drained and exhausted by the process of recovery and unskilled in communicating with children often fail to sufficiently prepare their children. As roles and patterns of functioning begin to change in the family system with recovery, family members respond with anxiety and fear (Brown, 1985). Even desired change can send members into a spiral of fear and foreboding. As a result, family members resist any change to the status quo, which appears illogical and at odds with the recovery process but is a remarkable testament to how addicting maladaptive patterns of functioning can become. The roles that have become so familiar—the parentified child, scapegoat, hero, lost child—lose their adaptive functions. Brown (1985) has postulated that the fear of change can be so great, family members can unwittingly attempt to sabotage the addict's recovery.

No one seemed to think I meant it. I needed to stop drinking. Every time I vis-
ited my parents they would push drinks on me and make jokes about AA.

Donna, in recovery from alcoholism

Children in recovering families can respond to their fear and uncertainty by developing or intensifying emotional or behavior problems, which often surprises newly recovering parents.

When I was using she was so good and took care of her brothers. Now she's
acting up all over the place.

Reggie, in recovery, describing her 5-year-old

Woven into this drama for children is their ongoing fear that the
addict may relapse, perhaps as a result of their inappropriate behavior. Children must take an incredible leap of faith to accompany
a parent on the remarkable journey of recovery, which always sets
off a roller coaster ride of emotions—everchanging feelings children
have about themselves, their parents, their families, and their futures. Recovery for children often means confusing and conflicting
feelings.

Daryll's angry and frustrated response to his recovering mother
is a profound statement about change in the recovering family.
Daryll was used to being in charge of the family and its rules. Daryll
was his family's enabler, but with his mother in recovery, that role
was changing. Although Daryll wanted his mother to stop using and
get clean, he was also overcome by anxiety. Daryll struggles with the
paradox of his role within the addicted family system. His role as enabler has both crippled and defined him. He desires to break free of
the trap of caring for his mother so he can have his own life, but what
is his life and his identity if not a caregiver? As Daryll's mother
develops an identity free of drugs in her recovery, Daryll is challenged to develop an identity free of caring for his mother. That self-
development is not easy when one's sense of self is so entwined in
the role of caregiver and enabler. Letting go of the power and perceived control possessed by the family enabler is an enormous challenge for Daryll.

The battle for control begins. Who is in charge now? Can Daryll
release his death grip on his perceived control of the family? Can he
make that leap of faith and restore balance in the family by letting
go of his need to be in charge? Will he still be valued and loved if his
role changes? How will he fit in? Can he trust? Can his mother let
go of her need to control and share family responsibilities with her

son? How do they resolve the control drama to meet both their needs?

Disruptions in Family Roles

Even children as young as 4 and 5 can have clearly prescribed roles within the family. Young children struggle to control people and the environment, especially in chaotic family situations. Children who are used to fending for themselves or caring for younger siblings see their roles changing with recovery. Very young children, however, cannot fully understand or communicate what is happening.

The paradox of family roles continues. Despite the obvious negative outcomes from adopting specific roles (e.g., shouldering so much responsibility as a parentified child at a young age, becoming "little mommies" or "protectors"), children receive positive feedback from the family and a sense of identity from taking on that role. While the parent was using, children knew very clearly what their job was in the family. As that role changes with the family's recovery, young children in the early stages of identity formation can become scared, puzzled, and angry about the shifting roles.

Without interpretation, young children have limited ability to understand, communicate, and sort out their feelings about this complex process. Recovering parents may not have the energy or skill to function as guides for their children and may be left puzzled by and frustrated with a child who acts like a child one day and a mommy the next.

I gotta watch him and keep him safe; he gets into a lot of things. You know how kids are. I gotta show him the right way to be.

Anthony

Anthony, a 7-year-old, took great pride in being his 2-year-old brother's protector. Although this dynamic between brothers is often healthy, in the extreme it is destructive. Anthony felt responsible when his brother was abused by a family member. He was blamed by family members, as well, which is a heavy burden to bear for anyone, especially a young child. As his mother became more available to the family in her recovery, Anthony compulsively defended the familiar role he had taken on. He gruffly reported that he was no longer a child and rejected his mother's attempts at mothering and affectionate contact. Anthony's affection for and care of his brother seemed to reflect Anthony's desire for the care he never received. He continued to voraciously monitor his 2-year-old brother at the expense of his own feelings and needs. He would come home from school instead of playing with friends so he could check in with his brother and rarely let the 2-year-old out of his sight. Anthony's worries about his brother were certainly legitimate, given the family history, but he also didn't know how to trust others, which prevented him from breaking out of old patterns.

Transformed Relationships

Children raised by addicted family members may develop disordered relationships and attachments to the addicted caregiver. Because of the disease and its associated pathology, many parents lose custody of their children, thereby paying the ultimate price for the family's disease by forever altering the parent–child relationship. Very young children, if separated from the addicted parent early in life, may not have the opportunity to develop an attached relationship with the parent.

I'd been away from my [3-year-old] daughter so long because of drugs, she didn't even know me . . .

Rose, a mother in recovery

When an addicted family member enters recovery and progresses to a stage where she is making connections and new relationships, things change dramatically for children (Brown, 1985; Nelsen, Intner, & Lott, 1992). Children who were neglected or abused by addicted family members are asked to rethink their relationships with those members. Children who had a clear understanding of how the actively using addicts behaved and how to act with them are confused by the drastic changes.

I knew to be quiet and stay in my room when he was drinking. Now he wants to talk all the time. What's that about?

Mark, age 12, describing his recovering father

Children in the recovering family are challenged to repair relationships ravaged by addiction, which may be overwhelming. Children may be harboring mistrust, anger, and resentment toward the recovering parent (Nelsen et al., 1992).

Anthony never seemed like mine because I didn't take care of him when he was a baby like I did the others. He doesn't know me.

Tara, a recovering addict

Children may still blame themselves for the parent's addiction or be so defeated, scarred, and disillusioned that they do not want a relationship with the recovering family member at all. This is a difficult and stressful position for a child, especially when the recovering family member desperately wants a connection and reunion.

Upended Rules

When the family enters recovery, whether enthusiastically or reluctantly, the family map changes. Rule systems that once supported the survival of the addiction are redesigned to accommodate the changes that will accompany recovery. Establishing limits and rules is a challenging task for anyone. It can be particularly daunting to individuals in recovery. As a result, family members may struggle with control issues as parents try to create healthy guidelines for functioning. Recovering addicts, especially early in recovery, may not have worked through their compulsive need to control their environment and relationships. Children, accustomed to having too much control in managing their lives or no control at all, can react intensely and unpredictably to parents, responding with fear, anger, resistance, excitement, sadness, or hope. If only one parent decides to change the rules, children quickly learn how to get what they want by aligning themselves with the appropriate parent, creating a highly charged family drama.

Very young children, especially toddlers, crave ritual and routine as a way to feel safe and secure and have an enormous capacity to resist change. A spirited toddler can communicate "no" in countless ways. They resist change because they are confused and scared. They may have no idea what a consistent routine is, only knowing to expect the unexpected. They may have slept at all hours and in different places. Mealtimes may have been sporadic and in different locations. While the parent was actively using, children may have fed themselves. Ultimately, the children survived in part by being in charge of at least some aspects of their own care. Through the process of recovery, the parent resumes his place in the family and exerts new power by setting limits, making rules, and establishing routines. Children, despite their innate need and desire for limits, resist and reject the parent's attempts. Change means loss for children: loss of the familiar, which is scary no matter how healthy the change.

Children living in chaos seize anything that they can control. A feisty toddler, secure in the knowledge that his older brother always fed him and that they always ate in front of the television, wails in protest when Mom wants the family to sit at the dinner table. Older children, left to fend for themselves with their homework, grumble and gripe when newly sober Dad establishes "homework time."

My ma says I have to put my toys away before I can watch my show. She used to let me before.

Sara, age 4, talking about her mom in recovery

Parents who struggle with this new way of functioning in the family make mistakes, which may confirm children's fears and further worsen the situation. Parents may make rules too restrictive or developmentally inappropriate. Children may lose their voice in the family and be banished from participating in rule making—particularly difficult for older children who are used to "running the show." Accepting and living by the new family rules is a struggle and a challenge to children at any age in the recovering family. The leap of faith children need to participate in this process is enormous.

Vacillating Emotions

Children experience a roller coaster of emotions as they face such enormous changes in their lives. Anger, hope, fear, elation, sadness—emotions come and go, grow and change, in the process of redefining the family and the self. Perhaps the child has never felt safe enough before to express anger and frustration. Anger and resentment that have been dormant and unexpressed begin to surface (Nelsen et al., 1992) and are unleashed on newly recovering parents. Anger can also contribute to children's destructive and acting out behavior. Not only are children anxious about the change in their lives, they are enraged at what has taken place in the past (Nelsen et al., 1992). These feelings come together in a gestalt: The sum is greater than the parts. This anger can grow into a toxic rage that overwhelms and consumes the child. Children faced with this overwhelming affect are often unable to manage it. The intensity of emotions may surprise them and their parents. Children, faced with these intense emotions, may not have been taught how to express anger appropriately and newly sober parents may lack the skill and energy to help children. As a result, children may act out inappropriately or internalize their anger and become depressed and withdrawn.

Even the youngest members of the family are not immune from feelings of intense fear and anger. Anyone who has been to a grocery store and witnessed a toddler being refused his desire for candy will agree that toddlers *get mad*. It is difficult for very young children, in their limited capacity, to express anger in a way that doesn't push adult buttons. Young children don't have the cognitive and linguistic ability, let alone the impulse control, to say, "I'm mad because you left me" or "I'm confused and upset because my routine is changing." Young children express their anger, fear, and confusion with their hearts and bodies. Babies scream, toddlers throw themselves to the floor, preschoolers refuse to eat. Children have countless nonverbal ways to express their anger. It is the adult's task to interpret and respond, while accepting and tolerating the child and guiding him to express it in socially acceptable ways.

It is important to remember that anger expressed by children is most often accompanied by fear. These emotions work in tandem. Children are afraid of loss and change and react in anger when they feel threatened. Parents who enter treatment programs and leave young children in the care of others report that their young children throw tantrums, hit them, and cry when they see their children again.

> I couldn't believe it. Here I was, back home after being in a 28-day (treatment) program, and all my 3-year-old could do was push me and hit me. I felt like he was rejecting me, telling me to get away from him.
>
> Rona, in early recovery from alcohol and cocaine abuse

It was quite painful for Rona to experience what she felt was her son's rejection at a time when she needed support and encouragement. She didn't understand that her son was communicating his fear and anger about their separation, not dislike for his mother.

It can be excruciatingly painful for parents who want to reconnect with young children after long separations in their relationship when the children don't seem to know or remember them. A parent in recovery attempting to reconnect with a young child may be met with rejection, not because she is an addict, but because she is a stranger. Time and consistent contact are needed for parent and child to reconnect. Children do respond, but they may respond very slowly.

As children grow and become more verbal, they may be better able to communicate their anger through words but may continue to resort to more primitive methods of expressing anger if they are overwhelmed or know no other way. Family routines, eating, sleeping, and homework schedules are arenas where parents' and children's anger and fear can be acted out. As they begin to move in the larger social circles of school and community, the stigma and shame they experience socially can also prompt intense rage at the parent. Beginning around the sixth year of life, children become more cognizant of rules and appropriate moral conduct (Damon, 1983).

Everyone knew my father was a druggie, a loser. He'd steal an old lady's purse if he thought it would get him his drugs. No one thinks he can change.

Mark, age 12

As children get older, they learn more about the roles and functions of family members from school and communities. As they interact with peers, they become aware of who has mothers, who has fathers, and who has both. Children become more curious about who they are and where they come from. They ask questions about family members and how they relate to them. As a result, children begin to understand more about disconnections in relationships and hunger for an explanation of what happened to their parents. They may desire a reconnection with a recovering parent but struggle with conflicting feelings of anger and resentment. They may vacillate between wanting a relationship with the recovering addict and flatly refusing contact. This confusion of feelings is understandable given the enormous risk children take in opening up their hearts and minds to a parent who was not there for them in the past.

Extended family members or foster families caring for these children who are at odds with the recovering addict may contribute to a child's confusion and ambivalence about renewing a relationship with the addicted parent. Out of concern for the child and sometimes out of anger toward the addict, they may keep the child from knowing the addicted parent at all. Or, extended or foster families may express negative opinions about the addict, sending confusing messages to the child. Foster or extended family members caring for children of addicts, fearing that they may lose their places in the lives of the children, struggle with their own desires to keep the children and the children's desires to be with their parents.

My mom thinks my dad is no good, but he's been sober for a year. I mean, he's my dad.

David, age 17

It is heartbreaking for children to be torn between two families, trying to connect with and remain loyal to each, especially if adults are at odds over care and custody. Fear of loss and change can be so great that foster or extended family members may painfully harbor a desire for the addict to relapse and return to their addiction. One family seemed to intentionally sabotage their daughter's entry into a drug treatment program by abruptly returning her three daughters to her the day before she was to leave, reporting that it was time she took some responsibility for the children. Other children report being torn between a recovered parent and a parent estranged from the relationship.

Losses that Build and Multiply

Losses in relationships can be numerous and profound as the child moves through the recovery process. Children can experience the loss of their idealized image of "the family that stays together" if the family breaks up during recovery. Children experience the concrete losses of caregivers and family members when they are removed from their care to be reunited with the recovering parent. Other losses may include friends, schools, neighborhoods, and familiar life routines. Children can grieve for these losses even while wanting the family to recover. Even though the potential for healing and growth in recovery is great, it exacts a price from families (e.g., loss).

Shattered Trust

As is typical of early recovery, many addicts relapse again and again before they get a foothold in the recovery process. Although relapses can be learning experiences for the addict, they are confirmations for the child that Mom or Dad will always drink, no matter how much she or he promises not to. Children in addicted family systems have a trail of broken promises between themselves and the addicted family member (Bradshaw, 1990; Nelsen et al., 1992), which include promises to quit, promises to behave better, promises to stop hurting them, and promises to change. Entering recovery may be a sign of hope for some children; for others, it's just another opportunity to not believe. Relapses confirm suspicions. Each relapse can erode whatever hope or trust might be left. Children respond cynically to addicts in recovery and wait for the relapse to happen again. Brown (1985), in *Treating the Alcoholic: A Developmental Model of Recovery*, retells the story of a family who would sit "on pins and needles" waiting for the recovering father to relapse. The mother described her "relief" when he finally began drinking again, because at least they weren't waiting every moment for it to happen. The status quo had been restored.

Very young children, just beginning their developmental journey, are especially vulnerable to shattered trust. When children are exposed to the family disease at a very young age, they have less opportunity to develop trust. Their internal representations of the world and the people in it have been created by destructive experiences and mistrustful relationships. When young children are exposed to a parent's early recovery, which may include relapses and the accompanying disruptions and inconsistencies in care, the child's sense of safety and trust is further eroded. Very young children don't understand the recovery process. They only know that things are changing.

Older children who can understand that addiction is a disease, may be able to comprehend that recovery is about "getting better." Cognitively, they understand that relapse can accompany recovery, but emotionally, they respond with fear, anger, blame, and hopelessness. In many ways, they struggle with the same issues as adult family members do. Can we trust that the addict means it this time? Will the addict be able to do it? Will my behavior cause the addict to relapse? Is another relapse just around the corner?

It takes an incredible leap of faith for children to trust not only the addict but themselves as well. Children battered by addiction often struggle to trust themselves and their abilities. Their reservoirs of faith have been drained by their experiences. Despite a lifetime of mistrust, children must trust the process of recovery and take the incredible risk of facing change head on. It is not easy.

~ Hope in Healing ~

It is hoped that all children in recovery are able to heal from the damaging experiences of familial addiction. Seeing the disease for what it is, grieving, finding power, reconnecting with others, integrating the experiences, and moving on in peace are steps in the recovery journey. Each individual can make that journey—it is within every child's grasp. Children, as they grow, can choose recovery even if the family has not, countless stories from ACoAs testify to that. The promise of recovery is that there is a light at the end of the tunnel and better days ahead. Developing new relationships with a family member now free of drugs, creating ways of being in the family by adapting old roles to new experiences, and cultivating trust in a historically mistrustful system are the daunting tasks of children in recovery. It is only by being open to the challenges of recovery that every member can truly benefit and grow into healthy individuals in a healthy system.

~ References ~

Alcoholics Anonymous (AA). (1976). *Third edition of the big book*. New York: Author.

Bollerud, K. (1990). A model for the treatment of trauma-related syndromes among chemically dependent inpatient women. *Journal of Substance Abuse Treatment, 7,* 83–87.

Bradshaw, J. (1990). *Homecoming: Reclaiming and championing your inner child.* New York: Bantam Books.

Brown, S. (1985). *Treating the alcoholic: A developmental model of recovery.* New York: John Wiley & Sons.

Damon, W. (1983). *Social and personality development.* New York: Norton.

E., S. (1985). *Women in AA: Recovery together.* Center City, MN: Hazelden.

Edward, J., Ruskin, N., & Turrini, P. (1981). *Separation-individuation: Theory and practice.* New York: Gardner Press.

Fraiberg, S.H. (1959). *The magic years.* New York: Charles Scribner & Sons.

Gorski, T.T. (1989). *Passages through recovery.* New York: Harper & Row.

Gorski, T.T., & Miller, M. (1984). *The phases and warnings of relapse.* Independence, MO: Herald House–Independence Press.

National Institute on Drug Abuse (1994). *Clinical report series—assessing drug abuse among adolescents and adults: Standardized instruments* (NIH Publication No. 94-3757). Rockville, MD: U.S. Department of Health and Human Services.

Nelsen, J., Intner, R., & Lott, L. (1992). *Clean and sober parenting: A guide to help recovering parents.* Rocklin, CA: Prima Publishing.

Piaget, J. (1970). Piaget's theory. In P. Mussen (Ed.), *Carmichael's manual of child psychology* (3rd ed.). New York: John Wiley & Sons.

Prochaska, J.O., DiClemente, C.C., & Norcross, J.C. (1992). In search of how people change: Applications to addictive behavior. *American Psychologist, 9*(47), 1102–1114.

Sutherland, L.A., Weaver, S.N., McPeake, J.D., & Quimby, C.D. (1993). The Beech Hill Hospital eating disorders treatment program for drug dependent females: Program description and case analysis. *Journal of Substance Abuse Treatment, 10*(5), 473–481.

Tabor, C.W. (1965). *Tabor's cyclopedic medical dictionary* (10th ed.). Philadelphia: F.A. Davis.

Winnicott, D.W. (1953). Transitional objects and transitional phenomena: A study of the first not-me possession. *The International Journal of Psychoanalysis, 34,* 89–97.

Young, E.B. (1990). The role of incest issues in relapse. *Journal of Psychoactive Drugs, 22*(2), 249–258.

~7~

Everybody Finds Their Power

Supporting Resiliency in Children and Families

The ability to survive, and grow and heal despite enormous pain and adversity, has fascinated researchers and clinicians and given hope to thousands who suffer great hardships in their lives. There are countless stories of men and women who have lived through debilitating poverty, abuse, violence, discrimination, family disruption, or familial substance abuse as children to grow into healthy, well-functioning adults. Anna and Cheryl are survivors. They found ways to protect themselves and grow strong. How did they do it? Why do some children overcome terrible hardship while others facing similar circumstances do not? Can one identify and nurture those qualities that help someone survive adversity?

Cheryl, an ACoA: Somehow I made it. Despite all of the craziness that has gone on in my life, I made it. I survived. Not just survived, I have healed. I have grown. I am stronger now than I ever was before. But I guess I was always strong, there was always something strong inside me, because I made it.

Anna, an ACoA: From a timid shy girl, I had become a woman of resolute character who could no longer be frightened by the struggle with troubles.

185

⌒ Resiliency Theory and Research ⌒

The Children of Kauai

In 1955, Dr. Emmy Werner began what was to become one of the seminal studies of resiliency in children. She and a multidisciplinary team of professionals set out to conduct a prospective study of all children born that year on the island of Kauai, following their development into adulthood. Among those studied were a small cohort of children exposed to a number of medical, educational, and social risk factors. What the researchers discovered as they followed these children over time offered a wealth of insight into resiliency and protective factors that mediate risks.

Werner (1989) was able to document that, despite facing identifiable risks to their development and well-being, one out of three vulnerable children fared quite well as they grew into adulthood, becoming competent adults who "loved well, worked well, and played well" (p. 108). Werner defined children as "vulnerable" if they faced four or more risk factors (including poverty, parental alcoholism or mental illness, abuse, or perinatal complications) before the age of 2.

Werner identified "protective factors" within the children themselves, their homes, and their communities that appeared to buffer these resilient children against the life stressors they faced. The resilient children in Werner's study appeared to have strong cognitive abilities and temperamental qualities that elicited positive responses from others. They were identified as independent, popular, and likable, and a majority were even identified favorably as newborns by their caregivers (Werner, 1989, 1990).

Werner identified protective factors in the environment, as well, that appeared to have served as buffers for these children against stress. Within the family, the resilient children of Kauai had a close bond with at least one nurturing caregiver during the first few years of life. This relationship provided them with the opportunity to develop trust and a secure base of attachment, an experience that helped these children as they grew (Werner, 1989, 1990). Outside of the family, the resilient children were able to find emotional support in the community, typically in an informal network of close friends, neighbors, school personnel, and others who helped in times of need (Werner, 1989, 1990). The children created safe havens away from their chaotic homes in their schools and religious and community centers. A majority of resilient children reported that religion and faith played an important role in their lives (Werner, 1990).

The resilient children in Werner's study grew into successful, competent, well-adjusted adults. The majority had steady employment, were in stable relationships, and reported a strong religious faith and a sense of hope and overall happiness with their lives.

⌒ Resiliency and Protective Factors ⌒

The *Merriam-Webster Dictionary* defines *resilience* as "an ability to recover from or adjust easily to change or misfortune" (Woolf, 1974, p. 596). Although sometimes thought of as an intangible ability to overcome seemingly unmanageable hardships, the concept of resiliency has emerged as a phenomenon that has been studied and used in therapeutic intervention. Werner (1990) reports that Anthony first described the resilient child as the "psychologically invulnerable child" (p. 98), comparing the resilient child to a doll made of steel. Despite being struck by a hammer, a steel doll remains unscarred and impenetrable much like an invulnerable child remains free of scars and untouched by trauma.

Rutter urged researchers and clinicians to move away from the term "psychologically invulnerable," arguing that "invulnerable" erroneously implies that children can be absolutely resistant to the effects of trauma when resilience is, in fact, relative (Rutter, 1993; Werner, 1992). Rutter also argued that the concept of an "invulnerable child" implies that invulnerability is some innate, individual trait that is static over time and circumstances.

Rutter (1987) continues to clarify the concept of resiliency by suggesting that resiliency "cannot be seen as a fixed attribute of the individual" (p. 317). A person's resistance to stress is variable and can change over time. What might be manageable for a person now may be less manageable at another point in her life. Rutter uses the term *protective mechanisms* to describe those factors or processes that reduce the impact of the stressor, reduce the likelihood of a negative chain reaction from the risk experience, promote self-esteem and self-efficacy, and provide positive opportunities for growth (Rutter, 1993). These factors or mechanisms, Rutter postulates, can exist within the child, family, and community.

Werner (1990) describes the concepts of *resilience* and *protective factors* as "the counterparts to the constructs of vulnerability and risk factors" (p. 97). She uses the term *resilience* to describe a character trait of the individual, whereas *protective factors* are conceptualized as individual and environmental characteristics that buffer the impact of stressors faced by the individual (Garmezy, 1987; Rutter, 1987; Werner, 1990). See Table 1 for a listing of protective factors. Garmezy separates protective factors into three categories: 1) dispositional attributes or personality characteristics of the individual; 2) family attributes such as cohesion, availability of support, and lack of conflict; and 3) the availability of external support systems such as schools and communities (Luthar & Zigler, 1991; Rutter, 1993).

Individual Characteristics

Resilient children tend to have temperamental qualities that elicit positive responses from others (Hauser, Vieyra, Jacobson, & Wertlieb, 1985; Luthar & Zigler, 1991; Werner, 1990). Resilient infants have been described by caregivers as active, alert, responsive, good-natured, and sociable. Toddlers and preschoolers identified as re-

---

Table 1.   Protective factors that foster resiliency in children

Individual characteristics

Positively regarded temperament
Cognitive competence, good problem-solving skills
Good verbal skills
Strong self-esteem
Internal locus of control
Goal directedness
Ability to use adults as resources
Spiritual or religious faith

Family characteristics

Availability of a stable, nurturing caregiver
Consistently enforced family rules within a framework of well-balanced discipline
Existing family rituals, structured family activities
Low parental tension, minimal family discord
High parental self-esteem

Community characteristics

Positive, nurturing school experiences
Availability of supportive adults to serve as role models and caregivers
Cultural connection, value, and identity

---

silient were noted for their self-confidence and independence as well as their sociability.

Chuck, an ACoA: I was really good at escaping what was going on at home. I would create these fantasies with a detailed plan about getting away, living somewhere else. I always made sure I had a plan.

Margaret, an ACoA and abuse survivor: I think having friends helped a lot. People seemed to like me. And I was determined to have a better life than the one my mother had. I kept going no matter what because I deserved better.

Resilient children tend to be goal directed in their play, self-reliant, and able to use adults as resources when needed (Werner, 1990). Researchers have also discovered that resilient children have good problem-solving skills and communicative abilities (Hauser et al., 1985; Luthar & Zigler, 1991). They tend to possess an internal locus of control, feel powerful rather than powerless, and believe they can effect change in their environment. Resilient children often have senses of humor, flexible coping styles, and a generally positive outlook on life and are adaptable to change. Religious or spiritual faith figures prominently in the lives of many resilient children.

Werner reported that resilient children tend not to have stereo-typical gender-specific character traits but are more androgynous in their style of competence (Werner, 1990). Both boys and girls may be nurturers, risk takers, independent, and/or socially expressive (Werner, 1990). Overall, resilient children tend to have strong self-esteem and positive self-regard.

Family Characteristics

One of the most significant findings of Werner's study is the important role caregivers play in fostering resiliency (Hauser et al., 1985; Rutter, 1993; Werner, 1990). Hauser et al. (1985) identified protective factors within the family that were related to parental attitudes, family structure, and the general home environment. Resilient children typically were able to form a secure, nurturing attachment to a significant caregiver during the first year of life, which afforded them

the opportunity to develop other attachments and a basic sense of trust. The resilient child often formed this close bond with alternative caregivers, such as grandparents or older siblings, if either parent was unavailable. These caregivers appeared to act as buffers to risks faced by the child.

My mother was the calming presence in my life. She was there. She understood. Everyone needs someone, and she was there for me.

Frank, an ACoA

Families in which there are consistently enforced rules and well-balanced discipline appear to support resiliency in children, as do family rituals and structured activities (Logue & Rivinus, 1991). Families with less discord, whose caregivers are supportive and respect individuality, also appear to act as buffers against risks (Hauser et al., 1985). Some research support the notion that good communication skills within the family support child resiliency (Hauser et al., 1985). Additional research links an internal locus of control and high self-esteem (two components of resiliency) in children to high parental self-esteem, emotional stability in mothers, low parental tensions and conflict, and a supportive family environment.

Protective Factors in the Community

Friends, teachers, neighbors, coaches, ministers, counselors, and countless others in the community can support resiliency in children and serve as buffers against stressors. Most studies report that resilient children like school and do well in school (Werner, 1990). Although resilient children tend to be cognitively competent, they are not necessarily gifted but do the best they can with the skills and abilities they possess. Resilient children often use school as refuge from home and develop supportive relationships with teachers. In fact, children most commonly identified teachers as role models outside of the family in Werner's study of resilient children (Werner, 1990). Teachers, friends, neighbors, and others who served as protective factors for children had the greatest positive effect on children if "they provide an organized and predictable environment for the young child that combines warmth and caring with clearly defined structure and rules" (Werner, 1990, p. 110).

John, an ACoA in recovery: Thank God there was school. I could go there every day to get away from my crazy family. When school ended every year for summer vacation, I was the only kid not racing through the door, shouting in joy and anticipation.

Ann, an ACoA: I found these neighbors. I just adored them. I wanted to live with them, I think I practically did! They seemed to be everything my family wasn't—safe, calm, predictable, and nice.

Culture as a Protective Factor Children of differing ethnicities who encounter risks to their development because of familial or community dysfunction are additionally challenged if they are not of the dominant culture. Racism and discrimination can tip the scales of risk and resiliency for these children, placing them in uniquely vulnerable positions, especially those who have been cut off from their histories and discouraged from identifying positively with their culture of origin (Vasquez, 1994).

Self-esteem is supported when children receive positive messages about who they are and where they come from. A strong racial identity may serve as a protective factor if it gives the child a sense of belonging and self-worth, as can a close attachment to one's ethnic community, which provides the child with supportive adult role models and mentors (Hodges, 1995). Vasquez (1994) has written that "la cultura cura" (culture cures) by acting as a protective factor against unhealthy behaviors. "La cultura cura draws attention to those aspects of culture that foster a caring, healthy, supportive, loving environment which in turn builds inner strengths within individuals and groups" (p. 5).

～ Fostering Resiliency in Families Affected by Substance Abuse ～

It seems easier to lie prone than to press against the law of gravity and raise the body onto its feet and persist in remaining vertical. There are many incidents which can eviscerate the stalwart and bring the mighty down. In order to survive, the ample soul needs refreshments and reminders daily of its right to be.

Maya Angelou (1993, p. 79)

Gina, a recovering addict, described herself as "a body with no soul, so sick I was." At the height of her drug abuse, she was empty, alone, and depleted. These feelings of emptiness did not begin with the drug use, however; they began long ago in her childhood. Gina was a lost child, living without protectors, without care, and without hope. Her soul was never fed in childhood and she grew into an adult feeling "soulless." Yet Gina survived her disease, and her soul came alive in recovery. She managed to evoke her resiliency to make it through the long journey. How was Gina able to do it? How could her innate resiliency have been supported in childhood to prevent her fall into drug addiction? How can resiliency be nurtured in the family affected by substance abuse? How can members feed and nurture their souls, their very selves?

Although numerous studies confirm the detrimental effects of familial substance abuse on children, not all children of substance abusers go on to develop addictions or other maladjustments (Alcohol Alert, 1990; Harter, 1991; Logue & Rivinus, 1991). Risk and resiliency in children specifically from addicted families are not completely understood or exhaustively researched, but much can be drawn from what is known about risk and resiliency in other high-risk populations, which paints a picture of both hope and concern for these children.

Children of alcoholics have been found to have impaired communication abilities and are at higher risk for antisocial behavior. They also score lower on indices of self-esteem and appear to be more likely to have an external, rather than internal, locus of control (Logue & Rivinus, 1991). Although school performance has been documented to be adversely affected by parental substance abuse, average or above-average intelligence or achievement appears to support resilience in children of alcoholics (Logue & Rivinus, 1991). Despite these troubling findings, children from substance-abusing homes can and do flourish. One of the most critical factors in the survival of these children is the family's entry into recovery. Even without this, resiliency can be supported and nurtured (see Table 2).

Nurturing the True Self

Building resiliency in children means building self-esteem and supporting the development of the "true self." When a child is accepted unconditionally for who she is and how she thinks and interacts with the world, her true self is allowed to grow and blossom.

In the addicted family system, the true self is often under attack. The disease requires the true self to hide and a false self to emerge. Children may not be allowed to "just be," but are expected to shape and form themselves in response to the needs of the addict and addicted system.

Table 2.   Strategies to foster resiliency in children

Nurture islands of competence

• Find something at which the child is good and nurture that ability.
• Encourage the child to teach his or her skills to others.
• Honor a child's talent at school with awards and special recognition.
• Plan a "Great Kid Day" and give every child a turn to be the focus of the day's events.
• Involve the child in activities and clubs that focus on positive self-development instead of perfection or competition.

Honor culture and ethnicity

• Provide opportunities for the child to learn about and celebrate his or her culture.
• Have special "cultural celebration" days during the school year in which children can share their cultural heritage with others.
• Use the children's birthdays to celebrate their uniqueness.
• Encourage children to research their own cultures and discuss biases and misperceptions.
• Use children's literature that celebrates and honors culture.
• Have children keep journals, make books, write letters, or tell stories about themselves and their cultural experiences.
• Connect children with community mentors or groups that share the child's cultural heritage.

Provide opportunities for play

• Explore interactive children's museums and amusement parks, even with teenagers.
• Give children more time among themselves to play with toys or board games.
• Stay outside a little longer at recess or visit a safe playground more often.
• Watch a funny movie together or put on a funny play.
• Organize a funniest joke or story contest where everyone wins.
• Toss around a ball or go for a walk with a child, even during a serious discussion. (Therapy doesn't always have to take place in an office.)

Opportunities to support self-esteem are essential to the self-development and well-being of the child in the addicted family system. Messages of "you're bad," especially for the family scapegoat, need to be countered with "you're wonderful just the way you are." Managing inappropriate behavior by expressing disapproval for the *behavior* and not the *child* is especially important for children trying to feel good about themselves. Praise for their abilities and encouragement for their struggles should be a constant for children from addicted families to stem the tide of negativism that can flow from the family.

Just as children need support for their fragile senses of self, other family members in the addicted system may need supportive encouragement for their own self-development. Low self-esteem may be a pervasive problem in the addicted system, and children's self-development may be impaired by caregivers who, themselves, feel incompetent and worthless. Praise and support for those who may be doing the best they can in the midst of tragic circumstances may help family members find their resilient core and move toward healthy change.

Building "Islands of Competence" Brooks (1994) writes that "because of their low self-esteem, many at-risk children seem to find themselves drowning in an ocean of inadequacy. However, every child has 'islands of competence,' areas that are (or could be) sources of pride and accomplishment" (p. 549). It can become the therapist's (or teacher's, coach's, counselor's, or neighbor's) role to help the child—and each family member—to find his own "islands of competence." Artistic abilities can be promoted, cognitive skills reinforced, and athletic talents challenged. It is possible for everyone to be successful and competent at *something*. The challenge becomes finding these islands and promoting them.

The codependent child in the addicted family system may be competent in her ability to care for younger siblings. Her caregiver role gives her identity and a sense of accomplishment. This "island" may serve as a positive function for her within the family and community, a way to get praise and attention. Caring for others can truly be a valuable gift and talent. The risk, of course, is that this role becomes unbalanced and unhealthy because the child gives up her own needs, her "true self," in the interest of others. Helping the codependent child find other islands of competence, unrelated to her caregiving role, may help to create a better balance for self-development.

The overachieving child creates islands of competence in school, at work, and in the community that can provide the positive feedback necessary for positive self-esteem and growth opportunities. School and work achievements are often the "ticket out" of a troubled family. Achievements can become a trap, however, if the child begins to feel that being perfect is the only to feel okay, thereby maintaining the family dysfunction. The child can "feel like a fraud," believing he can never be good enough, when he begins to define himself by the number of straight "A's" he makes and replaces his "true self" with a list of accomplishments. Islands of competence can be positive growth experiences for overachieving children when balanced with the messages, "you don't have to be the best," "mistakes are okay," and "you're loved no matter what."

Adult family members in the addicted system should also be encouraged to find islands of competence in order to nurture or rediscover their resilient selves. Finding a job, returning to school, or acquiring a craft or hobby can be a catalyst for growth and positive change. As one codependent partner said, "Going back to school helped me find myself again, and I began to realize what I wanted out of life, for *me*."

Supporting Cultural Identity and Connection Providing children with the opportunity to identify positively with their cultures of origin promotes self-esteem and supports a child's "true self." So often, especially when families have been decimated by discrimination, dysfunction, and discord, a child's history is lost. Children don't know where they've come from. They are disconnected from the family ancestors and the family stories that provide children with a sense of continuity and connection. If a child is from the non-dominant culture, she may only have learned negative, unhealthy, or pathological history about her culture of origin.

Activities at home, in school, and in the community that promote cultural pride and educate children may support resiliency in both the child and the family. Opportunities for the child and family to hear or participate in the retelling of their histories that correct misconceptions can be a powerful intervention to support resiliency. Matching children or families with role models or mentors who share their cultural heritage is yet another powerful way to support the true self and foster resilience through culture.

Using Humor, Having Fun

Resilient children are able to use humor as a buffer against stress and risk. Adult children of alcoholics often lament that they missed out on childhood. The intensity of growing up in an addicted environment and the difficulties encountered often trap individuals in a cycle of despair. Even treatment providers sometimes focus on the seriousness of the individual's experience and forget that humor and fun are a part of the human experience and must be nurtured and cultivated. Being able to laugh and see the humor in situations (although by no means minimizing their seriousness) gives the individual a chance to take a deep breath, step back, and bring a new perspective to the situation. "Laughter is the best medicine" carries a wise message to those who struggle to foster resiliency in children and families. Teaching children—and adults—how to *play* and giving them permission to have *fun* are valuable educational experiences.

Having a Plan

Children tend to fare better in the face of stress when they can make use of their cognitive abilities. Resilient children make the most out of the cognitive resources available to them to overcome adversity. They tend to be reflective problem solvers who feel competent in their abilities to effect change in their environment.

Individuals who face stress with a plan of action may feel more control over the situation and subsequently less stressed about their experience. Having a plan can help someone get through the most difficult of circumstances. Children, as well as other family members, can gain a sense of power and control by being proactive and formulating a plan. For instance, the child may need help in planning whom she will call if Mom starts drinking again or a plan for waking up in time for the bus in the morning if Dad keeps missing the alarm.

Family members also may need guidance in making plans for caring for and supervising children, especially if they have lived with or are living with the chaos of addictive disease. Family outings can feel much less stressful and more empowering when families make a plan. Making plans for doing household chores or managing a budget reinforces a sense of competence and control. Having a plan for leaving an addictive relationship can be a significant step in finding the resiliency needed to make a change.

Talking, Trusting, and Feeling

Fostering resiliency in children from addicted families means breaking the cardinal rule of the addicted family: "Don't talk, don't trust, don't feel." Resilient children tend to have good verbal skills, be attached to others, and are reflective and socially expressive. Children in addicted families learn to keep quiet, be mistrustful, and ignore or suppress their feelings. If these rules change, it may provide an opening for resiliency to flourish.

Children from addicted families may have lost their voices. Family rules and rigid roles have replaced true interaction and communication within the family. The child's internal reality and voice of truth is in conflict with the external reality of the family disease. Communication may be more about falsehoods, lies, and distortions than about connection and interaction. Children need to learn the language of emotions and find the power in honest communication. Recognizing and labeling emotions for children and helping them interpret their affective world serve to validate, clarify, and normalize their experiences. Listening to and hearing what they are feeling and letting them know that it is okay to feel and share can be liberating for children from addicted family systems.

Providing children with opportunities to develop nurturing relationships with caregivers within or outside of the family system gives them a chance to overcome the "don't talk, don't trust, don't feel" message. Children who are able to seek out supportive adults and ask for help tend to be more resilient. Asking for and accepting help is a critical skill in coping with stress and trauma, a skill that

is typically extinguished in the addicted family. Even the family overachiever often accepts the family rule and resists reaching out; after all, he doesn't need anyone, he can do it alone. Modeling asking for help and encouraging human connection are important interventions for promoting resilience.

It is important to keep in mind that learning to talk, trust, and feel can be a scary process for children and adults who have been indoctrinated into this rule system. Believing that you can speak the truth without dire consequences, that other people can be trusted, and that feelings are natural, manageable, and accepted are major cognitive leaps for those living with addiction. The process of changing the cognitive blueprint can be a long and challenging process for the individual.

Resiliency Mentors

Weinreb (in press) compares *resiliency mentors* to the notion of Segal's (1988) charismatic adults. *Charismatic adults* are the significant adults with whom children develop important and nurturing relationships. Resilient children in addicted families often look to the stable adults within or outside of the family for care and guidance. Weinreb postulates that resiliency mentors can foster resiliency in children by translating protective factors into active interventions for children.

Resiliency mentors may be teachers, therapists, clergy members, outreach workers, recovering addicts, neighbors, or relatives. They can come from all walks of life, but they often share resilient characteristics. Effective resiliency mentors were perhaps resilient children themselves. They can recognize and nurture their own resiliency and translate their experience into supportive work with others. Resiliency mentors effectively create a healthy balance in their own lives and model for others how to find power, peace, and healing in the midst of pain.

Resiliency mentors can provide necessary "parenting" if the caregiver is unavailable. Mentors can recognize and foster islands of competence to promote self-esteem. They can interpret and support the child's affective experience and expression of emotion. They can help the child "make a plan" and provide the structure and healthy rule systems children need to manage behavior. Mentors can model what it is like to use humor in stressful situations and to have *fun*. Mentors can instill a sense of hopefulness in discouraged children and help them see the potential in the future. Resiliency mentors can also guide adults in similar ways.

~ Finding Power ~

Resiliency, at its core, is about internal power. Resilient children tend to have an internal locus of control. They feel power at the very center of their beings. They believe that they can effect change in their lives, they feel hopeful about their situations and their futures, and they feel "in charge." A hostage held by a terrorist group poignantly described this internal sense of power, saying that, although his body was at the mercy of his captors, they could never have his mind. Perhaps resilient children in addicted families have a similar experience. Their bodies may be trapped by their circumstances, but their spirits and minds remain their own; at some level, they remain free.

Children who have been in control of some aspects of their lives will transfer these external experiences of power into an internal locus of control or sense of power. This may even begin in the earliest years when a child's basic needs are met at her command. Children who are given the respect and opportunity to make decisions appropriate for their age may grow in their resiliency and inner strength.

Children living in the chaos of the addicted family may not have the experiences necessary for developing a healthy internal locus of control. They may witness impulsive and out-of-control behavior. They may grow to feel victimized and powerless. They may allow themselves to be defined by their victimizer (the caregiver or the addiction) and, thus, be diminished in strength and power. The disease or the addicted caregivers may wield all the power in the unbalanced family system, leaving the child and other family members feeling hopeless and powerless.

To foster resiliency in children from addicted family systems is to help the child or other family members find their power by making supportive relationships with children and other family members, supporting self-esteem, helping individuals become proactive in making plans rather than reactive in a crisis, helping individuals to find their voices and speak the truth, and honoring an individual's true self.

~ References ~

Alcohol Alert. (1990, July). *Children of alcoholics: Are they different?* Rockville, MD: National Clearinghouse for Alcohol and Drug Information.

Angelou, M. (1993). *Wouldn't take nothing for my journey now.* New York: Bantam Books.

Brooks, R. (1994). Children at risk: Fostering resilience and hope. *American Journal of Orthopsychiatry, 64*(4), 545–553.

Garmezy, N. (1987). Stress, competence and development: Continuities in the study of schizophrenic adults, children vulnerable to psychopathology, and the search for stress-resistant children. *American Journal of Orthopsychiatry, 57*(2), 159–174.

Harter, M.W. (1991). Resilient children of alcoholics. *Dissertation Abstracts International, 52*(3), 1720-B.

Hauser, S.T., Vieyra, M.A., Jacobson, A.M., & Wertlieb, D. (1985). Vulnerability and resilience in adolescence: Views from the family. *Journal of Early Adolescence, 5*(1), 81–100.

Hodges, V. (1995, March). *Supporting and preserving families: A strengths based approach.* Paper presented at the Child Welfare League of America National Conference, Washington, DC.

Logue, M.E., & Rivinus, T.M. (1991). Young children of substance abusing parents: A developmental view of risk and resiliency. In T.M. Rivinus (Ed.), *Children of chemically dependent parents* (pp. 55–73). New York: Brunner/Mazel.

Luthar, S.S., & Zigler, E. (1991). Vulnerability and competence: A review of research and resilience in childhood. *American Journal of Orthopsychiatry, 61*(1), 6–22.

Rutter, M. (1987). Psychosocial resilience and protective mechanisms. *American Journal of Orthopsychiatry, 57*(3), 316–331.

Rutter, M. (1993). Resilience: Some conceptual considerations. *Journal of Adolescent Health, 14*, 626–631.

Segal, J. (1988). Teachers have enormous power in affecting a child's self esteem. *Brown University Child Behavior and Development Newsletter, 4*, 1–3.

Vasquez, H. (1994, Fall). La cultura cura: A protective factor. *Messenger,* 4–7.

Weinreb, M. (in press). Resiliency mentors. *Young Children.* Washington, DC: National Association for the Education of Young Children.

Werner, E. (1989, April). Children of the garden island. *Scientific American,* 106–111.

Werner, E. (1990). Protective factors and individual resilience. In S. Meisels & J. Shonkoff (Eds.), *Handbook of early childhood development* (pp. 97–116). Cambridge, MA: Cambridge University Press.

Werner. E. (1992). The children of Kauai: Resiliency and recovery in adolescence and adulthood. *Journal of Adolescent Health, 13*, 262–268.

Woolf, H.B. (1974). *Merriam-Webster dictionary.* New York: Simon & Schuster.

~ 8 ~

Treatment for
Substance Abuse and Addiction

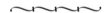

Trishia, in recovery from cocaine and alcohol abuse: I knew that I had to go into treatment, but I didn't know where to go or who to call. I spoke with a hotline worker who gave me a number to call. That person gave me the numbers of a whole bunch of places. By the time I finished calling four of them, I was so confused I felt like giving up. But I didn't. I did go into a residential program after I finished detox. I'm glad I stuck with it, but it wasn't easy to find a place.

The treatment possibilities for those with substance abuse or addiction problems vary dramatically, depending upon who they are, their addictions, and their resources. In fact, treatment programs themselves offer a range of services in different settings. There is no one definitive treatment program for people who wish to embark upon the recovery journey, however, and no general consensus on any one best type of treatment.

This chapter explores the various types of options that currently exist in the field of traditional substance abuse treatment and the

---

Much of the information in this chapter has been abbreviated to avoid cumbersome and complicated material. Some less popular treatment modalities have been excluded, but the many references cited provide excellent, in-depth information for those who are interested in further research.

relative strengths and weaknesses of each. The ways in which one can determine what type of program is best suited for a particular individual are also discussed. Finally, this chapter presents the groundwork for understanding the family-focused model of intervention (see Chapter 9).

∿ The Goals of Treatment ∿

The fundamental goal for any type of traditional addiction treatment program is abstinence from the substance or process of abuse (Brown, 1985). The success of any treatment is largely dictated by the assumption that the person at least recognizes that she has a problem and needs help. Learning alternatives to drug use, how to handle cravings, and how to establish a healthy lifestyle and positive relationships are also common goals of treatment. As a related goal, many programs also attempt to return the person to a life that is not only free from addiction but satisfying and productive. These programs emphasize abstinence but also believe that recovery is a process of ongoing growth and change.

∿ Different Treatment Options ∿

Didi, in recovery from cocaine abuse: And I noticed, too, there is a lot. If one center doesn't suit you, there are others. There is more than one place you can go. You are bound to find one that you are comfortable with, or where you can stay longer, or have your children with you. You can go to a halfway house and see your children on weekends.

Virtually everyone can find a treatment program with which they are comfortable among the variety of interventions available. Although programs vary widely, most can be classified as belonging to one of several types of structured interventions:

- Acute medical management
- Detoxification
- Methadone maintenance programs
- Pharmacotherapy
- Short-term inpatient treatment
- Residential treatment

- Partial residential or day treatment
- General outpatient treatment
- Family therapy
- Case management and advocacy
- Self-help programs

Acute Medical Management

Steve, in recovery from cocaine abuse: All I remember is taking that last hit and feeling like my heart was going to bust out of my chest. The pain was unbelievable, and I remember just before I went out that I realized that I was probably having a heart attack. I woke up in the emergency room and there were tubes in me and I was hooked up to machines and people were running all over the place. They knew I had used coke because the person I was with got scared and told them. I was lucky that time, I almost died. They told me that my heart rhythm was going crazy when they first brought me in and they had trouble getting it to beat the right way.

There are times when a person's drug use can lead to a medical or psychiatric emergency, inducing dangerous behavior to the self or others. Violent or self-destructive behavior, as well as severe anxiety, paranoia, and toxic- or drug-induced psychosis, can occur when a person is intoxicated from one of many drugs (Arif & Westermeyer, 1988). The most acute emergencies occur when addicts, either inadvertently or pointedly, overdose. At these times, individuals require medical management in an acute care setting, such as an emergency room, often involving monitoring and treatment to stabilize the crisis. A combination of medication and psychological support is typically used to treat the addict's symptoms.

Unintentional withdrawal caused by the cessation of a drug, such as alcohol or a sedative, can lead to seizures and other acute medical problems. Additional medical problems include heart arrhythmias, brain hemorrhages, lung abscesses, subacute bacterial endocarditis (infection of the lining around the heart), septicemia (generalized infection of the bloodstream), and pneumonia (infection in the lungs) (Arif & Westermeyer, 1988). In addition, someone may

be seriously injured secondary to his intoxication, in a car crash, for example. More disturbing are injuries to others, such as unintentional ingestion of drugs by a child or injury or illness caused by neglect or abuse.

A person who requires hospitalization to treat medical problems can be simultaneously detoxified or can be transferred to a detox program once the medical problem is stabilized.

Detoxification

Gina, in recovery from alcohol abuse: In my experience, it was the first time I went into a detox and after that I went to a rehab hospital, and I stayed there for 21 days. I didn't know what was going on and I was really judgmental. I was so scared. People came from all walks of life and it didn't matter who it was, we were able to go in there.

Ida, in recovery from heroin addiction: When I get up in the morning, a lot of times I'm in a real rotten mood. I don't want to hear anybody, I don't want to see anybody. I get into the shower, and once I'm out of the shower, we have an early meeting at 8:30 in the morning. We have to state who we are, what our drug is that we choose, and from there we say a little prayer, and we also say what our goal is going to be for that day and how we want it to go. By the time the meeting is finished everybody is in a good mood. We are wide awake, we are ready to get going, we have a lot of encouragement and faith, and we hug each other. We hold hands. We give each other uplifting that we need every day—not just one day but every day. There is a lot of loving, you can feel it when you walk into the building or into the room, you can feel the comfort, you can feel the energy that we all carry.

Well, being in detox is actually encouraging. It makes you feel good. They help you bring out a lot of things that you have been hiding. They help you admit things to yourself; they help you realize that it is not your fault, what has happened in the past. There are people around who help you feel good about yourself. An average day for me is going to meetings. There are regular meetings, the meetings I go to are focused on the 12 Steps, and also on honesty and admission, open mindedness, and willingness. If we break down, they are there so we don't fall back. We end up picking ourselves up to go forward instead of taking two steps back.

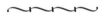

Detoxification (detox) is primarily a medical intervention to safely clear a person's body of a substance and stabilize her both physically and mentally. Detox can take place in an inpatient setting or on an outpatient basis, depending upon the drug of addiction and the severity of withdrawal syndrome. When a woman is pregnant, withdrawal from alcohol and certain other drugs can be dangerous to the fetus (Center for Substance Abuse Prevention, 1993; Chasnoff, 1989; Glantz & Woods, 1991; Zuckerman et al., 1989). Pregnant women are often hospitalized for detoxification or sent to a detox program that is specially equipped to monitor the pregnancy. Most detox programs are structured and the patients medically monitored. Patients are treated for withdrawal symptoms as well as any complications that arise from the addiction or the detox. Generally, individuals stay in detox from a few days to 3 weeks. Medication can be used to manage withdrawal symptoms that can be dangerous or extremely uncomfortable.

Some drugs cause physiological addiction, meaning the body has developed a physical dependence on the drug and withdrawal symptoms emerge upon cessation of the drug, some of which are life threatening. Sedatives and hypnotic drugs such as alcohol, tranquilizers, and barbiturates are physiologically addicting and require a carefully monitored detox that uses medication.

Withdrawal from narcotics, such as heroin, is extremely uncomfortable and although a person can stop suddenly (i.e., "cold turkey") without risking serious physical harm, many choose to enter a detox program. Symptoms of narcotic withdrawal begin to occur in 4–24 hours after the last use depending upon the narcotic. Symptoms reach a peak after 1–3 days, and acute symptoms can be expected to end within 4–10 days, again depending on the drug (Arif & Westermeyer, 1988). Withdrawal symptoms can include increased drug craving, agitation, depression, stomach cramps, nausea, vomiting, diarrhea, muscle cramps, fever, inability to sleep, yawning, and runny nose and eyes (American Psychiatric Association, 1994; Khantzian & McKenna, 1979). Many people describe this experience as "the worst flu I've ever had."

Withdrawal from stimulants and cocaine falls somewhere in between a physiological and psychological withdrawal syndrome. Although it is not physiologically dangerous to detox from these drugs, because the body is not dependent upon the drug, difficulty arises from the central nervous system's response to the cessation of the drug (Gawin & Kleber, 1988). The withdrawal syndrome can cause severe psychological symptoms, such as depression, irritability, sleep disturbance, psychosis, and acute suicidal ideation (Arif & Westermeyer, 1988; Gawin & Kleber, 1988). Monitoring a person's mental status through the first few days of abstinence in a safe environment is very important.

Other drugs such as marijuana, hallucinogens, inhalants, and PCP do not cause a physiological addiction, but often users have developed a psychological dependence that necessitates a detox period to wean them from the habit. People who have been using drugs for any length of time build up a tolerance (Arif & Westermeyer, 1988). And, although their bodies are not dependent, their minds and spirits are.

Trishia, in recovery from cocaine and alcohol abuse: I never thought it would feel so different, to be clean. I didn't get sick or anything like some people I know, but I still felt really bad. It was like I was in a fog. My head was all weird and I felt kind of lost. I wanted to use real bad because I couldn't stand the way I felt those first few days. I went into a detox for a week. They didn't give me anything [medication], but they watched me real carefully and I went to a lot of groups, and I talked a lot and I learned how to do these relaxation exercises when I felt like using. It helped me a lot. I think if I hadn't gone in I would have gone right back out there.

Even without serious physical symptoms, withdrawal from any drug can cause psychological difficulties, including depression, anxiety, or mood instability. In some cases, a person can become acutely psychotic or suicidal and require psychiatric treatment. At the very least, a detox program removes people from their usual environment, giving them a haven from the "people, places, and things" that contribute to their addictions. Adequate nutrition and sleep, along with counseling and support, are important components of a detox program.

Once a person has been stabilized in detox and is abstinent, he can choose from a number of other treatment options to maintain sobriety and continue in recovery. Completing detox does not mean a person has completed a treatment program for the addiction; it is usually just the first step in treatment. Many people are confused about this and believe that detox is "the treatment" for addiction.

Acupuncture Detox Acupuncture detox is a contemporary addition to treatment options. Acupuncture is an ancient technique used in Chinese medical practice that typically involves applying special needles to specific points on the ears, arms, hands, and/or feet. These points are believed to be associated with receptor sites related to pain, anxiety, and other physical or emotional conditions (Brumbaugh, 1993; Center for Substance Abuse Treatment, 1994; McLellan et al., 1993). When the needles pierce these points, they are thought to release blockages and realign the flow of energy through the body (Brumbaugh, 1993).

Although there is no general agreement on a standardized practice for acupuncture detoxification, the techniques reported most often employ the use of needles at key points on one or both ears (Brumbaugh, 1993; McLellan et al., 1993). Acupuncture can be used to treat a person for withdrawal symptoms in any setting and can be an adjunct to other forms of treatment. Other basic services such as a limited medical screening, supportive counseling, and referral are also offered in some acupuncture detox settings. Treatment duration is 1–2 weeks and includes about six treatments a week initially to manage acute withdrawal symptoms. Maintenance treatment can continue for several months with 2–3 treatments per week. Treatment usually lasts for about 1 hour, and people are encouraged to relax during this time.

Methadone Maintenance Programs

Methadone, a synthetic narcotic, is commonly used both for acute detox and maintenance with individuals addicted to heroin or other narcotics. It is a tightly controlled substance produced legally by a pharmaceutical company and must be prescribed by a physician.

Methadone is given in regulated doses to replace the use of heroin and can prevent withdrawal symptoms while maintaining a person in an alert and active state. Methadone is a long-acting, oral medication that can be administered only once daily (Arif & Westermeyer, 1988). A person can choose the duration of methadone maintenance she receives. One must be detoxed from methadone by slowly lowering the dosage while monitoring for withdrawal symptoms.

The use of methadone as a long-term treatment for narcotic addiction is somewhat controversial. There remains much disagreement as to the overall effectiveness of this treatment, what the treatment goals should be, the merits of total abstinence versus methadone maintenance, effective dose levels, and whether a person who is on methadone is considered to be in recovery (D'Aunno & Vaughn, 1992). Yet, arguments for the use of methadone as a way of preventing the spread of HIV infection are compelling. Many believe that methadone improves social and psychological functioning as well as physical health. The use of methadone also helps to reduce the crime rate among those who cannot tolerate abstinence (Arif & Westermeyer, 1988).

Because drug-involved pregnant women are at a higher risk for medical complications, most women who are pregnant and addicted to heroin are detoxified and placed on a methadone maintenance program. Sudden withdrawal from opiates can be dangerous and life threatening to the fetus, due to spontaneous abortion and premature labor. Still, when an infant is born to a mother who is taking methadone, that infant is born methadone dependent, requires careful monitoring, and may require detoxification.

Since the late 1980s, some hospitals have been safely detoxing addicted pregnant women from heroin without placing them on a methadone maintenance program (Carr, 1989). Pregnant women are also beginning to be detoxed from methadone. This requires that the woman is very highly motivated for treatment and will receive careful monitoring.

Pharmacotherapy

There are times when the use of medication is indicated either to help to manage symptoms related to addiction and withdrawal or to treat psychiatric conditions that coexist with addiction. A psychiatrist or physician prescribes the medication and well-trained professionals help to monitor the patient carefully. Medication can be used alone but is usually only one part of a coordinated treatment plan.

General goals of using medication include blocking, diminishing, or reversing the "high"; managing the toxic symptoms associated with intoxication; managing the withdrawal symptoms; reducing craving; reducing symptoms related to protracted abstinence; and treating underlying psychiatric disorders (Banys et al., 1994; Benzer, 1990; Dougherty & Gates, 1990; Giannini, Loiselle, Graham, & Folts, 1993; McDuff et al., 1993). Naltrexone, disulfiram (Antabuse), Clonidine, nicotine replacement, and psychotropic medications are all commonly used medications.

Naltrexone Naltrexone is an opioid antagonist, which blocks the effects of opioids in the central nervous system (Arif & Westermeyer, 1988). If an addict is given naltrexone, he or she will not experience the desired "high" of an illicit opioid (Arif & Westermeyer, 1988), which may discourage use.

Disulfiram Disulfiram, popularly known as Antabuse, is used to treat alcohol addiction. This drug causes a physiological response in a person if she drinks alcohol, causing her to become acutely ill. Severe nausea, vomiting, headaches, and mood swings can occur. Any amount of alcohol, even the small amount contained in medication, mouthwash, or aftershave lotion, can precipitate physical illness (Arif & Westermeyer, 1988). Disulfiram acts as a powerful deterrent for someone who is motivated to stop drinking but is having trouble doing so.

Clonidine Clonidine is a medication traditionally used to manage high blood pressure, but it is also capable of reversing the symptoms of opioid withdrawal. Clonidine's sedative effects can be

magnified by opioids, necessitating that the person stop using opioids. The treatment is short term, lasting about 2 weeks, and seeks
to restore a person to a completely drug-free state.

Nicotine Replacement Nicotine replacement provides an addict with nicotine without the harmful effects of smoking or chewing tobacco and prevents craving and uncomfortable withdrawal
symptoms. It can be administered in the form of chewing gum or a
patch that is worn on the skin.

Psychotropic Medication Psychotropics, which include antide-
pressant and antianxiety medications, are used to treat coexisting
psychiatric conditions, such as depression and severe anxiety disorders, in people who are addicted. Treating any underlying psychiatric disorders can help a person to remain abstinent by removing or
reducing his need to self-medicate feelings of depression, despair, or
hopelessness. Other psychiatric disorders, such as psychosis or bipolar illness, can also be stabilized with psychotropic medications,
which reduce the risk of relapse due to self-medication in an attempt
to ameliorate disturbing symptoms. New medications surface frequently and offer new options for treatment. Refer to a medical text
to keep abreast of changes.

The term *dual diagnosis* refers to the presence of both an addiction and a diagnosed major mental illness. Reported statistics vary
about the comorbidity of addiction and mental illness; however, the
incidence seems to be fairly high, ranging between 30% and 53%
(Boyd, 1993; Chavkin, Paone, Friedmann, & Wilets, 1993; Regier et
al., 1990; Schwartz et al., 1993). People who have a dual diagnosis
require a specialized setting for recovery, capable of treating both the
addiction and the psychiatric condition. Treating a person with a
dual diagnosis can be quite complex, depending upon the severity of
either or both of the conditions (Schwartz et al., 1993).

Short-Term Inpatient Treatment

Short-term inpatient treatment (STIT) programs are located in
hospital-like settings and offer intensive and comprehensive treatment. STIT programs differ from detox and residential programs in
that the patient's stay is shorter but the treatment more intensive.
The average length of a stay is 3–4 weeks, hence the popular titles
"21- or 28-day programs." Addicts can be detoxed in STITs or enter
the program after detoxing elsewhere. Medical care, psychological
assessment, and early stabilization are all components of this treat-

ment method, as are individual and group counseling and other types of educational and self-care groups.

Residential Treatment

The purpose of residential treatment is to remove a person from his usual environment for an extended period of time and to immerse him in treatment. A residential program allows a person to focus primarily on recovery. Addicts learn about their disease, about themselves, and techniques for staying clean and sober. Residential treatment provides a safe place in which people can explore their feelings, begin to change old behavior, and continue the healing of recovery. The length of stay varies depending upon the program and can range from several weeks to 2 years, sometimes longer. Almost all residential programs require that the person complete a detox first and/or have proof that she has been clean for a period of time.

Residential programs are located in a variety of settings. They are located in medical or psychiatric hospitals or are freestanding; some are privately housed in neighborhoods. Some programs are mixed, accepting men and women, and some only take same-sex clients. A few programs accept pregnant women and allow them to keep their babies in the program with them after delivery, and a small number accept parenting women with their children.

Didi: A typical day in the house that I am in starts out early. We get up early in the morning and we all have chores that we do and that need to be done by a certain time. We have groups where all of the women get together with a senior person who directs the groups on different things like feelings: how we feel that day or how we feel about anything. We also have 12-Step groups that teach us the 12 Steps of the program. For me, it is different because I have my baby with me. I have to learn how to schedule my son around the program, or should I say my program and then my son. Because before he came, I had to work my program, and now that he is here, we have to do it together. It is not easy some days. I am new at this; this is my first time having a baby clean and sober so it is a different experience for me. But I go to parenting classes that teach me and help me to learn how to take care of my baby today, something I didn't know how to do when I was out there.

Even though I thought I was doing it right. We have staff people in the house who help you learn how to take care of your baby, and they give you ideas. We also have a nutrition class where a specific woman comes and teaches you how to eat so that you can be healthy and so you can take care of your baby.

～～～～～

Each program has its own philosophy, structure, rules, and treatment methods, which vary from extremely structured and rigid to relaxed and informal.

Therapeutic Communities   Therapeutic Communities (TCs) were one of the first long-term residential treatment programs developed and have very specific treatment philosophies based upon the belief that negative, antisocial behavior and thinking must be changed in order to treat the addiction. These programs are drug free, meaning that patients are not allowed any type of medication. Highly organized and structured, TCs have very strict rules and consequences. TCs are the most rigid of the treatment programs and are considered the "toughest" to get through. Several other residential programs have developed their own treatment philosophies by borrowing from and modifying the ideology behind the TC.

Halfway Houses   A halfway house is a type of residential treatment that more closely resembles a community or sober living house. People sometimes enter a halfway house directly from detox; others enter after completing another type of residential program. Halfway houses are long term and are usually located in a "homelike" atmosphere. Most patients are expected to attend jobs, school, or training programs during the day and outside group or individual counseling as well as 12-Step meetings during the evening. Halfway houses provide people with a safe environment in which to practice their recovery skills and prepare them to reenter society clean and sober.

Homeless Shelters   Those individuals who are addicted as well as homeless face many obstacles. Many shelters for the homeless have residents who are actively using alcohol or other drugs or who have a known history of drug abuse or addiction. Some have a limited capacity for helping an addicted resident, while others will not accept a client who is actively using. There are shelters that offer walk-in services; others require that a person apply and be accepted for longer-term housing. Seeking more permanent shelter and treatment, however, can be nearly impossible.

Particularly problematic is housing homeless, addicted women with children. Although a few shelters have been developed to house women who are addicted and their children, usually they require that a woman first complete a detox program and continue in ongoing treatment as a prerequisite of entering the shelter. These new facilities provide safe shelter for women and children and offer groups on recovery, parenting, and life skills; they also help women find permanent housing. Children are ensured medical care, education, and other services they may need.

Partial Residential or Day Treatment

In the 1990s, day, evening, and weekend treatment programs have grown rapidly. Clients attend these programs during some part of the day or evening but are able to sleep at their homes. For those who work, evening or weekend programs provide treatment without interfering with their jobs. Quite beneficial, these programs allow people to receive intensive treatment while maintaining their homes, their jobs, and contact with their families and communities.

A few partial residential and day treatment programs have been designed to meet the needs of pregnant and parenting women. These programs provide child care and parenting groups for the mothers in addition to regular services.

General Outpatient Treatment

There is quite a bit of variability in outpatient treatment. Outpatient treatment centers are located in public or private clinics, are within a hospital setting, or are freestanding. Private therapists, psychologists, social workers, nurses, psychiatrists, and mental health counselors can all provide treatment. Treatment can be for an individual, a family, and/or a group. Outpatient treatment can also include the use of urine screening, case management, and advocacy.

Family Therapy

Family therapy not only helps the individual but also addresses issues in the larger system. For someone experiencing much difficulty in the family, working with the individual in isolation can be fruitless and counterproductive. (See Chapter 2 for an in-depth review of the various family therapy techniques that are used and the theories that inform the practice.) Family therapy can be combined with individual and/or group therapy. Most treatment programs include family therapy as part of the intervention.

Case Management and Advocacy

The concept of *case management* refers to clinical activities aimed at helping to locate, link, coordinate, and maintain services for clients. Originating from the field of social work, the concept and practice has been adopted by other clinicians and is now widely used in both psychiatric and substance abuse treatment.

A case manager develops a relationship with the client with the goal of providing support and advocacy. In this treatment component, the case manager provides a number of supportive interventions for an individual or family without requiring any talking therapy, often linking, coordinating, and referring the client to a variety of other services. This coordination minimizes fragmentation of services and enhances treatment (Graham & Timney, 1990). An important duty of a case manager is to provide outreach and follow-up to clients who have finished treatment or who have dropped out.

The nature of the case management service depends largely on the system of care within which it is embedded; but, generally, efforts are aimed at improving the efficiency of services through advocacy and coordination. In the long run, effective case management serves everyone's best interests. The clients benefit from coordinated and enhanced services, and care providers benefit by the linkage of various services, which reduces duplication of staff time. This intervention is also cost effective because it minimizes the need of one agency to "do everything." Following is a vignette describing how case management can be incorporated into traditional models of care:

At Boston Medical Center's pediatric primary care clinic, a new service, Pediatric Pathways, has been developed to provide case management and advocacy for the families it serves. Traditionally it had been the role of the clinic social worker who carries a huge caseload and usually has time to deal only with acute or emergency situations. A multidisciplinary team of professionals works to provide assessment, intervention, and referral. This team includes a family advocate, a child development specialist, a lawyer, and a mental health clinician, as well as the primary care provider and clinic social worker. In addition to their roles on this team, all—except for the family advocate—function in other areas within the institution.

The family advocate sees all incoming families who have a newborn, conducting psychosocial and legal needs assessments. Factors such as housing and entitlements are reviewed as well as general family functioning. Upon completing a needs assessment, the advocate works with the family, the clinic social worker, and the primary care provider to assist the family in getting their needs met.

Mrs. D came to this pediatric clinic with her newborn son. She also had three other children, ages 2, 4, and 7. She was new to the area and was currently living with her brother in the rundown family home. She had moved to get away from an abusive relationship but now had few resources to help her and did not know anyone except her brother. During the assessment, it was learned that she did not have entitlements in place for her children, and so the advocate was able to help her connect with the appropriate agency to get those in place. The advocate was able to help enroll the 4-year-old in a Head Start program. The infant seemed to be doing well; however, the primary care provider had some concerns about the 2-year-old who was not gaining weight and had developmental delays.

During the assessment, the advocate learned that the client often did not have enough food to adequately feed her children and that the house was in very poor condition. The 2-year-old was kept in a playpen because he was getting splinters from crawling on the wood floor. Furthermore, the mother seemed depressed and overwhelmed by her situation.

The advocate referred the mother to a food pantry and did a home visit to assess the living environment. The advocate then consulted the lawyer. The lawyer had the house inspected by the health department, which condemned it as unlivable. The 2-year-old was referred to the failure-to-thrive clinic within the pediatric primary care clinic—a linkage the advocate helped to make. He was also referred to the child development specialist who completed an evaluation and referral for early intervention. The mental health clinician saw the mother to evaluate her depression and referred her to a parenting support group, also within the clinic, and to counseling services.

Self-Help Programs

Self-help groups have well-organized chapters throughout the world that offer meetings, support, and sponsorship. The sense of shame and isolation is decreased within the fellowship of self-help. There is no membership fee or cost to attend. Membership is voluntary and based on anonymity. Anyone who wishes to stop his or her addicted behavior is welcome to attend. Meetings are widely available and vary in how they are structured: Some are general discussion groups, some use the 12-Step format to order their discussion, some rely upon speakers, and some are a combination of these three formats.

Gina, in recovery from alcoholism: The meetings that I go to are focused on the 12 Steps. The 12 Steps teach me about how to believe in a higher power and how to develop my spirituality. When I was a beginner on the 12 Steps, I didn't understand these things and I was in denial in that area around spirituality. I didn't want to deal with no higher power. They told me that the 12 Steps would get me to know who I really am. And I never knew who I was, so I was interested. The 12 Steps taught me who I am now, who I want to be, and whether or not I like myself. I don't have to hang on to old things, resentments. The past is no longer there; it's only today. I can't think about tomorrow because it hasn't come yet. It's simple.

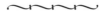

Patty, in recovery from alcoholism: For me, if I don't apply the 12 steps in my life and have a personality change then I will go back out there and use. Alcoholism and addiction are symptoms of something underlying. And the steps are there, they've helped me, and still help me today to deal with those underlying causes, to bring them out, to make amends where I was wrong, and to look inside of myself. I could get dressed up on the outside and feel horrible on the inside. It's the internal vigilance from the 12 Steps of AA, NA, any 12-Step program. Applying them in my life is what saved my life, because the person that I was would not stay clean and sober.

Alcoholics Anonymous (AA) provided the model upon which almost every self-help group is based. (See Chapter 1 for a discussion of the philosophy of AA.) The concept of AA, however, has grown to include myriad self-help groups, including Narcotics Anonymous (NA), Cocaine Anonymous (CA), Adult Children of Alcoholics (ACoA), Gamblers Anonymous (GA), Co-Dependents Anonymous (CODA), Sex and Love Anonymous (SLA), Al-Anon, Al-Ateen, Al-Atot, Incest Survivors Anonymous, Parents Anonymous, and Smokers Anonymous. (This is only a partial listing; see Appendix D for further information.)

Each of these groups is based upon the theory of admitting powerlessness and letting go. The central belief of loss of control as the key to understanding addiction requires that a person transform his or her belief system. Members of self-help groups often clash with proponents of controlled use. Self-help teaches that controlled use sidesteps the issue of loss of control and thus fuels denial and the inner argument over control, which can prevent people from shifting and changing basic beliefs about themselves and their beliefs.

Letting Go

To "let go" does not mean to stop caring; it means I can't do it for someone else.

To "let go" is not to cut myself off; it's the realization I can't control another.

To "let go" is not to enable, but to allow learning from natural consequences.

To "let go" is to admit powerlessness, which means the outcome is not in my hands.

To "let go" is not to try to change or blame another; it's to make the most of myself.

To "let go" is not to care for, but care about.

To "let go" is not to fix, but to be supportive.

To "let go" is not to judge, but to allow another to be a human being.

To "let go" is not to be in the middle of arranging all the outcomes, but to allow others to effect their own destinies.

To "let go" is not to be protective; it's to permit another to face reality.

To "let go" is not to deny, but to accept.

To "let go" is not to nag, scold, or argue, but instead to search out my own shortcomings and correct them.

To "let go" is not to adjust everything to my desires, but to take each day as it comes and cherish myself in it.

To "let go" is not to regret the past, but to grow and live for the future.

To "let go" is to fear less and love more.

Author unknown

Competing or Cooperating: The Controversy Historically, the rift between professionals treating addiction and self-help groups has been pronounced. Professionals, such as physicians, psychiatrists, social workers, and psychologists, criticize the self-help philosophy of treatment, viewing it as simplistic. Some professionals have been judgmental and devaluing, posing a serious dilemma for those who wish to benefit from treatment in both arenas (Bell & Khantzian, 1991; Khantzian & Mack, 1983).

The belief in a "higher power" is one major area of controversy and disagreement. Many who do not fully understand this concept see it as "religion." Many professionals have incorrect and inaccurate information because they have distanced themselves from the self-help programs and, as a result, do not encourage their clients to attend meetings and may even discourage it.

Fortunately, much progress has been made in repairing the rift, and more and more professionals are joining self-help treatment modalities in working partnerships (Brown, 1985). Efforts at increasing the understanding of various treatment modalities across disciplines and combining treatment interventions are ongoing.

～ Therapeutic Treatment Approaches ～

Successful individual treatment relies upon the successful development and maintenance of a therapeutic relationship in which a person is safe to explore painful feelings and learn how to manage his addiction. The mutual goal is relief from distress and movement toward a meaningful life free from addiction (Millman, 1986). Therapist and client work together as a team to determine goals and develop a useful treatment plan that enables the client to remain drug free. There are several different therapeutic approaches that one can use, either in individual or group treatment, including behavior therapy, cognitive therapy, behavioral-cognitive therapy, and psychotherapy. Many programs combine these approaches or use varying approaches at different stages of treatment.

Behavior Therapy

Behavior therapy is a commonly used treatment technique that uses psychological learning principles to directly change behavior (Arif & Westermeyer, 1988; Kadden & Mauriello, 1991). The focus is on current behavior, not on psychological dynamics, and the goal is to change the behavior, not necessarily to understand it. Behavior therapy techniques work best when a person is motivated and has admitted to having an out-of-control addiction.

Within behavior therapy, there are several commonly used techniques. *Contingency contracting* targets specific behavior for change by identifying reinforcers for positive behavior and consequences for negative behavior. It is often used in residential treatment programs. Before clients enter some programs, they are given an explicit treatment contract to which they must agree. Agreement and cooperation with treatment are directly linked to the privilege system. One attains privileges by following the treatment plan and loses privileges if one does not. Serious breaches in the treatment agreement can result in expulsion.

Relaxation training is another behavioral technique that teaches a person how to systematically achieve a relaxed physical and mental state. Relaxation can help a person deal with anxiety, stress, and anger and can be employed in difficult situations that may trigger a desire to use. Other behaviorial techniques teach people to use mental images, certain key phrases, or specific behaviors to cope with difficult situations and, thus, serve as a substitute for old and maladaptive behavior.

Cognitive Therapy

While behavior therapy is aimed at changing behavior, cognitive therapy is aimed at changing negative and destructive thinking (Brown, 1985). The most crucial cognitive shift takes place when denial crumbles and a person can begin to think of himself as an addict. Examining, constructing, and reconstructing thoughts, ideas, and perceptions helps a person to develop new and healthier ways of thinking and behaving. Often, this form of intervention includes the use of educational groups, films, and literature to increase knowledge about addiction and recovery. With this type of therapeutic approach, a person can begin to develop new language and healthier coping skills.

Behavioral-Cognitive Therapy

As the name implies, behavioral-cognitive therapy uses techniques from both modalities to encourage a change in behavior and thinking. Therapists who use this combined intervention believe that addiction is both a behavior and thinking disorder and that treatment must address both areas of function (Brown, 1985; Center for Substance Abuse Treatment, 1994).

The development of new knowledge and language is directly linked to behavior change, which in turn increases learning opportunities. People in recovery use concrete behaviors such as carrying AA literature or medallions as behavioral cues and also attend meetings or therapy to learn and talk about their addictions. Practicing new behaviors and cognitive skills eventually leads to increased proficiency and strengthens the recovery process. Behavioral-cognitive therapy that is specifically aimed at relapse prevention systematically teaches a person to recognize and manage triggers. This helps a client avoid relapse by replacing old, maladaptive thinking and behavior. Sometimes talking about an issue is most helpful; other times no words or cognitive skills are useful. In times like these, learned behavior responses can make all the difference, which are planned and practiced in anticipation of difficult situations.

Shania, in recovery from cocaine abuse: No matter how much I talk about it, every time I get into that situation, I get this funny feeling in my stomach and I feel like I have to use. I did use a couple of times when this happened in the past. Now, I have a plan for when that happens so I don't feel so helpless. I try to stay away when I can, but it is hard to avoid my family all of the time. When I'm there, I hang with my cousin Fran who does not use. I don't go there if I feel upset or if I know that certain family members who use will be there. I carry my sponsor's phone number so I can call her, and I talk with her before I go. I remember what I have learned in counseling and in meetings; I say the serenity prayer.

Incorporating behavioral-cognitive techniques is extremely useful in early recovery but can be employed and combined with other techniques throughout the course of treatment.

Psychotherapy

Psychotherapy is a general term that refers to a psychological intervention that employs an array of therapeutic techniques used in individual, group, or family therapy. The therapist and the client(s) work at developing a relationship, which is then used to help the client find relief from emotional and psychological problems.

Many forms of psychotherapy aim to uncover and examine unconscious material in order to help the client resolve conflicts, improve functioning, and change maladaptive thinking and behavior. Some schools of thought support a time-limited form of therapy aimed at solving specific problems. Others believe that many individuals who experience disturbing feelings or behaviors require longer periods of treatment in order to resolve conflicts and promote growth and change.

Psychoanalysis Psychoanalysis, or psychoanalytical psychotherapy, is based upon the work of Freud and is often called *talking therapy* or *the talking cure*. Its techniques include the examination and interpretation of unconscious thoughts, feelings, dreams, and fantasies to uncover psychological conflicts. The therapist uses himself as a "blank screen," remaining fairly neutral and inactive while the client responds to inquiries and talks freely about what she is thinking and feeling.

Joining together in exploration, the therapist and client develop a relationship that can help the client work through past difficult issues and serve as a model for healthy relationships. Examination of the past pays special attention to parental relationships in early life. The therapist can interpret the material and formulate a hypothesis about the connection between the material presented and the client's emotional difficulty.

This form of therapy can be quite intensive and expensive. Strict psychoanalysis requires that a person attend sessions several times a week. Modified forms of this therapy have a client attending once or twice a week.

Insight-Oriented Psychotherapy *Insight-oriented psychotherapy* is a modification of psychoanalytical psychotherapy that lends itself to several psychological theories instead of adhering to a fairly rigid theoretical structure. Again, the relationship between the client and the therapist is used as a way to help the client resolve issues and conflicts, and the therapist and client work together as a team. The client is encouraged to talk about thoughts and feelings, both past and present. The therapist is often more active in this type of therapy, interacting with the client more during sessions.

Supportive and Expressive Psychotherapy Another form of "talk therapy" is called *supportive and expressive psychotherapy.* This therapy focuses on the present situation, with far less emphasis on past events and unconscious material. The therapist does not necessarily work toward helping the client gain insight, although it is not discouraged and often happens as a by-product of the treatment. The client is encouraged to talk about thoughts and feelings related to his current situation, and the therapist actively supports the client by helping him problem-solve and develop coping strategies.

∽ Psychotherapy and Addiction ∽

The usefulness and efficacy of employing psychotherapy as a primary treatment modality for addiction has long been a point of contention. The disagreement is most sharply felt between the schools condoning traditional psychiatry and self-help groups. Ongoing debate includes discussion about what types of interventions are necessary, what is useful, what is effective, and what is ineffective.

Krystal (1985) argues that the difficulty of using psychoanalytical therapy with an addict lies in the assumption that the discovery of underlying fantasies and conflicts can relieve addiction in the same way as it relieves neurosis. For years, the use of psychoanalysis with addicts was practiced with poor results; the addicts kept on using while in therapy. (Remember, the failure of traditional psychiatry to successfully treat alcoholism is one of the primary reasons that AA was started.)

Treating a person in psychotherapy while she is still actively using tends not only to be ineffective but, in some cases, can worsen the situation by uncovering difficult memories and feelings that can fuel continued use. Every effort should be made to ensure that a person has stopped using drugs and is stabilized in recovery before engaging in therapy that is explorative and insight oriented. Those who have already developed cognitive and behavioral skills to support their sobriety, however, often find individual or group psychotherapy very helpful in resolving conflicts. One study of narcotic addicts in methadone treatment reported that patients who were afforded behavioral-cognitive or supportive and expressive therapy fared better than patients who did not receive psychotherapy (Millman, 1986).

Others believe that, although supportive therapy is useful in helping to enhance abstinence, in-depth therapy aimed at exploring deeper issues is necessary for a good long-term outcome (Schiffer, 1988). In-depth therapy can get at some of the more serious issues and the person can explore, heal, and change.

The therapist who is treating a person with an addiction or history of substance abuse must be knowledgeable about the process of addiction and recovery and have an appreciation for the many different types of treatment modalities. It is essential that the therapist adopt an empathetic and nonjudgmental attitude with the client; model a relationship of honesty, trust, and consistency; and provide a "holding environment" in which the client can grow away from reliance on alcohol or other drugs (Schiffer, 1988).

∼ A Letter From Elaina ∼

When Elaina began treatment, she had just finished a 21-day detox program and a short-term residential treatment program for her cocaine and alcohol addiction. In her 21 years, she had been in several serious accidents, two of them life threatening, and all but one were related to her addiction. She was in an abusive relationship with a man, she had not finished high school, and she was not working. Despite a family history that included alcoholism (both parents and two brothers), the death of her oldest brother in a car accident in which she was a passenger, a mother who was depressed and unavailable, a father who was sadistic and controlling, and evidence suggestive of early sexual abuse, she initially reported having no particular family problems and expressed that she felt quite close to her father.

She presented as a frail-looking and depressed young woman who was plagued by a variety of somatic and emotional symptoms, which she found disturbing and incapacitating. Over the course of the first 4 years of treatment, she had a complete neurological evaluation because her symptoms were vague and persistent and suggestive of a possible neurological problem. The neurological workup did not find any problems. She was hospitalized in a psychiatric hospital on three occasions for depression and suicidal ideation—twice during the earlier part of her treatment and once in her last year. Several medications were tried, primarily antidepressants, but after a short trial of each, she stopped using the medication, complaining of side effects and insisting the medication was not helping her.

Psychological testing was done during her first hospitalization and repeated again during her last hospitalization, a span of about 4 years. The first battery of testing found her to be of borderline to low-average intelligence, with many serious emotional and cognitive difficulties predictive of a limited capacity to fully function in life. The last battery of testing reported an IQ score increase into the average to high-average range, with a dramatic decrease in disturbing emotional and cognitive problems.

Throughout treatment, she attended a variety of self-help groups including AA and ACoA. She joined a church and completed her high school education. She stopped dating the abusive man and later developed a relationship with a man who was working, was not abusive, and was in recovery from alcoholism. She later had a child by him, and, although their relationship did not continue, they worked out a co-parenting arrangement that was mutually satisfying and in the best interest of their child. Elaina still struggled for a very long time with accepting that she was an alcoholic. She drank on several occasions in the first 3 years, each time for a brief duration.

Following is an excerpt from a letter Elaina wrote to her therapist several months after terminating 6 years of individual psychotherapy, in which many psychotherapeutic techniques were employed, from behavior and cognitive therapies to supportive and expressive therapy. Elaina was encouraged to attend self-help groups and to identify other sources of support. With her dual diagnosis of depression, she was also encouraged to have regular check-ups.

> Well, I've been missing you and my old therapy. It's very amazing to me!!! How much I learned in therapy. At the end, I was "banging my head off of the walls" when we were stuck. I knew it was time to go. I was scared and I hated the thought, but it wasn't until I left that I could SEE. While I was seeing you, I always asked, "What is happening?" "How is this working?"

"Oh, this isn't working." I really couldn't see what was happening to me. You used to say, "It's our relationship that will help you to get better." I didn't understand. I thought it was me who had to get me better, that somehow you would teach me how to make me better. The whole time, without me ("Oh smart me with all of the answers"), I, we, were developing a relationship. A good, healthy, caring relationship that has changed my life, I hope forever.

I never thought that I would think or be different, I never thought I could change and be a real person, but I am and it is amazing. I can now see "clearly" all of the work we did "together." You gave me a great, the greatest gift I ever got—ME. I came in there a mess: confused, scared, mindless, hopeless, no values. I had no clue what normal was. Today I have: Hope, Trust, Peace of Mind, Values, God, Friends, and most important—Me.

People notice the changes in me now. I have grown up a lot. Even better news: Remember I couldn't even be in a room with more than five people for 2 minutes? Well, I'm in college and in my third semester. So far, I have gotten A's in my first four classes.

Well, this letter sends a great deal of Love, Thanks, and Appreciation. I know that all of what I wrote sounds very positive and hopeful, but as far as I have come I still have a very long way to go in recovery.

⌒⌒⌒⌒⌒

⌒ Does Treatment Work? ⌒

Some people believe that addicts should be handled through the criminal justice system, which attempts to stem drug use and abuse with interdiction. Others believe that addicts are best managed with treatment, not criminal sanctions. Still others believe that to do either without providing early and extensive drug education and prevention is analogous to "shoveling sand against the tide."

To measure the effects of treatment, it is useful to think about success in terms of remission rather than a cure, which is rooted in the understanding of addiction as a chronic and relapsing disease. *Remission* means that there is a significant reduction or amelioration of symptoms and an improved ability to function. With remission, there is also a reduction in the cost to society in terms of health care, criminal justice, and personal productivity when a person is successfully treated for an addiction (Substance Abuse and Mental Health Services Administration [SAMHSA], 1994).

In the 1980s, the Reagan administration approached the drug problem with aggressive interdiction and criminal justice sanctions. Although there was no appreciable improvement in the rate of drug abuse and addiction in the United States during that administration, the criminal justice system was overwhelmed with drug-related cases and the prison population swelled (Califano, 1995). A parallel prevention campaign headed by Nancy Reagan, the "Just Say No" movement, had more promising results in terms of educating American youth about drug use (Califano, 1995).

Joseph A. Califano, Jr. (1995), president of the Center on Addiction and Substance Abuse at Columbia University and former Secretary of Health, Education, and Welfare, argues against criminal sanctions, citing that, despite all of the money that has been poured into the criminal justice system to curb drug abuse and drug trade, the number of arrests for drug offenses has soared from 30,000 in 1960 to over 1 million in 1989. The United States, among industrialized countries, ranks second behind Russia in the number of people imprisoned for drug-related crimes. More people have been incarcerated for drug crimes than for all violent crimes committed, and most violent crimes are committed by substance abusers. The judicial system, as well as law enforcement agencies, is overwhelmed.

Califano (1995) also notes, however, that only 25% of those in need of alcohol or other drug treatment enter a program. On average, one fourth complete treatment, and one half of those people are substance free 1 year later. In other words, of those who enter treatment, one in eight will be drug free 1 year later, success rates that do not instill confidence in treatment. Califano and others argue that money must be invested in research, prevention, and treatment, and legislature and laws addressing criminal justice issues must be changed to require drug treatment to be incorporated into the conditions of probation, parole, and release from prison, in order to curb the rates of addiction in U.S. society.

Accurate information about the effectiveness of drug treatment is greatly hampered by the complexity of the issues related to addiction, the variety of treatment, and the lack of high-quality research (Apsler & Harding, 1991). Some of the difficulty in looking at treatment success rates lies in the demographics of the population studied, the drug of abuse, and the treatment modality employed. For example, much of the published research has focused on narcotics addiction and the use of methadone (Apsler & Harding, 1991) or treatment success rates for alcoholism as opposed to those for other addictions. Although one must be careful to avoid making generalized statements, there is information available that can help to put this issue in perspective.

The Bad News

There exists a phenomenon in which substance abusers "mature out" of drug use, abuse, and addiction; as addicts grow older, they stop using. Also, the older a person is, the less likely he or she is to begin to abuse drugs or develop an addiction. In one well-known longitudinal study, Valliant (1983) followed men with alcohol problems for 40 years and found no significant differences in remission rates between treatment and nontreatment participants. In another well-known study, Valliant (1973) followed 100 heroin addicts admitted to a federal prison hospital. After 18 years, the death rate among participants was higher than expected for their ages, and among those living, there was a significant increase in abstinence from heroin. In other words, the heaviest drug users died. Several studies comparing intensive treatment to a brief advice intervention found no significant difference in success rates between the two groups (Miller, 1992), which may mean that 1) nothing works well; or 2) anything, including nothing, has equal results.

Reason for Optimism

The SAMHSA (1994) cited the following statistics, which seem to indicate that treatment on demand may stop the progression to more serious problems with substance use and abuse. While waiting for treatment to become available for cocaine addiction, participants in one study reported accelerating problems in employment and support, severity of medical complications, and substance abuse. In another study, after 1 year of methadone treatment for heroin addiction, nearly three fourths of the injecting drug users had stopped injecting heroin.

In another study of the effectiveness of treatment provided in four private programs serving employed and insured cocaine- and/or alcohol-dependent males, McLellan et al. (1993) reported significant and pervasive improvement at a 6-month follow-up visit, as confirmed by urine screening and breathalyzer tests. More than 50% of the group were completely abstinent, 80% were working, and less than 10% required retreatment. This study also compared success rates among the programs and found that programs that provided more services directed at particular problems had the best outcomes. These researchers concluded that the quantity and range of treatment services delivered is one of the major factors accounting for the difference in the effectiveness of treatment programs.

It is also interesting to note that Condelli and Hubbard (1994), in a study of clients in a variety of residential programs, found that those who stayed in treatment for a longer period of time had lower rates of drug use and criminal behavior than those who stayed in treatment programs for a shorter duration. One program that provided outpatient follow-up services for people treated for alcoholism reported an abstinence rate of 51%. Available research cites that approximately 35% of those who participate in an AA program achieve sobriety (Arif & Westermeyer, 1988).

Cost Effectiveness One year of untreated addiction costs society approximately $43,200 in criminal justice costs, medical costs, loss of labor, and results of crime (SAMHSA, 1994). Treatment for some addictions seems to be far less expensive than other alternatives. One year of methadone treatment for heroin addiction costs $3,500. One year of incarceration for the same person costs $39,600.

Most of the women who come into publicly funded drug treatment programs are welfare recipients. The cost of treatment and recovery for one woman with two children in a residential treatment program is approximately $26,266 for 1 year. Specialized foster care for children who have been drug exposed is estimated to cost $23,000 per year, per child. Another source reported that the cost of foster care for 1,194 infants exposed to drugs for 1 year was about $7.2 million or $6,030 per child (U.S. Government Accounting Office, 1990). At one hospital, the median cost of care for infants exposed to drugs was $5,500, while the median cost for nonexposed infants was $1,400 (U.S. Government Accounting Office, 1990). In addition, women who return to society after recovery can care for their children, get off of welfare, and be productive.

Savings are also seen in the reduction of criminal justice and incarceration costs, medical care, and the cost of crime to society in general. Nearly one third of people in one outpatient methadone treatment program reported that they had committed at least one predatory crime in the year prior to treatment. One half of all those arrested for assault and homicide test positive for illicit drugs, and two thirds test positive for alcohol (Wish, Klumpp, Moorer, Brady, &

Williams, 1989). In one treatment program for incarcerated felony offenders, only 35% of them were rearrested and 79% were employed upon release, compared with the rearrest rate for all offenders, which is 63%.

In regard to personal productivity, the SAMHSA (1994) reports that an estimated 59% of the adults who reported using illicit drugs during the past month were employed at the time. One study found that after treatment, job-related problems such as absenteeism, tardiness, injury, and errors all declined. Another study found a 20% reduction of accidents on the job following intervention by an Employee Assistance Program.

Substance abuse treatment can also help to slow the spread of HIV and STDs and decrease the health costs related to treating conditions associated with alcohol and other drug abuse and addiction. Without treatment, alcoholics spend twice as much on health care as people without alcohol abuse problems (SAMHSA, 1994). One study documented a 40% reduction in the health care costs of participants 2 years after completing treatment for substance abuse.

Prevention

Efforts at prevention, which include public education, early intervention, and public policy making, have intensified since the 1980s. Prevention is primarily aimed at keeping people from abusing alco-

hol and other drugs or becoming addicted but can also be aimed at stopping an occasional user from developing a more serious problem. Tertiary prevention is aimed at using treatment to reduce the risk of relapse and continued use (Center for Substance Abuse Prevention, 1993).

In order to develop effective prevention strategies, public health officials gather information about such things as the role that alcohol and other drugs play within a community, the nature of consumption, what constitutes harmful consumption, the context in which the choice to use drugs is made, indicators of drug abuse, and natural sources of prevention already in practice (Arif & Westermeyer, 1988). Public policy toward substance abuse has an impact upon general public attitudes and can further the making of laws that govern the use of alcohol and other drugs. Public health agencies also conduct campaigns to increase awareness and influence behavior change.

For example, rigorous anti-tobacco, "quit smoking" campaigns and the increased availability of smoking-cessation treatment programs have helped to decrease the number of people who continue to smoke and the number of people who start to smoke. These anti-smoking campaigns, which include research that shows direct evidence of the devastating health problems that result from tobacco smoking, have also educated the general public about the general ill effects of smoking as well as the burden of costs associated with smoking-related health problems. As a result, negative public attitudes toward smoking in public places have put sanctions on people who smoke, which encourages smokers to quit. There are now strict rules in many places that restrict or prohibit smoking. In addition, laws limiting cigarette (and alcohol) advertising have reduced the exposure that these products receive. Taxes on cigarettes and alcohol place an added burden on those who buy these products and help to fund many of the early education and prevention programs that discourage tobacco and alcohol use.

School-based smoking prevention programs, in place since the 1980s, and the abundance of anti-smoking curricula available for all grades have contributed to the one third decline in smoking rates among youth since the 1970s (National Cancer Institute, 1994). More recently, government grants have been awarded to support the development of education and prevention programs in public schools, which discourage drug use while teaching students of all ages about the effects of alcohol and other drugs and techniques for handling peer pressure. Student clubs such as Students Against Drunk Driving

(SADD) provide peer education and support. Unfortunately, the economic climate has created significant budget cuts, forcing some of these prevention programs to close.

Other examples of successful public campaigns include educating the public about safe sex, the transmission of HIV infection, and the danger of sharing dirty needles. Although these campaigns may not be able to directly change public behavior, they provide necessary and vital information to people of all ages.

Another type of prevention focuses on early detection and treatment for abuse and addiction. At-risk populations, as well as the general public, can be screened for evidence of alcohol and other drug problems. By asking a few questions, a health care provider can often determine whether a person is at risk or currently abusing alcohol and/or other drugs. Early detection can help prevent a person from experiencing more chronic and debilitating consequences of addiction. Medical professionals who can detect, diagnose, and treat complications of drug abuse and addiction early on greatly help individuals and society. Some caregivers, however, do not feel comfortable asking these types of questions or do not know what questions to ask. Also, they may hesitate to ask because they do not know what to do with affirmations of difficulty. Appendix B contains examples of how to take a drug and alcohol history.

The benefits of treating a parent who is addicted can be felt not only by the parent, but also by the children who then stand a better chance of not repeating their parent's legacy. This has far-reaching implications for the immediate family and the larger community in terms of money saved and the increase in human productivity.

⌒ Future Directions ⌒

Regardless of the disparity in reported success rates, treatment for addiction is and can be effective. There are so many factors, it is often difficult to determine what treatment works best and for whom. Research is one way to improve treatment outcomes; by studying what works and what does not, more effective and efficient treatment can be developed. Another way to improve treatment outcomes is through training and education. Providing information and training about addiction and treatment to health care providers, educators, and social services workers can increase the chances that a person who is in trouble with alcohol or other drugs, or a child suffering from the impact of parental substance abuse, can be identified earlier and offered intervention.

Susan, an ACoA: If only one person knew what was going on when I was growing up, maybe I wouldn't have such problems now. I couldn't say, "Hey, my father is an alcoholic and beats my mother," but I think if someone asked me what was going on I might have talked to them, at least I would have felt that someone knew something was wrong. In school, I got into trouble all the time, and twice my mother brought me to the emergency room with her after my father hurt her. No one talked to me or asked me what was going on. I felt almost invisible.

Pediatrician from urban city hospital: There are times that I am aware that there may be a drug or alcohol problem but I don't know how to approach the person. I am not sure about whether I should say anything, how I should say it, or even if it is any of my business as the child's pediatrician. I received almost no training in addiction, mainly I learned about the medical complications, and I don't know what questions to ask to determine if there is a problem.

～ References ～

American Psychiatric Association. (1994). *Diagnostic and statistical manual of mental disorders* (4th ed.). Washington, DC: Author.

Apsler, R., & Harding, W.M. (1991). *Cost-effectiveness analysis of drug treatment: Current status and recommendations for future research.* NIDA Drug Abuse Services, Series No. 1, 58–81. Rockville, MD: National Institute on Drug Abuse.

Arif, A., & Westermeyer, M.D. (1988). *Manual of drug and alcohol abuse.* New York: Plenum.

Banys, P., Clark, W.H., Tusel, D.J., Sees, K., Stewart, P., Mongan, L., Delucchi, K., & Callaway, E. (1994). An open trial of low dose buprenorphine in treating methadone withdrawal. *Journal of Substance Abuse Treatment,* *11*(1), 9–16.

Bell, C.M., & Khantzian, E.J. (1991). Contemporary psychodynamic perspectives and the disease concept of addiction: Complementary or competing models? *Psychiatric Annals, 21,* 273–281.

Benzer, D.G. (1990). Quantification of the alcohol withdrawal syndrome in 487 alcoholic patients. *Journal of Substance Abuse Treatment, 7*(2), 117–124.

Boyd, C.J. (1993). The antecedents of women's crack cocaine abuse: Family substance abuse, sexual abuse, depression and illicit drug use. *Journal of Substance Abuse Treatment, 10*(5), 433–438.

Brown, S. (1985). *Treating the alcoholic: A developmental model of recovery.* New York: John Wiley & Sons.

Brumbaugh, A.G. (1993). Acupuncture: New perspectives in chemical dependency treatment. *Journal of Substance Abuse Treatment, 10*(1), 35–43.

Califano, J.A. (1995, January 29). It's drugs, stupid. *The New York Times Magazine,* pp. 40–41.

Carr, S.J. (1989). Ladies in waiting . . . for detox: Tacoma Hospital unit treats pregnant polydrug abusers. *Professional Counselor,* 42–60.

Center for Substance Abuse Prevention. (1993). *Pregnancy and exposure to other drug use.* (CSAP Technical Report 7, Publication No. SMA 93-2040). Rockville, MD: U.S. Department of Health and Human Services.

Center for Substance Abuse Treatment. (1994). *Assessment and treatment of cocaine-abusing methadone maintained patients.* (TIP Series 10, DHHS Publication No. SMA 94-3003). Rockville, MD: U.S. Department of Health and Human Services.

Chasnoff, I.J. (Ed.). (1989). *Drugs, alcohol, pregnancy, and parenting.* Hingham, MA: Kluwer Academic Publishers.

Chavkin, W., Paone, D., Friedmann, P., & Wilets, I. (1993). Psychiatric histories of drug using mothers: Treatment implications. *Journal of Substance Abuse Treatment, 10*(5), 445–448.

D'Aunno, T., & Vaughn, T.E. (1992). Variations in methadone treatment practices: Results from a national study. *Journal of the American Medical Association, 267*(2), 253–258.

Dougherty, R.J., & Gates, R.R. (1990). The role of buspirone in the management of alcohol withdrawal: A preliminary investigation. *Journal of Substance Abuse Treatment, 7*(3), 189–192.

Gaudenzia, Inc. (1991). *Cost benefit: Treatment of addicted women.* Harrisburg, PA: Author.

Gawin, F.H., & Kleber, H.D. (1988). Evolving conceptualizations of cocaine dependence. *The Yale Journal of Biology and Medicine, 61,* 123–136.

Giannini, A.J., Loiselle, R.H., Graham, B.H., & Folts, D.J. (1993). Behavioral response to buspirone in cocaine and phencyclidine withdrawal. *Journal of Substance Abuse Treatment, 10*(6), 523–528.

Glantz, J.C., & Woods, J.R. (1991). Obstetrical issues in substance abuse. *Pediatric Annals, 20*(10), 531–539.

Graham, K., & Timney, C.B. (1990). Case management in addictions treatment. *Journal of Substance Abuse Treatment, 7*(3), 181–188.

Kadden, R.M., & Mauriello, I.J. (1991). Enhancing participation in substance abuse treatment using an incentive system. *Journal of Substance Abuse Treatment, 8,* 113–124.

Khantzian, E.J., & Mack, J.E. (1983). Alcoholics Anonymous and contemporary psychodynamic theory. In *Recent developments in alcoholism: An official publication of the American Medical Society on Alcoholism, the Research Society on Alcoholism, and the National Council on Alcoholism* (pp. 67–89). New York: Plenum.

Khantzian, E.J., & McKenna, G.J. (1979). Acute toxic and withdrawal reactions associated with drug use and abuse. *Annals of Internal Medicine, 90,* 361–372.

Krystal, H. (1985). Some problems encountered in attempting psychoanalytic psychotherapy with substance dependent individuals. *Drug Abuse and Alcoholism Newsletter, 19*(1).

McDuff, D.R., Schwartz, R.P., Tommasello, A., Tiegel, S., Donovan, T., & Johnson, J.L. (1993). Outpatient benzodiazepine detoxification for methadone patients. *Journal of Substance Abuse Treatment, 10*(3), 297–302.

McLellan, T.A., Grissom, G.R., Brill, P., Burell, J., Metzger, D.S., & O'Brien, C.P. (1993). Private substance abuse treatment: Are some programs more effective than others? *Journal of Substance Abuse Treatment, 10*(3), 243–254.

Miller, W.R. (1992). The effectiveness of treatment for substance abuse: Reasons for optimism. *Journal of Substance Abuse Treatment, 9,* 93–102.

Millman, R.B. (1986). Considerations on the psychotherapy of the substance abuser. *Journal of Substance Abuse Treatment, 3*(2), 103–109.

National Cancer Institute. (1994). *School programs to prevent smoking.* (NIH Publication No. 94-500). Rockville, MD: Author.

Regier, D.A., Farmer, M.E., Rae, D.S., Locke, B.Z., Keith, S.J., Judd, L.L., & Goodwin, F.K. (1990). Comorbidity of mental disorders with alcohol and other drug abuse. *Journal of the American Medical Association, 264*(19), 2511–2518.

Schiffer, F. (1988). Psychotherapy of nine successfully treated cocaine abusers: Techniques and dynamics. *Journal of Substance Abuse Treatment, 5,* 131–137.

Schwartz, L.S., Lyons, J.S., Stulp, F., Hassan, T., Jacobi, N., & Taylor, J. (1993). Assessment of alcoholism among dually diagnosed psychiatric inpatients. *Journal of Substance Abuse Treatment, 10*(3), 255–262.

Substance Abuse and Mental Health Services Administration (SAMHSA). (1994). *Cost of addictive and mental disorders and effectiveness of treatment* (DHHS Publication SMA 2095–94). Rockville, MD: Author.

U.S. Government Accounting Office. (1990). Drug-exposed infants: A generation at risk. *Report to the Chairman, Committee on Finance, U.S. Senate* (GAO HRD-90-138), Rockville, MD: Author.

Valliant, G.E. (1973). A 20-year follow-up of New York narcotic addicts. *Archives of General Psychiatry, 29,* 237–241.

Valliant, G.E. (1983). *The natural history of alcoholism: Causes, patterns, and paths to recovery.* Cambridge, MA: Harvard University Press.

Wish, E.D., Klumpp, K.A., Moorer, A.H., Brady, E., & Williams, K.M. (1989). *Analysis of drugs and crime among arrestees in the District of Columbia: Final report.* Washington, DC: U.S. Department of Justice.

Zuckerman, B., Frank, D.A., Hingson, R., Amaro, H., Levenson, S.M., Kayne, H., Parker, S., Vinci, R., Aboagye, K., Fried, L.E., Cabral, H., Timperi, R., & Bauchner, H. (1989). Effects of maternal marijuana and cocaine on fetal growth. *New England Journal of Medicine, 320,* 720–768.

~ 9 ~

Family-Focused Treatment

Interventions for Families
Affected by Substance Abuse

*C*hild development, family systems, and addiction/recovery theory inform the family-focused interventions presented in this
chapter, which recognize the interrelatedness of all players in the
family drama. Family-focused interventions recognize individual
strengths, needs, and skills as well as familial strengths, needs, and
styles of functioning. The whole of the family is not lost to individual characteristics and functioning but remains of primary consideration when family interventions are designed.

The family-focused interventions presented in this chapter offer
principles, practices, and strategies on which to adapt, re-create, and
expand. They are not meant to be "recipes" to apply verbatim to
families but rather starting points for professionals designing *individualized* interventions for families. There is, in fact, no one "right
answer" or method that works with all families. A "cookbook"
approach to interventions for families in recovery—matching the
family to interventions—is the antithesis to family-focused care,
which offers interventions to meet individual and family needs (see
Table 1).

Developing and providing family-focused services constitute the
backbone of successful intervention and provide the philosophy upon
which effective interventions are based. Family-focused services aim
primarily to preserve family integrity, however "the family" is defined by the client, without sacrificing the healthy development of
individual members. There are many ways to make interventions

235

Table 1. Assumptions of effective family-focused treatments

1.	One of the best ways to help the child is to help the family recover.
2.	One cannot treat an individual effectively in isolation of the family system. The client is the family.
3.	Family-focused treatment offers something for all members, focuses on family strengths, and promotes family resiliency.
4.	Family-focused treatment acknowledges, honors, and promotes the family's culture.
5.	Family-focused intervention matches interventions to families, not families to interventions.
6.	A therapeutic relationship is essential to any intervention.
7.	A crisis is a window of opportunity.
8.	One does not empower people; rather one assists people in finding their own power.
9.	A multidisciplinary team approach to family intervention is critical.
10.	Recovery from substance abuse is possible for everyone.
11.	The goal is progress, not perfection. There is no such thing as a perfectly functioning family.
12.	Recovery is a lifelong journey where change can be a slow process.
13.	Family-focused treatment is prevention, because what goes around comes around.

family focused, ranging from making simple changes in traditional models of interventions to creating entirely new programs.

For the person with an estranged family, of particular concern for the homeless, those with chronic mental illness, and long-time addicts and children who have been moved about from one placement to another, all of whom may have few or no family connections, it may be difficult to identify a primary system to which they belong. Experience has taught that almost no person exists in complete isolation. People make connections with neighbors, clergy, teachers, shelter staff, peers, hospital staff, food bank volunteers, and corner store workers. Creative intervention broadly defines an individual's "family," which may consist of genetically unrelated individuals.

If members are separated from each other, connection is encouraged, if and when appropriate, through letters, telephone calls, or visits. Clinicians can act as liaisons when other agencies are involved to help make these connections. A woman's attachment to her children is supported through validating her importance to them, helping to maintain contact with the children when possible, and connecting her with the children's substitute caregiver. The feasibility of reunification should always be considered in tandem with the best interests of the individual and family. Family or foster parents who are caring for children are included in treatment and are encouraged to participate.

This model sees the family as a system but also respects the individual needs and differences of its members. Services therefore are designed to promote family integrity while being cognizant of individual needs and respecting the rights of and maintaining each individual's identity. There are times when what may be best for one member is not good for another. Rather than seeing this as an "either/or" situation, family-focused interventionists work to understand and support each individual while maintaining some balance for the system. This is hard to do, particularly when there are painful or dangerous dynamics involved.

The following vignette from Nicki's story serves as an example of how to work within a family-focused model. For the many different agencies and clinicians involved, this was one of the more difficult cases.

〜〜〜〜

Nicki's mother, a serious and stern "no-nonsense" woman, had been raised in a particularly strict household. She believed that children should be seen and not heard, be obedient, and eat whatever was served to them. There were absolutely no circumstances when "back talk" was acceptable. To make sure that the children understood that she meant business, she would often sit with "the belt" in hand.

Nicki's mother had often taken care of her grandchildren and had frequently taken care of Nicki when she was trying to stop drinking and drugging. Despite concerns about her mother's care of the grandchildren, Nicki and her children frequently relied on her.

Life at Nicki's house was usually confusing and chaotic: There were no set routines and rules were arbitrary. After Nicki's death, the children, now with their grandmother, were suddenly expected to follow a rigid set of rules. The grandmother was ambivalent about taking on the primary caregiving role with her grandchildren, was obviously upset about her predicament, and made her feelings known to all, including her grandchildren. Although she herself felt devastated by the loss of her daughter, she showed little emotion, even when she was told the disturbing details of Nicki's death. She was not able to help her grandchildren grieve the loss of their mother.

The two youngest boys, who could be delightfully mischievous and playful, appeared more often as painfully sad, withdrawn, and depressed. They also seemed frightened of their grandmother but clearly cared about her and saw her as their primary caregiver. They were quite attached to the staff in the therapeutic child care center, the therapist, the child development specialist, and the pediatrician. Everyone worked hard to maintain the grandmother's cooperation, knowing that this was the only care arrangement that existed for the children. The older children struggled as well. Charles was getting into trouble at school, and Kara was sullen and defiant at home. The oldest daughter got pregnant and moved in with her boyfriend.

The staff appreciated the challenges that these children presented to the grandmother. The staff were also painfully aware of the children's many losses and the impact of the recent and devastating loss of their mother. They also saw with some pain that the grandmother seemed to have little capacity for empathy for her grandchildren and was overly rigid and punitive. She did, however, provide a home and food for them and made sure that they kept medical and dental appointments. She continued to bring them into the clinic, where they were seen by the pediatrician and the clinician who had been working with Nicki. Despite her stern demeanor, the grandmother clearly loved these children and thought that she was doing the best that she could do.

The staff members were primarily concerned with how the grandmother interacted with and disciplined the children. She had very high standards for behavior and limited tolerance for limit testing, lack of cooperation, or behavior that was less than what she expected. The limits and rules she established would be hard

for the most well-adjusted child to follow. Her methods of punishment included verbally berating the children as well as striking them with the "belt" if they misbehaved. The staff members made numerous calls to Child Protective Services expressing concerns, but the custody plan did not change. The staff struggled as the situation worsened.

The pendulum swung back and forth as clinicians called for the "wisdom of Solomon" to help them to decide what to do. Staff had attempted to work with the grandmother on such issues as discipline, rules, and limits, but with little success. At several meetings, staff members wondered if the children should be removed from her care. Various team members were involved with different members of the family, but all worked closely with one another. Regular team meetings provided a forum for discussing this family and for formulating treatment goals. Often people became visibly anguished as the situation and the needs of different people were discussed, and it was clear that there was no way to serve the very best interests of all no matter what was done.

The grandmother needed and deserved support for what she had undertaken. She deserved acknowledgment for her sacrifices—she had given up much to take in her grandchildren. She did cooperate with much of the treatment plan even though it took her much longer than anyone was comfortable with. She loved her grandchildren and they did seem attached to her. Yet she was harsh and rigid and, at times, her methods of punishment were viewed by some as abusive. She kept the children under a tight reign and was quick to react with negative comments if the children strayed even slightly.

The team worked together to set up goals for each family member and to agree about what was acceptable and what was not. The child protective worker, the child care staff, the children's therapist, and the pediatrician were all involved in these decisions.

Staff actively supported the grandmother in her catering to the two youngest and worked very hard at convincing her to keep them in the program and in therapy. There were several times when she was on the verge of pulling them out of both interventions. At those times, staff members who had a relationship with her and the family were able to change her mind. The grandmother had, on many occasions, acknowledged the important relationships that Nicki and her children had formed with the staff members and how

helpful these connections were. Together, staff and family struggled forward, doing the very difficult work of caring for the fragile
children.

Typically, as in this case, professionals cannot easily determine
whether all that was done was for the best. It is clear, however, that
this intervention forged strong bonds among the family and the various clinicians involved and was able to sustain members through
the most difficult of times. This case study and countless others
highlight the excruciatingly difficult job of accepting and providing
a family-focused model of intervention.

～ Common Ground: Developmental Tasks of Recovery, Child Development, and Parenting ～

Here I am, a mother and an addict in recovery, and I'm learning to be a new
person at the same time.

DeDe

Recovery, child development, and parenting—each one of these life
experiences follows an ongoing, developmental continuum that
influences and alters each experience. Within each stage of development (early, middle, ongoing, and later) there are specific developmental tasks (e.g., cognitive/behavioral, emotional, relational,
spiritual) that, when successfully negotiated, pave the way for
growth and change. Included in each experience is self-development
and the acquisition of language and communication skills. As one
progresses, one grows in maturity and in the capacity to function
more effectively. Successfully traversing any one of the continuums,
an individual gains in health, maturity, and the ability to be a well-
functioning human being.

The following tables illustrate the stages and developmental
tasks of recovery, child development, and parenting. Table 2 outlines
early development; Table 3, middle development; Table 4, later
development; and Table 5, ongoing development. Within each stage
of development, specific tasks to be accomplished are listed, helping
to increase knowledge and understanding in all areas. This conceptualization can help one move among the four stages, integrating
information and synthesizing various components to use in a
family-focused recovery treatment model—complex and involved
developmental processes to be sure, but processes that can comple-

Table 2. Common ground in the early stages of recovery, child development, and parenting

Common developmental tasks	Recovery	Child development	Parenting
Cognitive and behavioral growth	• Break through denial. • Achieve abstinence. • Improve self-care. • Admit powerlessness.	• Get basic needs met (e.g., food, comfort, attachment).	• Prepare for new role as parent. • Ready the environment. • Provide for basic needs (e.g., food, comfort, attachment).
Trust	• Trust in a higher power (Step 2 of AA).	• Develop trust in caregivers to meet basic needs. • Develop trust in self and ability to get needs met.	• Foster trust through consistent nurturing and care. • Trust in own ability to parent.
Relationships	• Give up unhealthy relationships. • Get involved in counseling, therapy, anonymous groups, sponsors, and so forth.	• Develop secure attachment with primary caregivers. • Begin to create internal representations of healthy relationships.	• Foster bonding and attachment with child. • Readjust relationship with parent. • Reexamine relationship and experiences with own parents.
Communication	• Learn to express thoughts and feelings. • Rely less on behavior to communicate.	• Give behavioral cues (e.g., vocalizations, gestures, facial expressions) to communicate basic needs.	• Communicate needs, feelings, and experiences as parent. • Read and respond to child's cues. • Ask for help with parenting.
Self-image	• Change image of self. • Accept loss of control, which allows one to take control and separate from the addiction.	• Begin to develop sense of self as separate but connected to others. • Increase autonomy and independence. • Develop positive self-image through caregiver mirroring.	• Explore ambivalence about new identity as parent. • Examine issues of control and loss surrounding body and lifestyle. • Develop evolving sense of self as separate yet connected to child.
Emotions	• Learn to identify and manage feelings. • Depend less on outside sources for self-regulation.	• Increase ability to experience and express emotions. • Increase ability to self-regulate and manage states of arousal.	• Model healthy coping strategies and emotional expression. • Interpret emotions and feelings for child. • Manage range of emotions connected to new role as parent (e.g., fear, doubt, anger, joy, confusion, sadness, hope).
Spirituality	• Implement varying stages of spiritual belief and practice, and begin to use spiritual practice in recovery.	• Develop emerging awareness of spiritual/religious beliefs and practice.	• Reexamine spiritual and religious beliefs in relation to new role as parent. • Develop new spiritual beliefs or return to old practices.

Table 3. Common ground in the middle stages of recovery, child development, and parenting

Common developmental tasks	Recovery	Child development	Parenting
Cognitive and behavioral growth	• Reexamine behavior and feelings and make appropriate adjustments. • Continue to practice and learn new behaviors. • Prepare to have "defects of character removed" (Step 6 of AA).	• Increase independence in activities and tasks. • Use imitation, practice, and mastery motivation to learn new skills and abilities. • Develop range of behavioral responses to environmental and caregiver demands.	• Reexamine role as parent as child becomes more independent. • Develop skills in managing a range of child behaviors and needs. • Develop abilities to keep child safe while allowing exploration in the environment.
Self-regulation	• Internalize behavioral and coping strategies.	• Increase ability to manage conflicting impulses to "hold on" and "let go." • Develop ability to self-regulate through mutual regulation.	• Create a safe environment with structure and limits. • Manage own behavioral and emotional responses to child's behavior.
Relationships	• Continue to develop healthy relationships. • Prepare to move out into the world. • Form more interdependent relationships. • Follow guidance of therapists, counselors, and others. • Make list of those who were harmed and make amends (Step 8 of AA). • Make direct amends except when doing so would do harm (Step 9 of AA).	• Continue to separate from parents and move out into the world. • Develop relationships with peers. • Begin to learn social rules. • Join social systems outside family (e.g., school, child care, clubs). • Begin to understand right and wrong and the impact of one's behavior on others.	• Act as a guide for child in the world outside the family. • Interpret world to child. • Allow healthy separation. • Continue to examine and adjust role as parent to the changing needs of the child. • Acknowledge confusion and mistakes made as parent.
Communication	• Learn and use new language. • Admit the exact nature of one's wrongs (Step 5 of AA).	• Acquire and develop verbal language. • Communicate ideas and experiences in addition to needs. • Use language to interact socially.	• Model and teach language. • Communicate needs, feelings, and experiences as parent with others. • Ask for help in parenting.
Self-image	• Reconstruct identity as an addict. • Make a searching and fearless moral inventory of self (Step 4 of AA). • Shift dependence from addiction to other sources. • Learn new ways to behave and cope. • Practice abstinence.	• Continue separation and individuation as self-development. • Continue development of self in relation to others. • Begin to identify self in terms of gender and culture. • Increase positive self-concepts as skills and abilities mastered.	• Establish identity as parental authority figure. • Evaluate self as parent.

(continued)

Table 3. *(continued)*

Common developmental tasks	Recovery	Child development	Parenting
Emotions	• Be more aware of feelings and affect. • Develop empathy. • Gain mature defenses. • Use self-exploration.	• Develop empathy. • Develop capacity to identify emotions in others.	• Model and interpret expression of emotions and healthy coping strategies. • Continue to manage own range of feelings about parenting.
Spirituality	• Continue to develop and practice personal spiritual beliefs and use in recovery.	• Participate in family's cultural and religious practices. • Explore concept of religion/spirituality through questions and stories.	• Teach child about own cultural, spiritual, and religious practices. • Model spiritual practices and cultural rituals for child. • Explore and establish own spiritual beliefs and practices.

ment and support each other with appropriate intervention. Interventions begin with recognizing where each member is on his or her developmental journey, naming that experience together, and developing supportive strategies for growth. Understanding each process strengthens the understanding of the others in multidimensional ways, making it especially beneficial to conceptually combine these three processes. There is a dynamic feedback process that can occur with families as one develops and enhances one's knowledge base of recovery, parenting, and child development. Successful negotiation of tasks in one area may help with the resolution of tasks in the other areas. A parent in recovery may, for example, develop empathy for her toddler's strive for independence if she sees they share a common struggle to individuate and grow.

For both families and the professionals who work with them, finding the common ground of experience can break down barriers and promote learning. Professionals who can identify for themselves and model for their clients the common experience of developing trust, for example, can clarify the challenges they may be experiencing in developing a relationship. Understanding the common tasks provides a road map and a common language for professionals and families alike that may be used to translate experience, understand behavior, and create interventions.

Cognitive and Behavioral Growth

Recovery In the early stages of recovery, the individual is coming to terms with the disease, breaking through denial, and learning

Table 4.   Common ground in the later stages of recovery, child development, and parenting

Common developmental tasks	Recovery	Child development	Parenting
Cognitive and behavioral growth	• Practice abstinence. • Have new and healthier behavior in place. • "Continue to take personal inventory and when wrong promptly admit it" (Step 10 of AA).	• Become capable of more sophisticated, abstract thought. • Continue to develop and refine reasoning and problem-solving skills. • Increase ability to take multiple perspectives. • May question/test authority. • Allow school peers to take on greater significance in the learning process.	• Adjust to child's increased maturity and independence. • Balance child's and parent's needs to hold on and to let go. • Adjust structure, limits, and rules as they relate to maturing child. • Allow child to make more life decisions and take responsibility for his actions.
Relationships	• Engage in sharing and interdependent relationships. • Choose to be a sponsor or mentor.	• Allow peers and friendships to be primary influence. • Explore own sexuality, may have sexual relationship. • Redefine relationship with parents as one matures.	• Reevaluate relationships with partner, family, and friends as they relate to changing role of self as parent. • Adjust relationship with increasingly mature child.
Communication	• Actively use language to communicate and use language of recovery. • Talk with others. • Gain understanding.	• Communicate new identity as maturing individual. • Develop communication skills in negotiating evolving identity with authority figures.	• Work through challenges of communicating with maturing child; find common ground of understanding. • Communicate and exchange ideas with family, friends, and other parents. • Ask for help in parenting.
Self-image	• Have new personal identity in place. • Continue to refine self-image.	• Develop self in relation to emerging sexuality. • Evolve sense of self in relation to others and the world. • Continue to develop cultural identity.	• Reexamine self as parent in the face of an increasingly separate and independent child. • Accept separate identity of child. • Objectively evaluate parenting experience and attempt to resolve perceived failures.
Emotions	• Continue to gain insight and understanding. • Manage difficult emotions.	• Establish coping techniques to manage roller coaster of emotions. • Examine and refine experience and expression of emotions.	• Examine feelings about parenting experience. • Offer insight and guidance to child about her emotional experience.

(continued)

Table 4.   *(continued)*

Common developmental tasks	Recovery	Child development	Parenting
Spirituality	• Believe in higher power. • Have spiritual practice and use in recovery and everyday life.	• Be aware of others' spiritual beliefs and practices. • Embrace or reject spiritual practices of family. • Explore spirituality and practice.	• Turn to religion/spiritual beliefs for solace. • Model religious rituals/spiritual practices for child. • Continue to develop own belief system.

to live with abstinence. Cognitive and behavioral shifts occur as the individual focuses on staying clean, developing new coping strategies, and learning how to live without drugs. As addicts move through recovery, they continue to practice and learn new behaviors while their energy begins to shift toward relationships and community. Gradually, the individual is able to refine, enhance, and expand on new and healthier behaviors, employing new skills in managing and regulating behavior.

Child Development   Just as the individual in recovery develops new ways of thinking and behaving in her world, the child progresses from concrete, less sophisticated ways of thinking and interpreting his world to more competent and capable thinking. The young child is egocentric in thought and action just as the addict in early recovery is very focused on self. The child moves from being quite dependent to more independent in action and deed, similar to the addict in early recovery taking his first steps in a drug-free world. The child uses practice, imitation, and mastery motivation just as the addict incorporates those tools to progress through recovery. The child, as does the addict, becomes increasingly able to manage impulses and stimulation by developing and mastering self-regulatory abilities.

Parenting   Adults, according to Galinsky (1987), go through significant cognitive and behavioral shifts as they become parents. Parents are faced with reinterpreting themselves in their new role as parents and, as a result, reinterpreting their world and relationships. Parents prepare themselves for their new roles, ready the environment, and provide for the child's basic needs. As the child grows and changes, so do the parents as their roles are redefined in response to the child. Parents allow for their child's growing need for independence by giving more freedom. Parents learn new skills and behaviors in response to the changing needs of the child. In essence, the

Table 5.   Common ground in the ongoing stages of recovery, child development, and parenting

Common developmental tasks	Recovery	Child development	Parenting
Relationships	• Tolerate some intimacy. • Maintain healthy relationships. • Work out difficulties in relation to others (e.g., past relationships with family).	• Establish sense of self as separate from parents. • Maintain authority with self, not parents. • Become involved in committed relationship. • Create own family, separate from yet connected to family of origin.	• Reexamine and adjust important relationships. • Continue to let go and recognize child as separate adult. • Make amends for past conflicts and forgive. • Prepare for grandparenting role if necessary. • Develop new relationships in larger social world.
Communication	• Continue to use language of recovery. • Talk with others and communicate thoughts, feelings, and wishes. • Listen and respond to others.	• Communicate needs, feelings, and ideas within relationships. • Use communication to resolve conflict. • Use communication as a social/relational tool.	• Work through changing relationship with adult child through talking. • Resolve conflicts by communicating. • Pass on family history through stories and conversation.
Self-image	• Interpretation of self and others has evolved and has been integrated. • Consider self to be mature and responsible. • See self as part of the shared human experience. • Become capable of altruism, sponsorship, and volunteerism. • Go on commitments with 12-Step group. • Step 12 (AA): "Having had a spiritual awakening, we tried to carry the message and practice principles in all of our affairs."	• View self as mature, capable adult. • Establish gender and cultural identity. • Identify self in relation to job/career. • Identify self in relation to current family roles and relationships.	• Reexamine sense of self as older person. • Recognize own wisdom and knowledge as older adult. • Forgive self for perceived failures and old regrets. • Identify self as guide/teacher to younger generation.
Emotions	• No longer use hostile and immature defenses as usual emotional reaction. • Continue self-exploration as new feelings continue to emerge. • Become aware of feelings, continue to take personal inventory (Step 10 of AA). • Integrate feelings, affect, and behavior.	• Use healthy coping strategies. • Display mature system of defenses. • Display mature repertoire of emotional responses.	• Work through conflicting emotions about growing older. • Grieve losses. • Process feelings about life successes, regrets, and perceived failings.

(continued)

Table 5. *(continued)*

Common developmental tasks	Recovery	Child development	Parenting
Spirituality	• Actively pursue spiritual practice and use in recovery and everyday life. • Step 12 (AA): "Sought through prayer and meditation to improve our conscious contact with God as we understood God, praying only for knowledge of His will for us and the power to carry that out."	• Continue to explore spiritual beliefs. • Establish spiritual/religious practices. • View spirituality/religion as centrally important to life. • Use spiritual/religious beliefs as guiding life force.	• Explore religious/spiritual beliefs in the face of own mortality. • Turn to religion/spirituality as major guiding force. • Share spiritual/religious belief with younger generation.

parent grows and changes and learns new ways of living along with the child.

Relationships, Communication, and Emotions

Recovery One of the primary tasks of recovery is learning to connect and communicate in a world now free of drugs. In recovery, individuals give up unhealthy relationships and make room for new, healthier relationships. Trust develops in others as the individual learns how healthy relationships work. The individual in recovery moves out into the world as if for the first time, seeking out and making connections with others. The individual in recovery may adopt new roles in the family, community, and world of work. At the same time, the individual is learning a new language of recovery and new ways to communicate with others. Emotions become central in the individual's progress in recovery, as she is increasingly able to identify and cope with a range of emotions.

Child Development Children move from giving behavioral cues to expressing needs to learning the language of their family and community. As children develop and become more independent, they seek out relationships and connections outside the family, as does the addict in recovery. At the same time, children continue to need a secure attachment figure to return to as they become more social beings. Children learn to communicate in order to establish and maintain interactions and relationships. And just as the individual in recovery is learning the language of emotions, so too is the child learning to identify, express, and manage a range of emotions.

Parenting   A primary task of parenting is establishing a secure, nurturing relationship with the child. Providing consistent, nurturing care becomes essential to the child's development. The parent–child relationship serves as the child's model for how relationships work. Parents act as guides for the child as she moves out into the world, interpreting her experience and keeping her safe while she explores. Parents refine and adjust their relationship with the child as the child grows and matures.

Parents also serve as models for and teachers of language. Parents model how to use language to get needs met and how to communicate as social beings. Parents teach the language of emotions and guide children toward appropriate ways of expressing emotions and regulating behavior. Parents can serve as models for asking for help, using language to resolve conflict, and communicating about sensitive issues.

Self-Image and Self-Esteem

Recovery   A primary task of recovery is building a positive regard for self. Early in recovery, the individual is focused on getting clean and staying clean. As he moves through recovery with healthier coping strategies, he is able to tolerate more self-discovery and self-exploration. He releases his false sense of control over his disease and accepts support and help. The individual begins to reconstruct his identity as an addict and create new, healthier aspects of his personality. He begins to develop a sense of who he is in relation to others as well. The individual can also move toward forgiveness and acceptance of himself for who he is.

Child Development   As the child moves through development, a sense of self emerges from the care she experiences and messages received about who she is. She begins to develop a sense of herself as separate from but connected to others. The child may also begin to develop a sense of cultural identity. Just as the addict constructs a new sense of self and self-regard, so too does the child grow to regard herself and form impressions about her value and worth.

Parenting   As an adult develops a sense of self as parent, she begins to form a self-concept as it relates to her parenting role. Parents may judge their abilities as parents and their senses of self-worth may color their behaviors as parents. Parents establish identities as nurturers, authority figures, mentors, and teachers in response to parenting demands. Parents also function as mirrors for their children's sense of self and worth. It is through the parent's care and interactions with the child that the child's sense of self is established.

⌣ Principles of Family-Focused Intervention ⌣

During the interview, the young mother sat sullenly and responded to the clinician with downcast eyes and one-word responses. The clinician felt discouraged by the lack of connection and by the young woman's past history, which included early childhood sexual and physical abuse; a mother who was addicted to heroin, cocaine, and alcohol; many siblings who were addicted and/or incarcerated; a sixth-grade education; and a current relationship with an abusive man. She had lost custody of her other children due to her drug use and had no trust in "social workers who just want to take kids away from their moms."

The clinician explained the program to the young woman and invited her to join. The young mother showed a slight brightening of her eyes as the clinician explained to her that she would not only help her to "get clean," but she would also help with her children, her housing, and other family concerns.

The clinician later commented about this woman to a colleague: "She will never make it." Some time later, this clinician "ate her own words," learning a very important lesson about prejudging a person's capacity to grow and change.

The young woman who she had felt would "never make it" proved to be the most successful client in the program. With the exception of one relapse, she was able to stop using cocaine and alcohol and eventually quit smoking cigarettes. She brought her child in faithfully for appointments, attended group regularly, called often for support and advice, created healthy boundaries between herself and her family, left her abusive partner, and steadily worked toward reunification with her other children. She gave birth to another child who was not exposed to alcohol or other drugs and afterward made a decision to use birth control to prevent unintended pregnancies. She cooperated with having her children in early intervention and later placed them both in preschool. She is now attending literacy classes so she can further her education and hopes to find a job that will allow her to be self-sufficient.

She is a dedicated, warm, and loving mother who literally soaks up the care and support offered to her and her family. She not only surprised the clinician but herself as well when she became the group sage—modeling parenting in recovery for her peers.

Window of Opportunity

A crisis in a person's life can provide an opportunity to change. A family may enter treatment anywhere along a continuum of contact points. The key is to have the *window of opportunity* open for them when they arrive or help them see it when it presents itself. Whether they come as individuals or as a family, through pediatrics, the maternity ward, medical services, schools, drug treatment centers, homeless shelters, or the criminal justice system, the circumstances that brought them there are often a window of opportunity for intervention.

For pregnant addicts, the birth of a baby is a unique window through which one can offer help. It is a time when a woman is faced with the reality of her drug use and its possible consequences on her infant. While in the hospital, she is a "captive" audience for at least a short while and is often pressured by various people and agencies to get help. There may be a complaint of abuse and neglect filed with Child Protective Services based upon her drug use, and family members and partners may "realize" that she has a drug problem. Reaching out to a woman at this unique time in her life can give her and her family a lifeline not otherwise available to them. Experience has taught that pregnant women and women who have recently given birth are particularly open to receiving help for their drug problems. Professionals who can reframe the crisis as a window of opportunity for the client may help the client begin the work of recovery.

Assessment

Focusing on the family begins by assessing individual family members as well as the family as a system. Child development assessments serve as tools to gather information but can also serve as interventions to help teach the family about the child. Drawing a family diagram (see Appendix A) is often very useful in obtaining a feel for the family and its relationships and actively engages the client in a learning experience. In conducting a family-focused assessment, one begins to show the emphasis of the intervention on the family, sending the message that the family system is important and influential.

Over a series of interview sessions, the quality of family relationships should be investigated and the family's current level of
functioning explored (see Appendix B). It is important to ask who in
the family supports one another and who does not. Extended family
members and the community should be discussed with the individual to identify additional sources of support or contact.

General questions about each person's—and their ancestors'—
health status including any past or current alcohol and/or other drug
use or abuse should be asked. Questions should be asked to determine if there is current or past history of violence, sexual abuse, or
trauma for any family members, and the interviewer should be
skilled in responding to any difficult information revealed. Gathering this kind of information will present a snapshot of the family
and give the professional the information she needs to plan interventions. Asking a person what information she thinks might be
important about her family can often reveal things that one may
have never thought to ask about. Any assessment, of course, should
be conducted by trained professionals. On a multidisciplinary team,
each staff member may take the lead on conducting one aspect of the
assessment.

Co-locating Services

It is typically a losing battle for service delivery systems professionals to expect a parent struggling with addiction or in early recovery
to manage multiple appointments in multiple locations for herself
and family members. Parents in recovery are often expected to jug-
gle several appointments, remember numerous care providers, and
organize disparate information in a cohesive way. Managing a busy
life and schedule is much more realistic for a parent who is somewhat stable in her recovery or one with a strong network of support.
Inappropriate expectations for parents in recovery can be frustrating
for all involved. In reality, many recovering addicts live extraordi-
narily chaotic lives, even when clean, and may have few or no skills
in organization and time management. Coordinating and co-locating
services whenever possible may help a recovering parent organize
and simplify her life.

Balancing the Needs of the Family,
the Child, and the Recovering Parent

Perhaps the most challenging principle of family-focused intervention is that professionals must continually balance the needs of the
family with the needs of individual family members. In family-

focused intervention, the client is always the *family*, but individual members can have different needs at any given time, needs that often seem in conflict with one another's. It is perhaps most useful to shift one's thinking from polarized terms—the parent's needs versus the child's—to more inclusive terms. Accepting that everyone's needs are valid may help professionals from feeling as though they must choose one member's needs to the exclusion of another's.

A salient example of this shift is when a parent relapses and returns to drug use. Rather than seeing this as an irreversible failure, professionals can use the relapse as a learning experience for the parent. The parent and professional can discuss what triggered the relapse and what the client could have done differently. The relapse may become a window of opportunity for rethinking existing treatment strategies or building in additional supports. A parent's relapse, however, is not typically a learning experience for a child but is more likely a traumatic experience. Professionals may need to weigh what is in the best interest of the child and consider alternate caregiving arrangements, which may not be what the parent desires at all. Balancing family members' needs, however, does certainly not mean satisfying everyone's demands. Making a decision that is in the best interest of the child can be in the best interest of the parent's recovery as well. Communicating honestly with parents and reframing experiences can help the entire family see the wisdom in working for both the parent's recovery and the safety and well-being of the child.

Cassie relapsed. She left her young children home alone, after having them back in her care only 3 weeks. Professionals and family members alike agreed that the children needed to be removed from Cassie's care. Cassie fought hard to have them returned to her with the promise that her sister would move in with her and help with the children. Cassie's eldest daughter begged to stay with her mother. Although it was difficult for professionals, they stood firm in their demands that Cassie enter a more intensive treatment program. Twelve months later at Cassie's graduation from residential treatment, Cassie thanked her counselors for their perseverance. "I needed to go away," Cassie said. "I just didn't know it yet. I learned that you were there to support me, but you weren't going to let me or anyone else hurt my kids."

Multidisciplinary Team

Family-focused intervention is probably most successful with a team of clinicians from multiple professional disciplines with varied skills and experiences who come together to help the family. In addition to providing various services to families, the clinicians also teach and train one another. Clinicians eventually find that their knowledge and skills in areas outside of their own area of expertise expand, thus enabling them to be even more effective.

The mix of disciplines is less important than how the team works together. A health care provider, a substance abuse specialist, and a child development or family specialist can compose the core of the team, with other staff available as needed. The team should see itself as a system and hold regular staff meetings, case conferences, and regular clinical supervision, which contribute to building and maintaining team cohesiveness.

Members of a family-focused multidisciplinary team who work with families in recovery need a broad base of knowledge about all aspects of the recovering family. Professionals need to learn each other's professional language and teach others their own. Professionals should acknowledge and respect the disparate skills and experiences of team members and recognize that their way is not necessarily the only way. Clinical supervision and team building then become very important in creating a cohesive, well-functioning team and invaluable learning experiences for families.

The substance abuse therapist who uses a developmental model of recovery can readily translate this information to understand the developmental models of child development and parenting. In so doing, the therapist increases her capacity to be useful to the entire family. In addition, one can help to translate the experience of recovery for other professionals. Other professionals working with families and children who are affected by addiction can use their knowledge of health, child development, or family systems to understand the experience of recovery and parenting.

Professionals who come together to learn and share a common language can certainly improve services to families. Parents in recovery may be getting mixed or contradicting instructions from well-meaning professionals who do not understand the complicated process of parenting in recovery and are not talking to other involved professionals. Parents may be hearing from their substance abuse clinician that they must put their recovery first. They are told to put themselves first and that they must attend meetings and appointments regardless of child care concerns. A child development specialist, a pediatrician, or a family therapist who does not understand this concept may be telling the recovering parent something very different. Child protective workers may require that the parent do it all and do it right. Professionals can and should come together in order to truly balance the needs of the family, the child, and the recovering parent.

～ Relationships as Interventions ～

The process of working with families in recovery can be understood as "reparenting." It is through the therapeutic relationship, and the interventions used within the context of the relationship, that a family moves forward in the healing process.

Part of Elaina's letter to her therapist: Nicole [her daughter] is getting really big and she is doing great. She goes to school full time, too, and she has adjusted just fine. As I teach her about life and growing up, she teaches me about being a child. She teaches me about my inner child, and I try to love me as much as I love her. We're great for each other, I hope. I also know I couldn't be the mom I am, nor the person I am today without your help. . . .

At my worst moments when I feel completely alone, I still feel like you are there and always will be. I hope that this is true, at least until you are 85!

When things get too bad I still talk things out in my head, I think about what you might say sometimes. Although your ears don't hear, I know your heart does. Thank you for raising a well-functioning woman.

The Therapeutic Relationship

The cornerstone in any intervention plan—and perhaps the most powerful intervention tool—is the relationship between the professional and client (family, parent, and/or child). It is within the context of this relationship that all contact, communication, and intervention occurs. The nature of the relationship between professional and client sets the stage for the work of recovery and parenting. When the relationship works, interventions can work. When the professional–client relationship is not working, treatment is profoundly affected.

Typically, the initial goals of family treatment involve the fostering of a therapeutic alliance (i.e., relationship) between professional and client (Millman, 1986; Seval Brooks, Zuckerman, Bamforth, Cole, & Kaplan-Sanoff, 1994). Ingredients that define a therapeutic relationship include common ground; honesty; trust; nonjudgmental attitude; empathy; and rules, limits, and boundaries.

Common Ground Identifying the common ground between client and professional is an important first step in forming a relationship. Talking about anything of mutual interest can help to spark a relationship. It may be that the most obvious common ground between client and professional is the mutual concern shared for the children involved in the treatment. Connections around culture or similar life experiences can foster healthy relationships as well. As Millman (1986) writes, "It is my sense that it's often useful to talk about anything you both can talk about. Certainly, in the early treatment stages, the content of the conversations is a lot less important than the relationship" (p. 105).

Honesty Honesty is an essential ground rule in a therapeutic relationship. It should be clear from the beginning that participants in the relationship need to be honest with one another and accept that there will be consequences in the relationship if honesty lapses. Professionals need to follow through on commitments and agreements as do clients. Honesty is not easy, particularly for clients who have lied and manipulated for years to maintain the addiction and the family secrets. Consequences for dishonest behavior need to be made clear and remain consistent. Lessons in honesty and the consequences of dishonesty are important life lessons for the client in recovery.

Tara had been seeing a substance abuse treatment counselor for 3 years. Periodically, she was given vouchers to purchase food and diapers for her young children. When her counselor discovered that Tara was forging the vouchers and trading them for cash, she confronted Tara with the news. This incident became a treatment opportunity to discuss the need for honesty in a relationship, but was also an opportunity for Tara to feel the consequences of her behavior when the counselor set up a contract with Tara to make amends for her actions.

Trust   Trust is critical in any healthy relationship and is absolutely necessary in a therapeutic relationship. The client may never have experienced a relationship based upon honesty and trust and needs to develop an understanding of how it works. The development of trust is a primary task for the recovering addict, the child, and the family. The therapeutic relationship can serve as the classroom within which trust is created, taught, and fostered. Every action on the part of the professional can be the material with which a client can build trust. Professionals who consistently keep appointments, follow through with goods and services, and are available on the other end of the telephone help clients learn that they can put their trust in someone. Especially important are professionals who can tolerate the challenging behavior of clients and continue to be available to them within the therapeutic relationship even in the midst of inappropriate, acting out, or manipulative behavior.

Sheila was a recovering addict in an outpatient treatment program and parenting group. She participated regularly with eight other women in an ongoing group, developing close relationships along the way. Two years into the program, she began an affair with the fiancé of a fellow group member. When the group made this discovery, it made a painful group decision to terminate her membership in the group. Sheila's violation of the relationships within the group became too great to sustain the feelings of trust and safety that the group worked so hard to establish. Despite Sheila's termination from the group, her primary therapist continued to see her, working closely with her to process this difficult experience.

Nonjudgmental Attitude   Sheila's therapist continued to offer her the unconditional acceptance that is so important in a therapeutic relationship. Although Sheila's therapist rejected her *behavior* and supported her termination from the group, she accepted Sheila as a *person*. Presenting a nonjudgmental attitude toward clients can be extremely difficult but is required in a therapeutic relationship.

Remaining nonjudgmental requires the professional to separate the behavior from the person and to process the intense feelings that accompany the client's difficult behavior. Sheila's therapist was intensely angry that Sheila violated the group's trust, but by processing those feelings in supervision, the therapist was able to continue to accept and care about Sheila. Although Sheila no longer belonged to the group she was able to maintain ties with the therapist and other clinicians in the program because she had not felt personally rejected.

Empathy Empathy is a sometimes difficult but crucial ingredient to have in a therapeutic relationship. To walk in someone else's shoes, if only for a moment, is to see that person's world with great clarity. To step back and take a client's perspective can offer insight into the relationship and the treatment plan. Teachers who can step out of their frustration and anger to see a child's behavior as a cry for help and not as a deliberate act against them can then be available to help. Nurses who can see the realities of addictive disease can step out of their anger at having to care for yet another fragile drug-exposed baby and see the mother's need for support. Empathy helps to strengthen the connection in any healthy relationship. It is especially important to a parent struggling with addictive disease or a child who has been forgotten or misunderstood. When professionals receive the training they need to understand addictive disease and are given opportunities to process the intense feelings generated by the disease, they may create room for empathy to grow.

Rona was a teacher in a child care center that served children living in poverty. She often spoke out in frustration at parents who failed to participate in school activities. She grew especially angry at one young mother who hurriedly dropped off her child at the center and did not respond to any notes from the teachers. Over several supervision sessions, Rona began to see that the young mother was not neglectful but stressed and overwhelmed. Rona was reminded how she herself felt as a young mother struggling to care for her own children. By stepping into the parent's shoes, Rona was able to take a new perspective toward her relationship with the young mother.

Rules, Limits, and Boundaries   Healthy relationships typically
have clear rules, limits, and boundaries to define them. A therapeutic relationship with limits and rules that are clear to both professional and client can serve as a model for healthy relationships.
Rules such as when and how the client and professional communicate, what role the professional plays in the client's life, and how the
professional and client are expected to behave provide the structure
for the relationship.

In therapeutic relationships, professionals are cognizant of helping family members find their own power. Limits are set on how
much a professional does *for* a client and how much a professional
supports clients to do *for themselves.* Professionals need to set
boundaries for themselves in terms of how involved they get with
clients and must continually evaluate the appropriateness of this
involvement. This constant attention to relationship limits and
boundaries sets a healthy climate for all involved.

Lizzie, a young mother in recovery, wanted to return to work. She
appropriately asked her case manager for help making a plan for
finding a job and finding child care. Her case manager agreed to
help and pulled together some numbers for child care and job
counseling. Lizzie didn't make any calls for several days. When
approached by her case manager, Lizzie asked her to make the
calls because Lizzie was "too busy." Rather than making the calls
for Lizzie, the case manager suggested they call together. The
case manager noticed Lizzie's anxiety about making the calls and
was able to model for Lizzie how to investigate child care centers
and sign up for job counseling. Lizzie, with coaching, grew more
confident about her own abilities and took on more of the telephone calling. With her case manager's help, Lizzie found her own
power and developed new skills in reaching toward her goals.

This is a good example of a case manager who, together with Lizzie,
was able to form a secure, respectful therapeutic relationship. The
relationship began, as many therapeutic relationships do, around
arranging goods and services for a client. Being able to meet a client's
basic needs can build a foundation of trust between client and professional. What typically occurs over time, however, is that the relationship becomes more significant than the services rendered. As
Pharis and Levin (1991) write, "In helping people to develop in a

healthy manner, in the long run, relationships count for more than things do. People count the most, things count less" (p. 318). In a study to examine the effectiveness of a sophisticated intervention program for pregnant and parenting addicted women who are considered at the highest risk for parenting dysfunction, the participants were offered a host of goods and services. At the conclusion of the study, the participants were asked to evaluate the importance of various treatment interventions. The vast majority of these women ranked "having a person to talk to who really cares" as most important (Pharis & Levin, 1991).

Primary Attachment Relationships

Garbarino, Dubrow, Kostelny, and Pardo (1992) describe therapeutic relationships with children as "primary attachment relationships." These attachment relationships function as substitute parenting relationships with children in need of nurturing parental care. Like resiliency mentors (see Chapter 7), teachers, counselors, adult relatives, coaches, and others use these relationships of care, trust, and safety with children as primary intervention strategies to support children. Garbarino et al. draw from the research on resilient children and challenges schools and community groups to rethink how they provide services to children.

Garbarino et al. (1992) believe in the primacy of relationships and argue that schools and communities need to develop strategies that make primary attachment relationships available to needy children. Children need opportunities to develop relationships with caring adults, but these relationships take time and regular contact to develop. Schools and community agencies need to develop or redefine their service delivery so children can be with a primary adult over time and in substantial ways. Children who can stay with the same child care provider or teacher for more than 1 year, mentoring programs that offer children contact with adults for at least a year, or sports programs that match younger students with older students all provide opportunities for the development of primary attachment relationships. As Garbarino et al. (1992) write, "A favorite teacher appears to function for children in one or more capacities: as an instructor of academic skills, as a confidant, and as a positive role model for identification" (p. 154).

A child care center serving abused and neglected children reevaluated the way it provided services to the young children in its care. It adopted a resiliency model as the primary focus of program intervention. Staff prioritized the need for primary attachment relationships for all children in the program and structured the program around this goal. Children were placed in mixed age group classrooms where they could spend more than 1 year with the teacher. Teachers were given time in the schedule for one-to-one contact with identified children. Support staff were used as primary attachment figures when appropriate, so that each child received special care and attention.

Reparenting

One of the most powerful relationship interventions in family-focused treatment is *reparenting*—helping a recovering person parent a child by parenting that *parent*. The dual function of the reparenting relationship gives a recovering addict much of what he never received in a primary relationship, while teaching him to parent in healthy ways.

Reparenting occurs when the professional and client join together in a relationship of supportive treatment. Professionals provide the nurturing and structuring of a holding environment within which the client in recovery heals, grows, and develops a new way of living and being in the world. Through reparenting, clients receive the support and guidance that were lacking in their primary parenting relationships. Through this "substitute parenting," the client has the opportunity to develop new skills, behaviors, and relationships and perhaps a new self that can relate to the world in a more healthy and life-satisfying way.

The framework of reparenting encompasses most aspects of the intervention process with recovering *parents* as well. Unconditional care, self-esteem building, modeling, limit setting, problem solving, and self-exploration are all components of the reparenting process. Recovering parents, if they were never parented themselves, may lack the skills and empathy to parent effectively. Through the reparenting provided in treatment, parents can learn to be parents for the first time. Parents can then parent their own children, not through old destructive patterns of parenting, but through the new ways experienced in the reparenting relationship.

Unconditional Care   In a parenting relationship, unconditional care and acceptance of the child supports healthy development of the child's true self. In a reparenting relationship, professionals need to send a message of care and acceptance of the recovering parent, regardless of past or present behavior. That does not mean the professional accepts the parent's *behavior* or tolerates inappropriate actions. But just as a child needs a mirror within which he sees a positive expression of himself, so too does the parent need to feel acceptance and care reflected by the professional.

Supporting a Sense of Confidence and Competence   Parents in recovery need ongoing encouragement as they struggle to parent effectively. Parents who have not been parented themselves may literally have no idea how to parent or even know what parenting means. Parents with poor self-esteem may not feel up to the task of parenting and can become paralyzed in their roles as caregivers. Professionals reparent by building a parent's self-esteem through praising attempts to parent as well as successes. Professionals work to help parents find their own voices and power as individuals, so they can transmit that power to their parenting role.

Evangeline was a young mother with five children. When she brought her fourth child to the pediatrician for a routine well-child visit, she was asked if she played any nursery games with her infant daughter. Evangeline looked down in embarrassment, then shook her head no. "I want to" she said. "I just don't know how."

For a parent who feels confident in her parenting role, this vignette may seem shocking. An interaction that comes so naturally to many absolutely paralyzed Evangeline. She did not feel confident enough in her own abilities to simply play with her daughter, despite having four other children. Evangeline had few memories of her own childhood and had little guidance in figuring out what being a "parent" meant. Evangeline's story reminded professionals how unsure recovering parents can feel. Evangeline was slowly guided through the parenting process with continuous support and encouragement.

Modeling   Modeling becomes a natural tool for intervention and is very useful for the reparenting process. Modeling is useful because it is concrete, observable, and meaningful—experienced in real time and within a real context. Modeling uses teachable moments to instruct, clarify, and reinforce the behaviors and skills desired. It can be used whenever the client and professional interact.

Modeling can perhaps be most useful with recovering parents when professionals make modeling an active learning experience. Professionals can activate the learning process by identifying to a parent that they are modeling a targeted behavior, by talking about what they are doing, and by interpreting their actions. Recovering parents may need these additional cues to fully recognize and integrate the behavior being modeled.

During a parent–child group activity at a treatment program, the group facilitator began reading to a small group of children. Recognizing this as a teachable moment for parents, she called a few parents over and asked them to participate in the reading activity. As parents watched, the facilitator read a story aloud. She then began chatting with parents about how to get children involved in reading aloud. She gave them specific tips for engaging children and clarified them with examples from the observed reading session. As parents grew more comfortable, some began to read to the children themselves, giving the facilitator opportunities to praise and encourage.

A child care provider in a residential treatment program observed a young mother struggling to calm her very distressed infant. The provider quietly approached the mother and offered to help. Instead of taking the baby and calming him herself, the provider talked the parent through the process of swaddling and rocking the baby. The provider praised the mother's efforts and reviewed with her how and why the intervention worked.

Both of the above examples of modeling show how professionals may actively participate in the intervention without taking power away from the parent. Both professionals recognized and utilized the parents' power as part of the intervention and did not demoralize the parent by doing *for* the parent. Professionals can actively intervene with clients and model appropriate behaviors when they remain cognizant of the parent's need to have power and respect.

Another aspect of the use of modeling has to do with the clinician's own behavior. One cannot live by the "do as I say and not as I do" rule. Conducting one's own behavior in the way in which one expects the client to behave serves as a primary model within the therapeutic relationship and also teaches the client to do the same in her relationship with her children.

Teaching Parents How to Play   Many parents in recovery may have missed out on childhood experiences, often taken for granted. They may be children of alcoholics or survivors of childhood abuse, and the freedom of childhood and the joys of play may have been lost in the midst of the family trauma. For these parents, playing does not come easily or naturally. They may lack the confidence and skills to play.

Although recovery is seen as very serious business and one may not feel that it is appropriate to "play," learning in recovery how to play and have fun without the use of alcohol and other drugs is vitally important. In recovery, one may have a great need to revisit one's childhood. At times, these needs can overshadow the needs of their own children. Providing opportunities for parents to play meets their needs to learn about healthy play while teaching them how to play with their own children.

A substance abuse treatment program initiated a parent/child play group as a way to promote attachment and positive parent/child interaction. Group facilitators designed the group so that parents and children would be together for part of the session to play and separate for part of the session so that parents could meet as a group. The facilitators planned interactive play activities that were simple, inexpensive, and could be replicated at home.

One of the first parent/child group activities was making playdough. The facilitators' goal was to have parents play with their children. What actually happened was that parents largely ignored their children because they were so involved in playing with the playdough themselves!

Supporting the Development of Healthy Coping Strategies
Through reparenting, recovering parents can learn new ways to cope with stress and manage difficult feelings and can begin to model healthy coping strategies for their children. Professionals can help parents identify and manage their affective experiences. Identifying

and labeling stress and difficult feelings, normalizing those experiences, and developing strategies to manage the experiences are important exercises for parents struggling in recovery. By paying attention to patterns of behaviors and responses, one can make positive changes in how one copes with life's challenges.

Angie is the mother of two young girls and is in recovery from cocaine addiction. She lost custody of her girls three times because of her addiction and subsequent neglect of her children. When Angie had periods of sobriety, her girls were returned to her. Three times, she relapsed while the girls were with her. In treatment with her present substance abuse counselor, Angie and her counselor discovered that Angie became incredibly anxious when alone with her daughters. That anxiety triggered Angie's relapse into drug use. By putting the pieces of her experience together, Angie and her counselor were able to come up with an alternative plan for coping with Angie's affect.

Paul was a father of an active 2-year-old and in recovery from alcohol addiction. Paul struggled with his son's growing risk-taking behavior as his son exerted his increasing autonomy. Paul became anxious and fearful whenever his son climbed up the playground slide or ran energetically across the yard. Paul responded by restricting his son's activities and compulsively supervising his play. Paul became increasingly more angry at his son when he protested his father's strict limits and impulsively yelled at him on a number of occasions. With his therapist's input, Paul began to connect that, in response to his anxieties about his son's safety, he was attempting to compulsively control his son's behavior. With this information, Paul and his therapist were able to identify new strategies for Paul to cope with his stress and explore how his addictive behavior was affecting his parenting.

Dealing with a Parent's Guilt   One of the most difficult aspects of parenting in recovery is dealing with feelings of guilt that can continually crop up as a parent recognizes the impact of her addiction and witnesses it in the difficulties of her children. At times, this guilt can threaten to overwhelm and send a person hurtling back into using alcohol or other drugs. Helping a person accept and manage these painful feelings without distortion is a tricky but crucial intervention. Accepting the reality of "what was done" is a healthy step in recovery.

Patty, talking about her son, diagnosed with FAS: I was running on guilt. I couldn't be a parent to him because of the guilt. And what happened was, I was asking for a lot of help on it. I was asking my higher power, and I had to look at it much like the way I look at my alcoholism. I don't know whether I got it because my father was an alcoholic, because I was brought up in a dysfunctional family, because I was raped as a child and sexually abused. It doesn't matter where my alcoholism and my addiction came from. It's what am I going to do about it today. And that is the most important thing I could do. And what I had to look at was this little boy's fetal alcohol syndrome, not live with the guilt, but I had to look at what am I going to do about this today. And relief came; I was able to move on.

Clients are able to more easily accept reality if they can identify how they are working to make things different and the positive things that they have already done. Helping clients define areas of strength and concretely identify change can alleviate some of the power of the guilt. It is never useful to try and "absolve" a person or minimize his feelings.

In the manual *"Getting Sober, Getting Well"* the following guidelines are offered to help a substance-abusing mother deal with her guilt (Finkelstein, Duncan, Derman, & Smeltz, 1990):

1. Help her to understand that both she and her children have been victims of her addiction and that her behavior was neither deliberate nor intentional.
2. Listen with compassion to what she feels she has done wrong.
3. Help her to realize that during active drinking and drugging options and choices in parenting were limited.
4. Convey hope for change through recovery.
5. Timing of the work around the guilt is important; if a client is not ready to deal with it, she may relapse.

∼ Self- and Mutual Regulation ∼

Children exposed to drugs in utero and/or in substance-abusing environments may have difficulty managing their behavior and affective states (see Table 6). The capacity to self-regulate (i.e., manage both internal and external stimulation) begins in the newborn period but grows as children develop increased cognitive and behavioral functioning. Caregivers play a critical role in the development of self-regulatory abilities and can be instrumental in shaping children's ability to manage stimulation (Seval Brooks et al., 1994; Tronick, 1989). Parents in recovery, however, may have difficulty managing their own behavior, much less that of their children. In some families, both parents and children may need supportive interventions to help them regulate their affective states.

Through the process of reparenting, professionals can help families learn to self-regulate by providing modeling, feedback, and support and by building a meaningful relationship. Professionals can also help parents read and respond to children's cues. Parents can then engage with their children in the process of mutual regulation, which thereby enhances the child's ability to self-regulate. The process of mutual regulation typically refers to "the process by which infants thrive through the support and responsive interactions provided by their caregivers" (Seval Brooks et al., 1994, p. 212). Parents read and respond to a host of cues given by the infant in an interactive dynamic that can be mutually beneficial to both caregiver and infant. The parent and professional have a similar, interactive dynamic.

Strategies to Promote Mutual Regulation in the Recovering Family

Although the techniques outlined in the discussion of substance abuse treatment and reparenting (pp. 254–265) support the development of regulation in the recovering parent, following are specific treatment strategies of particular significance in the process of mutual regulation. They include reading and responding to cues, proactive planning, establishing family routines and structure, limit setting and positive reinforcement, and parenting groups.

Reading and Responding to Cues Professionals should teach clients to interpret their infants' behavior and affective states and provide them with knowledge of the following strategies to promote self-regulation in young infants:

1. Minimize stimulation in the environment. Turn down lights, reduce noise, and be selective with visual stimulation.

Table 6. Behavioral signs that may indicate decreased self-regulation in young children

Infants
- Color change in skin to red or mottled, evident in light-skinned infants
- Increased respiration and/or heart rate
- Sneezing, hiccuping, or coughing
- Jerky, uneven movement in arms or legs
- Gaze aversion, squeezing eyes shut
- Frowning
- Fussing, crying
- "Shutting down" and sleeping

Toddlers and preschoolers
- Inability to make or sustain eye contact (when culturally appropriate)
- Perseverative "circling" around a room, rapid motion without productive exploration of the environment
- An increased voice pitch with words or nonverbal utterances (screaming, screeching)
- Inability to focus for more than 30 seconds on a toy
- Excessive movement of arms and legs (fidgeting)
- Difficulty sitting for group activities, even with a mat or adult lap
- Excessive temper tantrums
- Frequent aggressive behavior directed at self or others
- Severely limited tolerance for frustration
- Excessive focus on one repetitive activity, which inhibits appropriate exploration
- Distress with transitions
- Atypical body postures (rigid body position, head averted, fingers splayed)
- Increased respiration and/or heart rate
- Quick to "blow up" or "fall apart"

Note: All children may display one or more of these behaviors at times. Concern should arise when a child exhibits them frequently, to the point that they disrupt learning and functioning.

2. Swaddle. Young infants can be wrapped snugly in a blanket with their limbs in flexion or "swaddled" by gently holding the infant's arms folded across the infant's chest with her legs in flexion.

3. Rock. Some babies like to be rocked vertically, some horizontally. Use slow, gentle, rhythmic movements.

4. Feed in a quiet environment.

5. Offer one kind of stimulation at a time. Infants may be better able to tolerate face-to-face interaction if the caregiver just looks without talking. Gradually, the infant may be able to tolerate both.

6. Encourage sucking. Pacifiers and fingers are great calming tools. Help an infant learn to suck her fingers by bringing her hand to her mouth.

7. Listen to the infant. Infants will let you know what kind of stimulation is acceptable. Look for signs of distress.

8. Know the infant's individual needs. Caregivers should find out what works for each infant.

There are also several strategies that can be taught to promote self-regulation in toddlers and preschoolers.

1. A structured environment that "speaks" to children with obvious uses for each area gives a child many opportunities to feel supported. It provides limits and direction without direct adult intervention.

2. Predictable routines and consistent schedules provide external support that helps to regulate a child's internal rhythms. Children can depend on the sameness, feel safe, and will eventually be able to predict what will happen next.

3. Clear expectations and simply stated rules with appropriate and consistent consequences are crucial to help children gain internal controls. Simple rules help children to say the rules themselves and help remind adults not to go into lengthy discussions about behaviors (which may confuse the child).

4. Carefully planned transitions provide support. Warn children about minor and major changes.

5. Real choices offer children some control. They can choose activities in less volatile situations and can choose between limited choices during struggles to avoid yes/no arguments.

6. Anticipatory guidance helps to avoid difficult situations or blowups. Anticipate problems before they happen and intervene.

7. Healthy self-esteem can be supported by respecting and celebrating the individuality of each child.

8. Frequent praise should be given throughout the day. Be specific about what you're praising and remember to praise effort as well as success.

9. Help children identify feelings by labeling them and modeling them. Give children permission and guidance to express a range of feelings.

Proactive Planning Recovering parents often operate in a crisis mode. When they were using, they ordered their lives around getting and using the next drink or drug fix. In recovery, they may still be ordering their lives around crises and chaos—bouncing from one crisis to another in a reactive mode. Through professional/parent mutual regulation, recovering parents may be able to move into a more proactive mode of relating to the world. Professionals can help parents *stop and think* instead of impulsively reacting without a thought about consequences or the next step. Professionals can process daily experiences with parents and help parents reflect on what happened and what they could have done differently. Professionals and parents can role-play stressful life situations and anticipate problems and solutions. Through proactive planning, recovering parents can feel less anxious and more in charge of challenging situations.

A parent/child group for recovering families took regularly scheduled field trips to local attractions and community events. The staff initially planned these trips as a way to provide drug-free recreational experiences for recovering families. They turned out to be object lessons in parenting and proactive planning.

It was clear from the staff's exhaustion after the first field trip that things had to change. Parents and children had been stressed and overwhelmed. It was not a pleasant experience for anyone. For the next field trip, staff and parents did more planning. Parenting sessions leading up to the trip were devoted to planning and role playing in preparation for the field trip. Lists of materials and snacks needed were drawn up and chores were divided up among participants. Participants discussed issues such as child safety, what to do if a child got lost or hurt, how to get to the field trip, and how long the trip should last. The group's second field trip was a little more organized and a lot more enjoyable.

Parents participating in this object lesson had the opportunity to learn the rewards of proactive planning, which may motivate them to apply the principles of proactive planning to other life situations. Parents can also recognize that no amount of planning guarantees a trouble-free experience, but it can minimize the potential for problems. Proactive planning can certainly reduce stress and maximize enjoyment of the parenting experience.

Establishing Family Routines and Structure Helping families establish family routines and structure provides an antidote to the often unpredictable and chaotic lifestyles of addicted families. Children can blossom in environments that are consistent, predictable, and ordered. As Nelsen, Intner, and Lott (1992) write, children living in chaotic, substance-abusing homes "don't develop a smooth rhythm to events of the day, they lack a sense of calm expectancy" (p. 65). Rituals, routine, and structure in a child's external world can help children develop trust and an internal sense of order and calm that supports self-regulation.

Routine and structure can also help the recovering parent regulate his own behaviors and affective responses. Creating a daily schedule can help recovering parents function effectively in a drug-free world. Keeping an appointment book for doctor's appointments, meetings, children's schedules, and important telephone numbers can help a parent order a hectic daily schedule. Structuring household duties and activities helps children know what to expect and how to behave. Posting chores; having regularly scheduled mealtimes, bedtimes, and homework time; or having designated areas in the home for eating and sleeping can be new concepts for recovering parents and their children (see Table 7).

Limit Setting and Positive Reinforcement Discipline is perhaps the most challenging task for the recovering parent. At no time is one's childhood baggage more clearly in evidence than in one's style of disciplining children. Parents make sincere promises to themselves to parent differently from the ways their parents did but often find themselves repeating old and destructive patterns with their own children. Two primary interventions for recovering parents in regard to discipline are ongoing parent support groups and psycho-educational parenting groups (Lief, 1985; Nelsen et al., 1992; Plasse, 1995). Parent groups can provide the structure, support, information, and relationships needed to break old patterns of behavior and learn and adopt newer, healthier ways of using discipline. Table 8 lists some key aspects of positive discipline that parent groups can convey to newly recovering parents.

Ongoing Parent Support Groups Asking for help and seeking outside support is a healthy coping strategy, not an admission of failure. Recovering parents may think they have to go it alone and avoid groups for fear that they will be labeled inadequate and inept, but parenting groups can offer the peer connections necessary to fight the feelings of frustration and isolation that so many recovering parents face. Recovering parents and group facilitators can act as coaches in the parenting process, offering suggestions and support and encouraging an honest evaluation of the parenting process.

Valerie was a young parent of two toddlers. She attended a parenting group weekly as part of her substance abuse treatment program. She was having a very difficult time managing her chil-

Table 7.   Tips for establishing family routines

1. **Focus on one routine at a time**—Bedtime and mealtime routines are good places to start, but choose only one area to begin.
2. **Discuss the plan with family members**—When family members are calm and not in conflict, discuss the plan together. Allow older children to have input in establishing the routine. Make sure adults in authority are in agreement about the plan.
3. **Consider the child's age and stage of development**—Older children and younger children probably need different routines to match their needs. A young adolescent and a toddler have different sleep schedules, for example, and the adolescent may not want a story before bedtime. All children in the family may have the same mealtime, but older children may have a more active role in meal preparation and cleanup.
4. **Make the routine fun**—Make reading aloud to young children a nightly ritual and part of the bedtime routine. Let older children plan and cook one of the family's meals. Make dinner time a sharing time when everyone can report on daily experiences.
5. **Post family routines**—Let children make posters or charts listing rules and routines.
6. **Reward cooperative behavior**—Routines aren't always fun. Praise, encourage, and reward behavior whenever possible. Let children earn privileges for good behavior.
7. **Be consistent and follow through**—Children may very likely test new limits and increase their noncompliant behavior before cooperating.
8. **Be patient**—Change happens slowly. Don't give up if you find yourself struggling to enforce new rules. Seek out other parents for support and ask for help.

Adapted from Nelsen, Intner, and Lott (1992).

dren's behavior and often complained that she had no time to herself. Group members acknowledged the stress she was under and worked to help identify solutions to Valerie's discipline problems.

During one session, Valerie admitted that she had "had it" with her children over the weekend and left them in the care of an unreliable boyfriend. Group members responded with concern and questioned Valerie about her judgment. They reminded her that she did have other choices that would have perhaps been better and that they as a group were available for her to call. The group gave a very clear message that Valerie's behavior was not okay and that she had jeopardized both her children and her recovery.

The recovering parents in Valerie's group intervened more successfully with Valerie than the group facilitators could. They spoke with a legitimacy born from "being there." The power of the group intervention was evident in the way Valerie listened to her peers. Parenting groups for recovering parents offer support, insight, and information but demand honesty, openness, and commitment. Learning how to parent and how to successfully provide rules and limits

Table 8. Key components of positive discipline

1.	**A child's behavior is a message**—Caregivers need to interpret what the child is trying to communicate before they can intervene.
2.	**Empathy is critical**—Caregivers who step into the child's shoes and see his or her experience can respond with empathy and care.
3.	**Anticipate**—Plan the environment and your behavior to keep discipline problems from occurring.
4.	**Children need and want appropriate limits**—Clear, consistent, and developmentally appropriate limits help children feel safe and cared for.
5.	**Be consistent and follow through with limits**—Children need to know that caregivers really mean what they say. Children almost always test by increasing acting-out behavior before complying.
6.	**Reward positive behavior**—Offer encouragement and support. Be specific about the behavior you are praising.
7.	**Ignore or redirect inappropriate behavior whenever possible**—Children want attention, even if it is at times negative attention.
8.	**Give choices**—Caregivers should offer an alternative acceptable behavior when they are attempting to eliminate an unacceptable one.
9.	**Replace physical discipline with talking, timing out, or removing privileges**—Hitting teaches children that it is acceptable to use violence to solve conflicts. Caregivers can teach children in another way.
10.	**Take a time out**—Caregivers should never discipline when their anger is out of control. Caregivers should always have a time-out plan for themselves in place.
11.	**Ask for help**—Caregivers can look to other parents and professionals for information and support.

for children often requires the kind of intense intervention that can be found in group work.

Psychoeducational Parenting Groups Psychoeducational parenting groups typically combine education with process-oriented reflection and self-exploration. Recovering parents may need concrete information about parenting, but they also need an opportunity to examine how their childhoods and addictions have shaped their parenting behaviors. Psychoeducational groups are typically time limited, but ongoing support groups are often available, which are particularly useful for recovering parents because of the long-term demands of recovery and parenting. There are a number of parenting curricula and training programs available that can be adapted for use with recovering parents. There are fewer curricula that are specific for parents in recovery, but some are available. Individual programs should investigate and evaluate available curricula for their appropriateness for the particular clients being served.

One report (Camp & Finkelstein, 1995) presented the results of implementing a parenting component in residential treatment. The outcome data demonstrated that the women who completed the parenting training had considerably improved in parenting knowledge and attitudes associated with positive parenting behavior. In addition, these women maintained a high quality of interaction with their infants throughout the first year of the infants' lives.

High Hopes, Realistic Expectations

An important point for professionals and parents to keep in mind comes from the philosophy of Alcoholics Anonymous—*"Progress and not perfection."* Those in recovery certainly know that recovery occurs one step and one day at a time, a philosophy that is easily translated to the parenting experience. Along with this comes the idea of identifying and praising positive steps. People in recovery learn how to evaluate their progress by identifying steps in the right direction and often receive verbal praise from fellow peers and concrete rewards in the form of "chips" and tokens. Sobriety anniversaries are acknowledged and celebrated, as are important events and markers in the recovery process. Families can be rewarded and should reward themselves for steps taken toward growth, attempts to change, and for every success, no matter how "small" it may seem.

～ Traditional Treatment ～

A busy mother has five appointments to keep in one afternoon. She has her two preschool-age children with her and needs to be back home by 3 p.m. to meet her older children at the bus. She must 1) take the two younger children to the pediatrician for routine check-ups, 2) take her oldest child for a development assessment, 3) see her substance abuse counselor and get a urine screening, and 4) make an appointment for a check-up and obtain birth control. She also needs to 5) investigate alternative housing options, as her current situation is unsuitable.

Arriving at the pediatric clinic on time, she is told that there will be "a little bit of a wait." Forty minutes later, the pediatrician sees her children. She is now late for the consultation with the child development clinician and must wait until the clinician is done seeing the child who was scheduled behind her child. During her child's assessment, this mother realizes that she is already 1 hour late for her own counseling appointment. She calls her counselor, who admonishes her for missing the appointment and not calling any sooner. The counselor goes on to say that she feels the woman is not organizing her time well and needs to learn to make better plans. Hanging up from that disastrous telephone call, the woman is feeling angry and unsupported and remembers that she still has two more appointments to keep. She rushes off to the OB/GYN clinic to see about scheduling a check-up and obtaining birth control. There is a long line in front of the family planning office and she cannot be seen, but she does make an appointment for a check-up. Looking at her watch, she realizes she must go home in order to meet the school bus and her oldest children. Stopping a nurse in the clinic she has seen before, she asks if it would be possible for the nurse to take a urine screening as she doesn't have time to go to the lab. The nurse replies that she cannot do that without an order or a consultation in the clinic. Now, the woman's children are crying, whining, hungry, and tired and the woman feels like drinking. She leaves for home feeling depressed and overwhelmed, asking, "What's the use?"

∽ The Women and Infants Clinic ∽

One-Stop Shopping

The Women and Infants Clinic at Boston Medical Center provided a one-stop shopping of family-focused intervention, which would have been invaluable for this woman, offering a number of needed services in one place and networking in the community for any other necessary services that could not be offered at the hospital. The Clinic was located in the nonstigmatizing environment of pediatric primary care, a place that felt safe for women and was easy to get to by public transportation. Child development services, pediatric care, family planning, substance abuse counseling, and case management services were provided during regularly scheduled treatment visits. One or two key professionals were identified as primary case managers for the family, minimizing confusion and allowing for relationships to develop. Several clinicians, however, worked together as a multidisciplinary team, often seeing a family together. During these joint visits, each clinician addressed his or her particular area of concern with the mother and each other. Often, clinicians were able to help each other frame a concern or topic to make it more easily understandable and broaden everyone's understanding of how to more effectively intervene. Primary emphasis was always placed on creating an individualized package of services to families and offering them to all significant family members.

Professionals in the Clinic used frequent contact and their close relationships with families to assist families in all aspects of the recovery and parenting process. Each point of contact provided an opportunity to support recovery, parenting, and/or child development. During regularly scheduled pediatric visits, children received books and toys, while professionals modeled developmentally appropriate skills, supported the mother's competence, and motivated the mother to stay in treatment. Many women repeatedly stated that they were "doing this for [their] bab[ies]," and professionals used this to secure the women's recovery. Parents gave urine screenings and their clean time (or drug use) was monitored and discussed during regular visits.

Interventions were both planned and spontaneous, and services were offered outside of the routine visits. Pediatric staff gave families appointment books to help them keep their outside appointments and develop their organizational skills. Parenting groups and individual parenting sessions were offered as needed. The children received more intensive primary care schedules, regular developmental screenings, and, if needed, referrals to early intervention.

As an example of the Clinic's philosophy in practice, during one visit the mother was sent to another clinic for a brief period of time. She was told that she could leave her children with the clinicians while she was gone. She walked out of the room without saying goodbye, initiating a torrent of tears from her 18-month-old daughter. Despite the staff members' efforts to calm the child, she continued to cry, stopping only upon her mother's return. The team saw this as a golden opportunity to do some work with the mom. Recognizing the positive, the child development specialist first commented to the mother about how attached her daughter was to her. When the mother asked how she knew this, the child development specialist described to her how her daughter cried for her until she returned and could not be comforted by anyone, which meant that the child was attached to her in a special way. The mother then said that her daughter did this all the time lately and she did not understand why; she felt annoyed by her child's crying. The child development specialist explained how children typically become attached to their mothers and how young children can experience separation anxiety when their mothers are out of sight. The mother was told that it would help a great deal if she would explain to her daughter each time she left where she was going and when she would return. She was also told that she should tell her daughter good-bye when she was leaving instead of just slipping away.

The mother was having trouble understanding this concept through her child's eyes, so the substance abuse clinician tried a different approach. She asked the mother what she remembered from her childhood about the comings and goings of her own mother. The client reported that she never knew when her mother, an alcoholic, was going to be leaving and whether she would ever return once she had left. When asked if she remembered how that felt, she said she often felt scared and angry and eventually stopped believing what her mother told her. The substance abuse clinician then used an example from their treatment relationship. She asked the client what she thought it would feel like if she could not count on the treatment team to keep appointments. The client began to see that explaining events was helpful to her and could be helpful for her daughter as well. The two clinicians were then able to work together to help this mother understand her daughter's distress at separation and the importance of telling her daughter what to expect. This intervention helped the mother to have empathy for her child. By recalling her own experiences, she was able to learn new skills to help her daughter.

Once enrolled in the program, families never "left." For those families or members who were not able to attend sessions, the connection was maintained through case management, telephone contact, letters, and home visits. Pediatric services were continued for children as often as possible, even for those women who went into residential treatment.

Families saw the clinic as their home base and the clinicians as their primary source of support. For 4 years, the Women and Infants Clinic worked with the same small group of women. The retention

rate for the first year was more than 75%, and families that might otherwise have free-fallen into the addiction abyss were held in various states of recovery. Some families generally dropped out of treatment because of the mother's inability to maintain abstinence. In these cases, the children were either placed in foster or kin (family) care, and the staff continued to work with the woman, her children, and the children's caregivers whenever possible.

In 1993, the Women and Infants Clinic at Boston Medical Center was closed because of its loss of funding and inability to procure new funds.

~ Lessons Learned ~

Several invaluable lessons were learned while working with the families of the Women and Infants Clinic. The families served as teachers, acknowledging what was right and illuminating what was not; they were pioneers blazing new trails in treatment intervention. Following is a general discussion of the most salient of these lessons and the basic assumptions that grew from the experience, which have become "truths" in supporting families.

Recovery from Substance Abuse and Addiction Is Possible

Many of those who work with individuals and families struggling with addiction do not know or believe that recovery from addiction is possible. Their attitude may convey a "no hope" message to their clients, who end up feeling hopeless and defeated. Granted, recovery from addiction is one of the hardest roads to walk, yet millions of people walk the road each day, and new people join all the time. There is hope in recovery for all who want to stop addictive and destructive behavior in order to grow and develop.

There Is No Such Thing as a "Typical Addict"

Each person is a unique individual, and each person who is addicted has her own unique issues. One cannot assume that everyone who is addicted struggles with the same issues, will respond to treatment in the same way, or will move through recovery at a particular pace. Recognizing this and learning what "makes a person tick" is important.

Walk in Their Shoes

The more one knows, the more one is able to help. One of the best ways to learn about addiction and recovery is to talk to people who are in recovery, hear their stories, and see the progress that they have made. Many 12-Step meetings are open to nonaddicts, which provides an opportunity to listen and learn firsthand. It is helpful first to acquire some basic knowledge and understanding about addiction and recovery, perhaps by reading and attending lectures. (See Appendix C for more educational references and Appendix D for a listing of addiction/recovery programs and resources.)

Attitudes and Beliefs

Even equipped with basic information, there are those who simply do not "believe" that recovery is possible. There are times when ideas and attitudes can be related to personal experience one has had or is having in one's life. Clinicians who have had or who are having personal encounters with addiction in their private lives can have much difficulty sorting out their experiences and emotional reactions. This "boundary" confusion can taint their professional work and interfere with their relationships with clients. In this case, self-exploration and engaging in one's own recovery can be very useful.

There Is No One Best Treatment Model

One must work to fit a treatment model to the person or family, not try to fit the person or family "into" a treatment model. Everyone has unique treatment needs, and success, measured in tiny steps, is unique for each person. Praising success and "catching" people doing the right things augment the difficult tasks of pointing out when a person is not doing what is best. Treatment interventions work best when they identify and promote strength and resiliency, not weakness. They also work best when one assists the person to find his own power instead of assuming that one can empower the person. One need not reinvent the wheel; however, much of what is "standard practice" is easily adaptable to create and enhance programs for families who are struggling with addiction.

Raising the Bottom

"Hitting bottom" is a term commonly used by addicts and addiction treatment clinicians. It refers to an arbitrary and idiosyncratic low point that a person "must" reach in her addiction before she begins to realize that she needs help. This concept also implies that those who could help must passively "wait" until the person reaches bottom to intervene. Imagine standing nearby when a person trips and begins to fall. One can either reach out and try to grab the person to break the fall or step aside saying, "Oh, well, she is already on her way down." "Raising the bottom" is actively intervening to help a person before he slides further down the slope of addiction. It means that no matter where a person is in her struggle with addiction, there are ways to help move a person toward better functioning.

⌒ References ⌒

Ainsworth, M. (1974). The development of infant–mother attachment. In B. Caldwell & H.N. Riccuti (Eds.), *Review of child development research* (pp. 1–93). Chicago: University of Chicago, Society for Research in Child Development.

Bowlby, J. (1958). The nature of the child's tie to his mother. *International Journal of Psychoanalysis, 39,* 350–373.

Brown, S. (1985). *Treating the alcoholic: A developmental model of recovery.* New York: John Wiley & Sons.

Camp, J.M., & Finkelstein, N. (1995). *Fostering effective parenting skills and healthy child development within residential substance abuse treatment settings.* Rockville, MD: Center for Substance Abuse Prevention.

Finkelstein, N., Duncan, S.A., Derman, L., & Smeltz, J. (1990). *Getting sober, getting well: A treatment guide for caregivers who work with women*. Cambridge, MA: The Women's Alcoholism Program of CASPAR.

Fraiberg, S. (1959). *The magic years: Understanding and handling the problems of early childhood*. New York: Charles Scribner & Sons.

Galinsky, E. (1987). *The six stages of parenthood*. Reading, MA: Addison-Wesley.

Garbarino, J., Dubrow, N., Kostelny, K., & Pardo, C. (1992). *Children in danger: Coping with the consequences of community violence*. San Francisco: Jossey-Bass.

Lief, N. (1985). Parenting and child services to drug-dependent women. In G. Beschner, B. Reid, & J. Mondanaro (Eds.), *Treatment services for drug-dependent women* (DHHS Publication No. ADM81-117). Rockville MD: Department of Health and Human Services.

Millman, R. (1986). Considerations on the psychotherapy of the substance abuser. *Journal of Substance Abuse Treatment, 3*(2), 103–109.

Nelsen, J., Intner, R., & Lott, L. (1992). *Clean and sober parenting: A guide to help recovering parents*. Rocklin, CA: Prima Publishing.

Pharis, M., & Levin, V. (1991). A person to talk to who really cares: High risk mothers' evaluation of services in an intensive intervention research program. *Child Welfare League of America, 120*(3), 307–319.

Plasse, B. (1995). Parenting groups for recovering addicts in a day treatment center. *Social Work, 40*(1), 65–73.

Seval Brooks, C., Zuckerman, B., Bamforth, A., Cole, J., & Kaplan-Sanoff, M. (1994). Clinical issues related to substance involved mothers and their infants. *Infant Mental Health, 15*(2), 207–217.

Stanton, M. (1979). Family treatment approaches to drug abuse problems: A review. *Family Process, 18*, 251–279.

Tronick, E. (1989). Emotions and emotional communication in infants. *American Psychology, 44*, 112–129.

Wilmes, D. (1988). Parenting for prevention: *How to raise a child to say no to alcohol/drugs*. Minneapolis, MN: Johnson Institute.

~ *10* ~

"Burned Out"

Support for Professionals Working with Families Affected by Substance Abuse

It doesn't matter how much you know. If you're too burned out, too fried out, you're no good to anyone.

                              Bridget, an educational supervisor

I feel like I'm in a lifeboat, trying to pull in as many kids as I can, and we've sprung a leak.

                             Claire, a mental health clinician

I am beyond exhausted.

                               Chris, a family advocate

Working with families affected by substance abuse, although challenging, rewarding, and important, can also be very difficult. Working on the "front lines" every day—guiding parents through treatment, negotiating the social services system, managing puzzling behavior in the classroom, and keeping children safe—can truly feel like combat. In many ways, although distressing, battling is an accurate analogy about the work professionals do with families affected by substance abuse. Professionals and families work together to survive a treacherous battle where the stakes are high, resources limited, and outcomes unclear. Both professionals and families can be casualties in this battle. The experience is felt deeply and profoundly by both, albeit differently. Why *is* this work so difficult? How can one carry on in the face of seemingly insurmountable odds? How does one remain hopeful and energized? How can professionals best take care of *themselves* so they can best care for the children and families they serve?

⌐ The Inherent Difficulties ⌐

A Lone Voice

Whenever professionals working with families affected by substance abuse are asked why the work is so hard, responses are typically numerous and heartfelt. So many families need help, the needs within each family are tremendous, resources are limited and sometimes inadequate, and each professional is only *one* person!

I'm just one person and I'm being pulled in a million directions. It feels like I've got all these people just hanging on to me, pulling on me.

Ellen, a treatment counselor

It is an unfortunate truth that there are many needy families and few resources. There is a constant struggle to simply maintain existing resources in the face of budget cuts and downsizing. Yet the need for services grows. It is also a difficult task to reconcile society's denial that alcohol and other drug abuse is a tremendous national problem in the face of reality. Professionals advocating for families often feel like their voices are carried off into the wind when the enormity of the problem is denied, budgets are slashed, and programs eliminated. Political debates about the needs of the poor and disenfranchised strike a sensitive chord as many professionals see the hurt faces of their clients when they hear political rhetoric and name calling. Frontline professionals may feel discouraged when they realize that the powerful majority must find compassion for the disenfranchised few—the children, the poor, the addicts—in order for there to be substantial change in policy and practice. This can often lead to feelings of helplessness and hopelessness, a breeding ground for professional burnout.

"You Do What?"

Professionals are often met with incredulous and confusing responses from others when asked about the work that they do. Professionals who work with troubled families can feel isolated from and unsupported by friends and family who don't want to hear or can't understand the difficulties of the work. Eyes glaze over, faces grimace, and hands go up in defense, leaving professionals feeling alone in their struggle. Professionals sometimes feel that their experiences leave them disconnected, even when family and friends do their best to be there for them. In fact, many professionals will attest to the fact that one cannot really comprehend the plight of these families without experiencing their pain firsthand.

Sometimes when I tell people what I do, it's a conversation stopper. And a lot of times I get the distinct impression that they want it to stop there!

Kay, a substance abuse counselor

Professionals can also feel unsupported by the larger culture or community because their professional roles are not given high status in society. Child care providers are derogatorily considered (and called) "glorified baby sitters." Teachers may be invalidated by the educational bureaucracy and assaulted by parents. Nurses may feel devalued by a medical hierarchy that gives physicians more power. Mental health workers may feel devalued as healers and health clinicians in light of budget cuts and changes in the insurance industry.

Overall, frontline professionals working with families receive little recognition for the invaluable work that they do. The typically low salaries of many human services professions reflects the value placed on the helping professions. Low salaries, tough working conditions, and lack of professional validation from society all contribute to feelings of exhaustion and burnout.

It Feels All Too Familiar

I realized that I was too wrapped up with this family I was working with. It started to feel too familiar. This was the role I had in my own family. To fix everything and make it all better.

Leslie, a case manager

Perhaps one of the most difficult aspects of working with families affected by substance abuse is bearing witness to the stress and trauma faced by each family member. The pain and hardship of the seemingly endless cycles of family dysfunction can demoralize even the most dedicated clinician or teacher, and for some families, substance abuse is only "the tip of the iceberg." Manipulating, confusing, and alienating behavior on the part of the addict, needy and troubled children, family secrets and distortion—any one of these issues alone is challenging; together they can feel overwhelming. The addicted family may bring all of this baggage with them.

Repeating Family Dramas Professionals, too, bring their own baggage to their work with families. In a society where alcohol and other drugs play such a central role, it is likely that everyone has been touched by them in some way. Personal experiences and attitudes and beliefs about alcohol, other drugs, and addiction color per-

ceptions of addicted families and affect the work professionals do, both positively and negatively. Professionals who have had bad experiences with alcohol or other drugs, or who have a family member with an addiction, may have unresolved anger and resentments that can cloud their work. At the same time, professionals who have been touched personally by substance abuse can be some of the most attuned and empathetic care providers.

Individuals who grew up in substance-abusing homes may find themselves drawn to the helping professions and to the field of substance abuse treatment. They may have been the family heroes (overachievers) and sacrificed much of their own self-development in the interest of caring for others. The role of caregiver feels familiar, validating, and self-affirming to the family hero, and one may naturally gravitate to a professional caregiving role as an adult. Former family heroes can be skilled, attuned, and empathetic caregivers who provide helpful and healing support to children and families. Because they've "been there," they can understand the experience in profound ways. Former family heroes are also at great risk for immersing themselves in unhealthy roles with the families in their care by reenacting their original family roles as heroes and caregivers. This dynamic is unhealthy for both professionals and clients. Dramas concerning enabling, power struggles, conflict resolution, and role responsibilities that professionals and clients replay are detrimental to everyone involved.

Kern (1986) postulates that even treatment agencies and intervention programs can develop dysfunctional systems within their programs that mirror the unhealthy familial experiences of individual staff members. Kern believes that programs can incorporate dysfunctional aspects of the alcoholic family such as denial, avoidance of confrontation, rigid role definition, and communication difficulties into their programs' style of functioning.

Triggering Memories The traumatic experiences faced by children and families can be disturbing reminders (i.e., triggers) of a professional's own difficult past experiences. If these triggered memories are dissociated, the professional may be especially troubled, struggling to cope with intense affect and anxiety. Bearing witness to the pain and suffering of families can be overwhelming to those professionals who are still struggling in their own recoveries.

The Need for Good Quality Clinical Supervision

Professionals working with families at high risk need the opportunity to process the intense affect that arises from the work with families and to reflect on their responses to this challenging work. Professionals need support, guidance, and respite from their difficult work. Good quality clinical supervision can provide the support and guidance professionals need to effectively care for themselves and effectively work with families. Unfortunately, not every professional has access to clinical supervision. All too often, professionals do not have this opportunity because their organizations and agencies do not offer adequate supervisory experiences.

In the traditional mental health profession, clinical supervision is an accepted and integral component. It is well understood that these professionals will be working with needy and troubled individuals and, as a result, will need support and guidance. Social workers, psychologists, counselors, and other mental health clinicians typically participate in regularly scheduled supervisory meetings where cases are discussed, interventions are strategized, experiences are shared, and feelings are processed. Clinical supervisors can offer a well-seasoned perspective on the clinician's experiences and guide a process of reflection and self-exploration, so important to professional growth and survival.

Children and families experiencing stress and trauma continue to be served by an increasingly broad array of programs and an increasingly diverse group of professionals. Teachers, early intervention professionals, family advocates, and other professionals from non–mental health professions are serving families with a range of needs. As a result, these professionals are wearing a number of hats as they struggle to support families. Teachers may function as social workers, substance abuse counselors may need to become child advocates, or family advocates may be faced with addressing concerns about familial substance abuse. The challenges of serving the diverse needs of multirisk families while experiencing the pain and stress that accompany this work can be very hard for professionals. Unfortunately, clinical supervision is often not a program component in the traditional models of educational, advocacy, and health care service delivery. If supervision does exist, it may follow a more traditional educational model, one that does not always address the feelings and emotional responses generated by this very challenging work. As the needs of families and children increase, the professionals who care for them face increased needs for specialized support in order to stay healthy and whole.

～ Professional Burnout ～

Anyone who has experienced *professional burnout* could most likely define the term with ease. It refers to the "psychological strain of working with difficult populations" (McCann & Pearlman, 1990, p. 133). Professionals who feel "burned out" are depressed, discouraged, or disheartened—exhausted and unmotivated by the work and filled with a growing sense of hopelessness and helplessness. Freudenberger and Robbins (1979) describe cynicism, boredom, loss of compassion, depression, and discouragement as symptoms of burnout. McCann and Pearlman (1990) summarize the research on professional burnout by reporting that professional isolation, ambiguous successes, the emotional strain of always giving and not receiving, and unrealistic expectations are all factors that appear to contribute to burnout. Burnout is a very real experience for many professionals and those working with multiproblem families may be at high risk for facing burnout at some time in their careers.

I am tired a lot. It seems as though there are endless numbers of children who need care and I feel so ineffective. They just keep showing up and we do the same old, same old. It just doesn't seem to make a difference.

Rob, an educator

I need a vacation, like for the rest of my life.

Joyce, a social worker

Vicarious Traumatization

Some researchers take the concept of professional burnout a step further, postulating that professionals working with victims of trauma are at risk for a unique set of symptoms and responses to the work that is distinct and perhaps more intense than the traditional description of burnout. McCann and Pearlman (1990) believe that symptoms of burnout reflect continued exposure to traumatic material that cannot be integrated or worked through. This difficulty with processing traumatic *material* is similar to the client's inability to process or manage the traumatic *experience*. Both parties can use numbing, avoidance, or other defenses to ward off the intense affective experience.

The term *vicarious traumatization* has been used to describe the responses to and symptomatology of professionals working with victims of trauma (McCann & Pearlman, 1990). Vicarious traumatization draws from the notions of secondary traumatization and countertransference. *Secondary traumatization* was observed in family members of traumatized individuals. Family members were displaying symptoms characteristic of trauma survivors (e.g., nightmares, anxieties, safety concerns) as if they "absorbed" the symptoms from their traumatized family members.

Countertransference refers to the phenomena that can occur within a therapeutic relationship when the client's affective experience is projected onto the therapist, which, in turn, triggers the therapist's own unconscious feelings, conflicts, and concerns. For example, a client may be expressing anxieties and fears about an abusive experience, becoming overwhelmed in the process. The client's feelings of being overwhelmed are then "transferred" to the therapist. The therapist may then feel overwhelmed by this transference and can respond with his own unconscious feelings. The intense affect that is generated between client and professional around traumatic material can confuse and trigger responses from both professional and client. Many times it becomes unclear where feelings are coming from and whose feelings they are. This intensity can be trying to the professional and can interfere with the therapeutic relationship.

Vicarious traumatization is different from burnout in the way in which it invades a person's cognitive and affective experience. The feelings that are generated by the work can be enormously intense, unsettling, and difficult to process. Professionals can also experience symptoms of trauma (e.g., sleep disorders, nightmares, mentally replaying traumatic events) that leave them anxious and exhausted.

Going home from work at night only to have a motion picture of the day's traumatic story replaying repeatedly in one's head, waking up at night thinking about the safety of a child, or having trouble sleeping at all are a few of the symptoms that a professional has vicarious traumatization.

Professionals experiencing vicarious traumatization may develop a changed view of the world and the people in it. The world that was once considered a safe, nurturing place may now be considered unsafe and unmanageable. People may be viewed with growing fear, mistrust, and suspicion. Professionals who once felt they possessed power and a certain invulnerability feel powerless and ineffective. The exposure to traumatic material through their work leaves an indelible mark on professionals and may change the way they view and interact with the world.

⌐ Strategies for Supporting Professionals ⌐

There are a number of things professionals can do to support themselves and a number of things programs can do to support professional staff. The remainder of this chapter discusses individual stress management strategies, peer support, clinical supervision, professional training, and learning to let go and embrace hope as tools to support professionals working with families at high risk.

Individual Stress Management Strategies

Stress management techniques to guard against professional burnout have gained wider interest and acceptance in the fields of health care, mental health, and education. Burnout prevention programs have incorporated stress management techniques into the curriculum with much success (Grasha, 1987; Greer & Greer, 1992; Sparks, 1983), by primarily focusing on recognizing stress and managing it through education, relaxation techniques, and proactive planning.

What Is Stress? Stress is part of the human experience, if viewed as any change that requires one to adapt or adjust (Davis, Robbins Eshelman, & McKay, 1993). Although stress is typically thought to be negative, it can certainly be a positive experience as one makes welcome adjustments or changes that are accompanied by stress. Children learning to walk for the first time feel the stress of growth and development. Moving to a new home or returning to school are welcomed life experiences but can certainly be stressful.

Stress is experienced on a number of levels by the individual: psychologically (in one's mind), physiologically (in one's body), and socially (in one's environment) (Davis et al., 1993; Kabat-Zinn, 1990). The mind experiences stress in the way it perceives and interprets events and experiences. When someone is faced with an event (stimulus), the mind takes in information about the event and decides whether the event is stressful. Based on the mind's perception, the mind and body respond in kind. A body can experience stress through illness, biochemical changes, pain, digestive upsets, sleep disturbances, and other signals that something is taxing the system. The environment—traffic, noise, personal interactions, and time pressures—places constant demands on both the mind and body to adapt and change.

Therefore, it is not always necessarily the event itself that is stressful but the mind's perception of that event. What is stressful to one may not be stressful to another. Some people, for example, feel that speaking in front of a group is extremely stressful, while others are perfectly at ease. Body and environmental stress aren't as easily controlled, making individual stress management techniques an important part of managing life stress and its potentially negative outcomes.

Body Response to Stress William Cannon and Hans Selye were instrumental in translating how the body reacts to stress (Davis et al., 1993; Kabat-Zinn, 1990). In Davis et al. (1993), Cannon is identified as the first to conceptualize the body's physiological response to stress as the "fight or flight response." Cannon described a series of biochemical changes that occur reflexively in the body to prepare the individual to respond to life-threatening situations, which he believed were biologically programmed in humans by primitive man who had to be prepared to respond to attacks. The body prepares itself to fight or flee by increasing the heart rate, respiration, and blood circulation and by tensing muscles in order to respond quickly and survive.

Selye (1974) detailed what happens in the body when the mind perceives a stressful event (real or imagined). The cerebral cortex (the thinking part of the brain) triggers the autonomic nervous system to respond by sending an alarm to the body, which includes the hypothalamus, the main switch for the stress response. The hypothalamus then sends a signal to the sympathetic nervous system, which triggers a series of chemical changes in the body. Adrenaline is one of the most well-known chemicals that helps the body "rev up" and prepare to respond.

The body, after this quick series of chemical changes, is able to regroup quickly and return to a more balanced (homeostatic) state once the mind perceives the stress or threat to be gone. Problems occur, however, when the mind and body experience and perceive chronic, ongoing stress. The body may be in a constant, hyper-aroused state that destroys the opportunity to return to a more balanced state of nonarousal. It is important to remember, however, that the mind determines when the body is under stress. Even if the stress is not being experienced at that moment or it is not real, the body will always respond to the mind reflexively with a biochemical stress response. Over time, the body feels the wear and tear of responding to chronic stress, becoming "worn down."

Professionals working with families at high risk can experience stress on a number of different levels, real and perceived, placing them at risk for being in a chronic state of hyperarousal. Thinking about work events or traumatic stories can trigger the body's stress response, even if the professional is not experiencing the event directly. It is this chronic state of physiological imbalance that places the individual at risk for physical problems, such as headaches, gastrointestinal disturbances, chronic pain, and other debilitating illnesses, and can compromise the body's functioning (Benson, 1975; Kabat-Zinn, 1990).

Techniques to Manage Stress Fortunately, there is much that can be done to manage stress and return the body to a more balanced state of wellness. Benson and others have documented the effectiveness of relaxation techniques such as practiced breathing, yoga, and meditation on heart disease, chronic pain, and lifestyle stress. Classes and books on these relaxation techniques are available in most communities and are often simple and inexpensive.

Saying "No" and Asking for Help Professionals working with families never have enough time in their day to do it all. Managing time more efficiently may help, but perhaps more important is learning to say "no," sometimes difficult for caregivers to do. They may have never been allowed to say no in their own families of origin and, therefore, don't know how to say it in their professional lives. It is important to support colleagues and be a team player; however, one human can only do so much. Setting limits on the demands of others, clarifying priorities, and being able to say "no" are components of taking care of oneself.

Professionals may also need to incorporate one more phrase into their language repertoire: "I need help." Again, caregivers may feel that they can and should do it all on their own, and asking for help may be thought of as a weakness. But needing help is part of being human. Asking for help can also be a great model for families, many of whom also need to learn this skill.

Good Nutrition, Sleep, and Exercise Eating well and getting enough sleep and exercise are stress management techniques that are widely known but not always practiced, especially when one is under stress. Professionals working with families are notorious for skipping meals, eating while standing up or moving, or eating nonnutritional foods. Eating energy-fortifying foods, taking time to eat, and eating regularly keeps the body fueled and prepared. Sleeping regular hours when at all possible also prepares the body and the mind. Relaxing with music, a book, or meditation (not the traumatizing late news) before bed can help the stressed-out professional get to sleep and stay asleep. Finally, some type of regular exercise—a walk, yoga, cycling—creates balance in the body and, most important, stimulates the body's nervous system to release calming chemicals that counteract the body's stress response.

Laughing Humor can be used to support resiliency in professionals just as it is used for children. As one educator said, "If you don't laugh sometimes, you'll cry." Humor can be a release from intense affect and can help professionals take a step back. Humor, of course, should never be at the expense of clients and families, but humor among professionals can be liberating and healthy. The term *gallows humor* is sometimes used to describe the strange and quirky humor that often emerges from the staff lunchroom or case conference room in response to the difficult and painful work.

Leisure Time Having a fulfilling life outside of work is probably the most precious gift professionals can give themselves. Taking time for family and friends can be rewarding and energizing. Setting aside time for a special hobby, sitting down to read a favorite book, taking a nice, warm bubble bath, or anything else one enjoys doing alone can also be extremely beneficial.

Too often, caregiving professionals create an imbalance in their lives. They busily care for others as they neglect themselves. They do not give themselves permission to take time for themselves. Perhaps they feel undeserving of the special care they give everyone else. It can be disheartening to witness the lack of respect that some professionals can have for themselves and the way that they deprive themselves of time for their own lives and their own passions. Nurturing oneself and taking care of one's own needs is the best gift to give.

Peer Support

Support from peers can be a healing and bonding experience for professionals working with families at high risk, helping them to combat the isolation and feelings of hopelessness that often lead to burnout. Other professionals may be the only other people capable of fully understanding what it is like to be a frontline professional. Working together, peers can validate feelings, commiserate, and formulate workable strategies for managing stress and burnout.

Peer Support Groups   Peer support groups can provide invaluable professional support. Meeting to share frustrations, information, materials, and laughs provides professionals with the opportunity to reduce stress through contact and connections. Peer groups usually meet at night, but some administrations support peer groups during work hours. Successful groups tend to be somewhat structured with regular meetings and members who make a commitment to attend the group. They are also flexible and nonhierarchical—group members collectively decide the group's rules and purpose. Group members may decide to have scheduled topic-oriented discussions or leave the agenda open. This approach is most successful when members share common experiences and have equal voices in group decision making. Of course, food is an essential ingredient as well!

Survival Bonding   *Survival bonding* is akin to a buddy system for professionals. A health care clinic serving families with HIV infection in New York was observed to have a naturally occurring buddy system among staff people (Wade & Simon, 1993). Researchers studied this phenomenon of one-to-one informal pairing and were able to document its effectiveness in preventing staff burnout and discontent. This study determined that programs serving families at high risk should create opportunities for staff people to connect in supportive relationships in order to buffer job stress. Each program is then challenged to operationalize these connections to meet program and staff needs.

Mentoring   Mentoring relationships, both informal and formal, can be valuable sources of professional peer support. In this relationship, the mentor typically has more experience and/or training than the individual being mentored (Fenichel, 1992). The mentor guides a process of education, interpretation, and reflection, while the mentored grows and develops from the shared knowledge and experience. A mentor listens, gives guidance, and offers support and encouragement. Yet those being mentored bring their own skills, interpretations, and insights to the mentoring relationship, thereby moving each party forward in his or her professional journey by learning from and sharing with the other.

Mentoring relationships can happen informally when professionals are drawn to each other because of similar styles or interests that create a bond or connection between them. These often occur between teachers with classrooms across the hall from each other or social workers who share the same office. Informal mentoring typically does not have an evaluative component, and parties define the relationship together. Mentoring relationships may also be set up more formally by program administrators or specific mentoring programs (Fenichel, 1992; Perry, 1992). Formal mentoring relationships are typically defined by the program, structured by some guidelines, and often have an evaluative component.

The formality or informality of the coupling as well as the presence of an evaluative component shape the personality of the mentoring relationship. Yet both types of mentoring relationships share characteristics that can contribute to their success. Characteristics of successful mentoring relationships appear to mirror characteristics of successful supervisory relationships—mutual respect, collaboration, confidentiality, regularity—and use process-oriented discussion (Fenichel, 1992).

Clinical Supervision

Good quality clinical supervision is of critical importance to professionals working with families at high risk (Fenichel, 1992). Unfortunately, not every professional has access to the specialized kind of supervision that seems essential for this difficult work. As discussed, the traditional mental health field typically builds clinical supervision into program designs and requires participation by staff. Non–mental health programs such as schools, child care centers, and early intervention programs often do not provide supervision or do not place a high priority on consistent, quality supervision, although these staff also work with families at high risk. Professionals trained in non–mental health professions may never have had experience with clinical supervision and may be unaware of how to provide it for themselves or other staff. As one staff person remarked, "I didn't know I was missing something very important in my previous job until I *had* supervision!"

According to the Center for Clinical Infant Programs Work Group on Supervision and Mentorship (Fenichel, 1992), effective models of clinical supervision should be safe and confidential. They should be process oriented with opportunity for self-exploration and reflection. The relationship between supervisor and supervisee should be collaborative and mutually respectful. Finally, supervision should be supported and promoted by program administration.

Safe and Confidential Supervisees should feel safe and supported throughout the supervisory experience in order to promote honest and thorough exploration of sometimes very sensitive issues. Confidentiality is essential, especially because supervisees may be sharing information about clients as well as themselves.

Process Oriented Some traditional models of educational supervision have typically been action and outcome oriented. Educators can be great "fix-it" people and move quickly to figure out a plan of action, often missing out on the rich and insightful experience of self-exploration and reflection. Although there is clearly a place for strategizing and making a plan, there also needs to be room to process the supervisee's feelings, attitudes, and perceptions. Process-oriented supervision recognizes the value of talking, listening, and reflecting on different aspects of the experience. One supervisee described the essence of process-oriented supervision perfectly: "There's not always an answer, but by talking about it, I begin to see the issue in a whole new way." Process-oriented clinical supervision can help the supervisee step back from an experience, look at it more objectively, and perhaps address it in a different way. Clinical supervision also gives the supervisee a chance to process the intense affect that is generated by the work and manage the associated stress. "I feel lighter after a supervision session," said one supervisee. "Even though we didn't make the problem go away, at least I got a chance to talk about it and I don't feel so alone."

Collaborative Relationship The relationship between the supervisor and supervisee is important to the success of supervision. There should be a climate of mutual respect, with both parties recognizing that each brings skills and experience to the relationship that deserve consideration. Power in this collaboration is shared mutually, albeit unequally. Even though the supervisor is a more experienced and senior guide, it is understood that the supervisee is the authority about her own beliefs and experiences. By listening, the supervisor validates the truth and importance of the supervisee's experience, in essence, mirroring the kind of relationship desired between clients and professionals.

Administrative Support Clinical supervision cannot thrive in an organization that does not support and nurture it. The administration needs to actively broadcast the message that supervision is critical and invaluable by building it into the program with regularly scheduled meetings, which may not be interrupted or canceled. Administrative support of supervision acknowledges that the work is important and hard and professionals are valued and respected by training supervisors in the skills they need to be effective.

Professional Training

Knowledge and skill can be powerful tools for combating burnout. When professionals feel confident and competent, they are less likely to develop stress and anxiety when faced with challenging tasks (Weder, Drachman, & DeLeo, 1992). Professional self-development through training experiences can give one a renewed sense of energy and commitment to the work.

Meeting Staff Training Needs   Training that meets the informational needs of the professional and matches the trainee's learning style can offer enlightening and enhancing experiences to professionals. Staff in-service training must grab the interest and excitement of staff who are at a variety of levels of experience and ability. Inexperienced staff may need basic information about the work and instruction on what *to do* to get them through the day. They may need concrete strategies and hands-on experience to learn the unfamiliar tasks they are faced with daily. More experienced staff may be interested in broadening their well-established base of knowledge and learning about new issues and strategies related to the work. Comfortable with their abilities, they are often ready to do more insight-oriented work and more interested in exploring other points of view or challenging established rules and practices. Experienced professionals may, in fact, be ready to conduct staff training themselves.

Matching Training to Learning Styles Staff may also use different learning strategies to gain information and knowledge. Passive learning and active learning techniques can be used successfully when designing in-service training. Passive learning—typically a lecture-style format—is often used in education and conditions individuals to sit and absorb knowledge for long periods of time. Passive learning may have limitations with individuals who have had more diverse experiences and have more diverse needs. Active learning—hands-on, experiential learning—can be quite beneficial to staff working with challenging families. Interactive discussions, case presentations, role playing, journal writing, and other exercises bring topics to life and can energize tired and overworked staff.

Cross-Disciplinary Training Cross-disciplinary training and teamwork give professionals the opportunity to share their unique skills and experiences while gaining a wealth of knowledge from other professional disciplines. Bringing together professionals from the fields of substance abuse, child development, medicine, and mental health helps to break down communication barriers, clarify treatment issues, and assist professionals feel connected and supported. Each profession has much to learn from the others in order to create a system that features holistic, family-focused treatment. Gaining a broader knowledge base can only help the professional best serve the family.

Professional Development Days Opportunities for staff to have professional days in which they observe other programs and conduct their own in-service training can benefit both program and staff. Staff can feel renewed, refreshed, and confident, helping the program grow and expand with their newfound knowledge and skills. Ongoing staff training—as opposed to isolated training experiences—can enhance the level of skills and information acquired by staff. A workshop series with related, staff-generated topics can be a rich learning experience for all participants and challenges programs to rethink traditional training experiences for program staff in lieu of training that focuses on the needs of individuals as well as the staff as a group.

Letting Go and Embracing Hope

Perhaps the most difficult challenge faced by professionals working with families at high risk is knowing when it's time to let go, which may mean that a family literally leaves one's care, or recognizing that the work that remains is out of one's control to change. For example, children may need alternative care, but the social services system can no longer support them. Individuals may have a drug problem but will not accept treatment. Families may leave programs when staff know they need to stay. Letting go is acknowledging the successes and accepting the outcome. Letting go is about coming to terms with one's own expectations for change and, instead, accepting the realities of what life is currently offering. Just as in the first two steps in Alcoholics Anonymous, letting go is about admitting powerlessness over some aspects of one's life.

Letting go is not about giving up, however; it is about giving over. Similar to the process of recovery, it is about believing in a higher, healing power and the strength of the human spirit. It is about trusting that something better may be just around the corner and healing can *always* happen. If one can learn to let go, one can embrace hope, believing that anything is possible, if not now, then someday in some way. Remember the thousands of miracles of recovery in which what once seemed impossible became possible. Professionals must only open their hearts and their minds and trust that miracles can and do happen . . . every day.

Darren is an athlete. He roller skates and does tricks on his bike. He is bright and outgoing and loves animals. Darren is 5. He is Nicki's son. Nicki's story begins *Families in Recovery*; Darren's story draws it to a close.

When he was born, exposed to cocaine and HIV, Darren and his mother joined the Women and Infants Clinic drug treatment program. With his mother, Darren struggled to grow and heal despite great odds. Program staff were drawn to him as they were drawn to Nicki. His quiet watchfulness and intelligent eyes seemed to reflect an inner strength and light.

Darren's life has been full of hardship as well as miracles. He did not contract HIV. He developed into an intelligent, verbal child with many skills. He drew to him people who nurtured and supported him. When his mother died, the treatment program staff and child care staff held him close and continued to care for him and his siblings.

For 5 years, the program staff struggled to give Darren and his brothers and sisters the support they needed to grieve for their mother and move on. Staff were angry and sad that Darren's grandmother, trapped in her own rage and depression, could not provide a healthier environment for them. Yet there was nowhere else for the children to go and no one who would respond to the staff's ongoing concerns. Miraculously, despite the tension between the grandmother and staff, she let her grandchildren stay in the program.

When it came time for Darren to leave the program and attend kindergarten, his therapists and teachers shared his pain in leaving. Darren struggled with the knowledge that he was leaving behind the people who gave him the nurturing his grandmother could not. Program staff fretted and worried about what lay ahead for Darren. It was hard to remain hopeful.

A few weeks before Darren's departure, he began talking about his older sister Kara, who had run away from home several months before. She had severed contact with her therapist and family, and no one could find her. Darren's therapist helped him write a note to his sister expressing his worry and desire to see her. For Darren, this was yet another profound and painful loss in his young life. It seemed more than he could bear, losing his sister just when he was leaving his caregivers and the program.

Neither Darren's nor Kara's therapists felt very hopeful about finding Kara. No one had heard from her in months. A week after writing the letter, Darren insisted on calling Kara's therapist to make sure she was looking for Kara. He left a message for the therapist on her answering machine. It was only a few minutes later that the therapist received another message on her machine. It was from Kara. Their voices side by side on the answering machine, Kara and Darren had found each other.

The lesson in this story is one of profound hope. If we can embrace hope despite harsh realities, we can see the small miracles when they come into our lives. That Kara and Darren found each other again at a time when he needed her the most gave his therapists permission to let go and gives us all a chance to believe. Darren's life and survival are miracles. He has come further than anyone ever expected. At this point, Darren's life path is unknown, but there is every reason to hope that his journey will be a healing one and that he will come full circle.

～ References ～

Benson, H. (1975). *The relaxation response*. New York: Morrow.

Davis, M., Robbins Eshelman, E., & McKay, M. (1993). *The relaxation and stress reduction workbook*. Oakland, CA: New Harbinger Publication.

Fenichel, E. (1992). Learning from supervision and mentorship to support the development of infants, toddlers and their families. In E. Fenichel (Ed.), *Learning through supervision and mentorship: A sourcebook* (pp. 9–17). Arlington, VA: National Center for Clinical Infant Programs.

Freudenberger, H., & Robbins, A. (1979). The hazards of being a psychoanalyst. *Psychoanalytic Review, 66*(2), 275–296.

Grasha, A. (1987). Short-term coping techniques for managing stress. *New Directions for Teaching and Learning, 29*, 53–63.

Greer, J., & Greer, B. (1992). Stopping burnout before it starts. Prevention measures at the preservice level. *Teacher Education and Special Education, 15*(3), 168–174.

Kabat-Zinn, J. (1990). *Full catastrophe living: Using the wisdom of your body and mind to face stress, pain and illness*. New York: Delta.

Kern, J. (1986). Adult children of alcoholics as professionals in the alcoholism field. In R. Ackerman (Ed.), *Growing in the shadows: Children of alcoholics* (pp. 197–207). Pompano Beach, FL: Health Communications.

McCann, L., & Pearlman, L.A. (1990). Vicarious traumatization: A framework for understanding the psychological effects of working with victims. *Journal of Traumatic Stress, 3*(1), 131–149.

Perry, J. (1992). A review of infant/toddler issues in supervision and mentorship based on instruction of the mentor teacher class. In E. Fenichel (Ed.), *Learning through supervision and mentorship: A sourcebook* (pp. 56–60). Arlington, VA: National Center for Clinical Infant Programs.

Selye, H. (1974). *Stress without distress*. New York: E.P. Dutton.

Sparks, D. (1983). Practical solutions for teacher stress. *Theory into Practice, 22*(1), 33–42.

Wade, K., & Simon, E. (1993). Survival bonding: A response to stress and work with AIDS. *Social Work in Health Care, 19*(1), 77–89.

Weder, S., Drachman, R., & DeLeo, T. (1992). A developmental/relationship in-service training model. In E. Fenichel (Ed.), *Learning through supervision and mentorship: A sourcebook*. Arlington, VA: National Center for Clinical Infant Programs.

Family Diagram

All members can participate in creating the family diagram. Drawing a diagram helps members see the relationships and creates an easy "map" to use. Try to elicit information from all who are present. If you can, trace back at least one generation from the oldest person in the family system. In other words, if the family consists of grandparents, parents, children, and grandchildren, diagram back to the parents of the grandparents or great-grandparents. It is quite effective to draw the diagram on a chalkboard or on a large piece of paper tacked to the wall so everyone can see it as it unfolds. Figure 1 is an example of a family diagram. Colored markers can be used to highlight certain details and make the diagram even more dramatic. Circle the person who is identified as being the reason for the evaluation. Then, for each person in the family diagram, write down his or her name, birthdate, and marital status (if married, indicate year). Briefly list any health, alcohol and/or other drug, emotional, or mental problems. In the case of divorce or separation, indicate the year and brief reason for the split. In the case of death, indicate year and briefly state the cause. Indicate new families, including stepfamilies, using a thick, solid line. Information written on the diagram should be basic and brief. If there are obvious gaps in information, for example, if a couple cannot remember when they were married or the birthdate of one of the children, indicate this with a question mark. Often, members will spontaneously offer stories and other details while the diagram is unfolding. While you are drawing, you can also take more detailed notes. Remember to transcribe the diagram to keep as a permanent part of the family's file. The family diagram is designed to elicit the following type of information:

- Name, gender, and age
- Occupation/school
- Named after anyone in family—if yes, ask why
- State of health, previous serious illnesses, operations, accidents
- Substance use/abuse—if yes, get details of history and any treatment
- Mental health history—list treatment and medications
- Criminal justice history with any current pending cases

～ Evaluating Family Function ～

The best way to begin evaluating family functioning is by learning some of the family's history. Just as every person is unique, so, too, is every family. Much can be learned simply by observing members as they relate their family history, prompted by questions in the areas of symptoms, relationships and boundaries, love and affection, authority and leadership, communication, problem solving, role flexibility, and family strengths.

Symptoms

What, if anything, is the family complaining about? Do they think there is problem, and, if so, what do they think the problem is? Is a child sick? Is a parent sick? Is there any physical, sexual, or mental abuse? Is there alcohol and/or other drug abuse? Is a child doing poorly in school? Are parents fighting? Are there healthy self-care habits? Are members generally healthy or are people frequently sick?

Relationships and Boundaries

Who composes the family and what are their relationships to one another? What are relationships like between family members? How

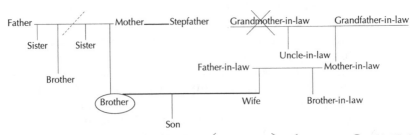

Figure 1.   An example of a family diagram. (Key: ⁄⁄ = divorced; ✕ = deceased; ◯ = identified person; ——— = new family.)

would the family characterize the relationships? Do they agree or disagree about this? Is there room for flexibility that will allow movement along the closeness/distance continuum as needed? Can the family as a system provide a safe and loving environment that supports its members while allowing independent action? What do the subsystems look like and how are they functioning? Are parents able to assert authority while encouraging growth? Can they make parenting decisions together without too much interruption from the children or the outside world? Are they paying attention to their relationship? Can the kids be kids? Do siblings harbor intense negative feelings about each other or can they cooperate with one another? Are there triangles or coalitions that are causing difficulties among members? Are relationships too close or too distant? What are relationships like with the outside world? Can members easily move back and forth between the family and the outside world?

Love and Affection

Are there open and appropriate expressions of love? Are members affectionate with one another? Do people feel loved and cared about? Is praise and positive reinforcement used for success or are people berated for mistakes? Do spouses model a loving and respectful relationship? Is there inappropriate fighting or abuse? Do members trust one another? Is jealousy, suspicion, or anger present?

Authority and Leadership

Who is in charge in the family: the parents or the children? What constitutes the parental system: Is there one parent or extended family involved? Are there clear lines of authority in the family? Who makes the rules, and is there cooperation and agreement about the rules among the family leaders? Are there clear and appropriate rules that are fair and apply to all? Are rules enforced, and what are the consequences of breaking rules? Are these consequences appropriate and consistent? Who makes important family decisions, and how are decisions made? Is individual freedom valued or are people manipulated and controlled?

Communication

How do members communicate with one another? Do people talk to one another, yell at one another, or ignore each other? Do they share feelings, concerns, interests, and accomplishments? Is there a "no-talk" rule? How do people listen and respond to one another; is it with respect or disdain? Do verbal and nonverbal expressions match; for instance, does the father smile when he is chastising a child for doing something "wrong," or does the mother look depressed and distant when she is expressing love for her husband? Is expression of feelings allowed and encouraged? How are people supported when they are upset? Do parents model appropriate expression of feelings for the children? Can people agree to disagree? Do disagreements or fighting regularly disrupt family function? Is there always one person who gets picked on or who feels left out? Are there any "family secrets"? If so, do members feel they can talk about the secrets?

Problem Solving

What does the family consider to be problematic and how do they react to problems? Do they work as a system gathering information and considering different ways of solving the problem or do they ignore problems and hope that they just disappear? Do parents expect children to try and find solutions to problems or do they always try to "fix it" for the child? Can the family ask for help if they need help?

Role Flexibility

Is the family system flexible enough to allow members to sometimes share in roles and tasks? Can the mother allow her child to help her prepare a special meal or does she have to keep the child out of "her" kitchen? Can Dad share a project with his child or does he need to do it all by himself? Can the wife allow her husband to help out with her usual tasks, and can the husband allow his wife to do the same? Are family tasks evenly distributed, or is one person in charge of everything? Is the family open minded or rigid and inflexible? Are new experiences allowed? What are the family traditions; are they passed from previous generations or created by the family?

Family Strengths

What are the positive attributes of each member of this family and the family as a system? Under what circumstances does the family best function? What are the strengths of this family? How does the family see itself in terms of strengths or weaknesses? Does the family accept responsibility as a system or are certain members scapegoated?

~ B ~

Taking a History of Substance Use

~~~~~~

The CAGE (Ewing, 1984) is a four-question quick evaluation tool:

1. Have you ever felt the need to CUT DOWN on your drinking or other drug use? If yes—why, when, what did you do, and what happened?

2. Have you ever been ANNOYED by criticism of your drinking or other drug use? If yes—by whom, how often, and what happened?

3. Have you ever felt GUILTY about your drinking or other drug use? If yes—what were the circumstances, and what did you do?

4. Have you ever had a morning EYE OPENER (used alcohol or other drugs first thing in the morning to get started)? If yes—how often, why, and do you get relief?

General Questions to Ask[1]

A "yes" answer to any of the following questions should raise concern and may indicate an alcohol or other drug problem. If there are "yes" answers to several questions, further evaluation is needed to determine the severity of the problem.

- Do you use alcohol or other drugs more if you are feeling upset, unhappy, or disappointed?
- Do you feel that using alcohol or other drugs helps you to function better on the job or in relationships?

---

[1]This section is adapted from Finkelstein, Duncan, Derman, and Smeltz (1990).

- Have you noticed that you are able to tolerate increased amounts of alcohol or other drugs?
- Do you ever wake up the "morning after" and realize that you cannot remember parts of what happened while you were drinking or using other drugs?
- Do you try to hide the amount you drink from others, drink less in public, or drink alone?
- Do you feel uncomfortable in situations where you cannot drink or use other drugs?
- Do you often feel that you would like to continue drinking or using other drugs even when others have stopped?
- Do you often regret things you have done or said while drinking or using other drugs?
- Have you tried switching brands of alcohol or types of drugs or making rules for when and how much you will use?
- Have you failed to keep promises about cutting down or stopping?
- Have you found yourself avoiding close people while you are drinking or using other drugs?
- Are you experiencing increasing work, school, or financial problems?
- Do you use more often than you used to?
- Are you experiencing a change in your tolerance (i.e., you cannot drink as much as you used to or you find that you cannot get the same effects you once got from drugs)?
- After periods of use, do you have shakes, depression, physical illness, or hear or see things that are not there (e.g., feel like bugs are crawling on you)?

～ Clinical Intake, Interview, and Assessment ～

The following areas should be explored and the information used in conjunction with Figure 1 to determine someone's status during a clinical intake, interview, and assessment:

1. **Personal history**—name, address, telephone number, age, sex, ethnicity, and citizenship status
2. **Family/social relations**—current living situation, sexual orientation, marital status, children (names, ages, birthdates, custody status, living arrangements, visitation), quality of relationships, drug use among family and friends (past and present), name, relationship, and telephone number of emergency contact

3. **Educational history**—current grade, high school diploma, general equivalency diploma, training or vocational programs, and college (list any degrees earned)
4. **Employment history**—occupation, current status, past status, date of last job
5. **Financial status**—current income and source (include public entitlements), amount of money spent on drugs and source of that money
6. **Treatment history**—provide names, dates, and outcomes

   Detox
   Residential treatment
   Halfway house
   Day treatment
   Outpatient treatment
   Methadone clinic
   Self-help, 12-Step programs (sponsor)
   Other

7. **Abstinence**—previous attempts, most recent attempt, and longest period
8. **History of withdrawal symptoms**—from what substance, blackouts, shakes, seizures, delirium tremens, "dope sick"
9. **Medical history**—current health care provider; any current medical problems (treatment and by whom); past serious medical problems (treatment and by whom); accidents; injuries; overdoses; hospitalizations; medications; dates of last physical exam; tuberculosis and hepatitis tests; and HIV education, testing, and status (Offer to provide information or resources about health care, safer sex, safer needle use, and testing.)
10. **History of physical/sexual/emotional abuse**—current abuse, safety concerns, need for immediate treatment, and perpetrators (These questions are not always appropriate for the initial assessment, which should be brief and fact focused.)
11. **Legal history**—any current charges pending, probation or parole (name and number), incarceration (date and length), warrants, court dates, court name, type of criminal offense, weapons involved, violence committed, under the influence, and driving under the influence
12. **Child Protective Service involvement**—for whom, dates, office and worker name and number, reason, and current status

Drug	Current use	Current rank	Past use only	Year/age of first use	Date of last use	Typical use (daily, weekly)	Amount
Alcohol (type used)							
Cocaine (IV or sniff)							
Crack							
Heroin (IV or sniff)							
Methadone (prescribed or street)							
Opiates/ painkillers (prescribed or street)							
Amphetamine/ methamphetamine (type of, IV, sniff, or smoke)							

Drug	Current use	Current rank	Past use only	Year/age of first use	Date of last use	Typical use (daily, weekly)	Amount
Benzo-diazepines/ tranquilizers (type)							
Barbiturates/ sedatives/ downers (type)							
Marijuana/ hashish							
Psychedelics/ hallucinogens (type)							
PCP							
Inhalants (type)							
Cigarettes							
Caffeine							
Other							

Figure 1. Sample substance use/abuse history form. For each drug, be sure to ask interviewees about effects sought and actual effects from use. Also ask participants about precipitants to drug use or if they know why they use. Additional information can be written in narrative or on reverse side of page. (Adapted from Kleber, 1994.)

309

13. **Psychiatric history**—any current treatment (include reason and diagnosis, name of treatment program, any medications), past treatment (include all treatment episodes, hospitalizations, medication), suicidal ideation (past and current [if current, the person will need to be further evaluated for safety]), suicide attempts (method and treatment), homicidal ideation (past and current [if current, person will need to be further evaluated; the evaluator will also need to be familiar with the "duty to warn" law]), and homicide attempted or committed (who, how, under what circumstances, legal status)

14. **Evaluation of mental status**—appearance, orientation to interviewer, date and place, level of alertness, mood and affect, quality of speech, confusion, psychotic symptoms, appropriate thought content, quality of judgment, and quality of insight (which requires some knowledge of evaluating a person's mental status)

∿ Other Assessment Tools ∿

Addiction Severity Index (ASI)

The Addiction Severity Index (ASI)—developed by A. Thomas McLellan, Ph.D.—rates the severity of key problems involving alcohol and other drug use, medical status, legal status, family and social relations, and psychiatric conditions in adults. It is a structured and easy-to-use index that can be utilized in a variety of settings.

National Clearing House for Alcohol and Drug Information (NCADI), Post Office Box 2345, Rockville, Maryland 20847-2345. Or call 1-800-729-6686 and ask for order number NCADI # BKD122.

Adult-Adolescent Parenting Inventory (AAPI)

The Adult-Adolescent Parenting Inventory (AAPI) is fairly short and can be given orally or completed in writing. It assesses parenting attitudes and child-rearing practices.

Family Development Resources, Inc., 3160 Pinebrook Road, Park City, Utah 84060. Or call 1-801-649-5822.

Beck Depression Inventory (BDI)

The Beck Depression Inventory (BDI) is a 21-item self-report inventory for determining the severity of symptoms of depression. It is not a diagnostic tool. It is short, simple, and widely used.

The Psychological Corporation, Order Service Center, Post Office Box 839954, San Antonio, Texas 78293-3954.

Michigan Alcoholism Screening Test (MAST)

The Michigan Alcoholism Screening Test (MAST)—developed by Melvin L. Selzer—is a simple and inexpensive screening tool that is widely used to evaluate for alcoholism. The full screening tool consists of 25 yes/no questions. There is also an abbreviated form consisting of fewer questions.

Melvin L. Selzer, 6967 Paseo Laredo, La Jolla, California 92037. Or call 619-299-4043.

Problem-Oriented Screening Instrument for Teenagers (POSIT)

The Problem-Oriented Screening Instrument for Teenagers (POSIT)— developed by a panel of expert clinicians to be used as part of an extensive adolescent intervention—is a self-administered yes/no assessment intended to briefly evaluate adolescents (ages 12–19) in 10 areas of functioning, including substance use and abuse, health, mental health, family relations, peer relations, school function, vocational status, social skills, leisure activities, delinquency, and aggression. It is easy to use and short and can be administered by a variety of people. It is not a full diagnostic tool, however.

The National Clearing House for Alcohol and Drug Information (NCADI) offers POSIT as part of the Adolescent Assessment/Referral System (AARS), DHHS Publication No. [ADM] 91-1735. Write to NCADI, Post Office Box 2345, Rockville, Maryland 20847-2345.

∽ References ∽

Ewing, J.A. (1984). Detecting alcoholism—the CAGE question. *Journal of the American Medical Association, 152*(14), 1905–1907.

Finkelstein, N., Duncan, S.A., Derman, L., & Smeltz, J. (1990). *Getting sober, getting well—a treatment guide for caregivers who work with women.* Cambridge, MA: The Women's Alcoholism Program of CASPAR.

Kleber, H.D. (1994). *Assessment and treatment of cocaine-abusing methadone-maintained patients: Treatment improvement protocol (TIP) series #10* (DHHS Publication No. [SMA] 94-3003). Rockville, MD: U.S. Department of Health and Human Services.

~ C ~

Bibliography of Children's Books

Children's literature can be a valuable source of intervention material for families and professionals. The following list is a sampling of the many helpful titles available for children who are affected by familial substance abuse. It is strongly recommended that each of these books be previewed for appropriateness. Many of the titles require informed and careful guidance when used with children.

~ Children of Alcoholics ~

Al-Anon Family Group Headquarters, Inc. (1977). *What's drunk, Mama?* New York: Author. (Available from Post Office Box 182, Madison Square Station, New York, New York 19755.)

This story explores the issues surrounding alcoholism in the family. Told from a young girl's point of view, this title attempts to answer the questions young children have about addiction and family recovery. For ages 5–10.

Black, C. (1992). *My dad loves me, my dad has a disease.* Burlington, VT: Waterfront Books. (Also available from ACT, Post Office Box 8536, Newport Beach, California 92568.)

In this interactive workbook, children share what it is like to live in an alcoholic family. Activities help children work through the complicated feelings experienced with the family disease. For ages 6–14.

Carbone, E.L. (1992). *My dad's definitely not a drunk*. Burlington, VT: Waterfront Books.

Twelve-year-old Corey wishes she had a "normal" life. Her dad, who drinks too much already, has begun drinking more and more. In this realistic and sensitive tale, Corey struggles to help her dad and discovers a way to help that is both healthy and self-affirming. For ages 9–14.

Children of Alcoholics Foundation. (1994). *The feel better book*. New York: Author.

An activity workbook for children who might have alcoholic families. Reproducible worksheets and suggested activities can be used to help children deal with feelings, build self-esteem, and ask for help from trusted adults. For children in grades 1–6.

DiGiovanni, K. (1986). *My house is different*. Burlington, VT: Waterfront Books.

Joe learns through a magical dream adventure with his dog that he did not cause his father's alcoholism and that he cannot fix it, but he can feel good about himself. For ages 4–7.

Sanford, D. (1988). *I know the world's worst secret: A child's book about living with an alcoholic parent*. Burlington, VT: Waterfront Books.

Elizabeth's mother is an alcoholic. Although she is very young, Elizabeth tries to take responsibility for caring for the family and struggles with the pain. She learns, however, how to grow and heal even when faced with such difficult challenges. For ages 4–7.

Vigna, J. (1988). *I wish Daddy didn't drink so much*. Burlington, VT: Waterfront Books.

One of the few preschool-level titles available, this well-regarded book tells the story of alcoholism in the family from the perspective of a young child trying to understand it all. For ages 3–6.

∼ Dealing with Feelings ∼

Avery, C. (1992). *Everybody has feelings*. Mt. Rainer, MD: Gryphon House.

This book, available in Spanish and English, helps children recognize their own feelings. Beautiful photographs of culturally diverse children illustrate the range of feelings children experience. For ages 3–7.

Crary, E. (1994). *I'm mad, I'm frustrated, I'm scared, I'm proud, I'm excited, I'm furious.* Burlington, VT: Waterfront Books. (Also available from Western Psychological Services, 12031 Wilshire Boulevard, Los Angeles, California 90025.)

Six little books, each of which tells a familiar children's story to illustrate feelings common to all children. Whether it's Katie who is furious at her dad for canceling their picnic or Tracey who is terrified of the neighbor's new dog, children can relate to the experiences in the stories and adults can learn how to help children cope. For ages 3–9.

Godwin, P. (1993). *I feel orange today.* Mt. Rainer, MD: Gryphon House.

Different colors feel different, and this wonderful, rhythmic text weaves a tale of a boy who feels "violet sad" or "quiet green." Illustrations and words stir the imagination to talk about feelings in a creative way. For ages 3–7.

Mayer, M. (1968). *There's a nightmare in my closet.* New York: Penguin.

This children's classic features a humorous approach to dealing with a child's fear of the dark. This nonthreatening story can help children process and master feelings of fear. For ages 4–8.

Viorst, J. (1972). *Alexander and the terrible, horrible, no good, very bad day.* New York: Simon and Schuster.

Young Alexander knew his day was going to be bad from the start, but he is reassured when he learns that some days are just like that. Children are really drawn to this story and its familiar themes. For ages 5–9.

～ Promoting Self-Esteem ～

Brown, M.W. (1942). *The runaway bunny.* New York: Harper & Row.

A classic tale of a mother's unconditional love for her child. Children can see that a parent's love can have no boundaries and that they are truly cherished. For everyone, infants to adults.

Chocolate, D. (1991). *On the day you were born.* New York: Scholastic.

This moving story chronicles the celebration of the birth of a child to a large and loving African American family. The captivating illustrations take the reader through the family's ritual of welcoming this precious new life. For all ages.

Kraus, R. (1971). *Leo, the late bloomer.* New York: HarperCollins.

This story follows the "growing up" of Leo the tiger, teaching children that everybody grows at their own pace and that they are okay just the way they are. For ages 3–7.

Simon, N. (1976). *Why am I different?* Mt. Rainer, MD: Gryphon House.

This book explores the differences in culture, physical makeup, and experiences among children using gentle, self-affirming text. It supports positive self-esteem by honoring an individual's uniqueness. For ages 4–8.

Groups, Organizations, and Resources

Adult Children of Alcoholics (ACoA)
Post Office Box 3216
Torrance, California 90510
310-534-1815

Al-Anon/Alateen Family Group Headquarters, Inc.
1600 Corporate Landing Parkway
Virginia Beach, Virginia 23454-5617
1-800-344-2666 (United States)
1-800-443-4525 (Canada)

Alcoholics Anonymous (AA)
World Services, Inc.
468 Park Avenue, South
New York, New York 10016
212-870-3400

Campuses Without Drugs
National Office
2530 Holly Drive
Pittsburgh, Pennsylvania 15235
412-731-8018

Center for Substance Abuse Treatment
Drug Abuse Information and Treatment Referral Hotline
1-800-622-HELP

Children of Alcoholics Foundation, Inc.
555 Madison Avenue, 4th Floor
New York, New York 10166
212-351-2680
1-800-359-COAF

Children's Defense Fund
25 East Street, NW
Washington, DC 20001
202-628-8787

Clearinghouse on Child Abuse and Neglect Information
Post Office Box 1182
Washington, DC 20013
703-385-7565
1-800-FYI-3366

Cocaine Hotline
1-800-COCAINE

CSAP National Resource Center for the Prevention of Perinatal Abuse of Alcohol and Other Drugs
9300 Lee Highway
Fairfax, Virginia 22031
703-218-5600
1-800-354-8824

317

Families Anonymous
Post Office Box 548
Van Nuys, California 91408
818-989-7841

Hazelden Educational Materials
Post Office Box 176
Center City, Minnesota 55012
1-800-328-9000

Healthy Mothers, Healthy Babies Coalition
409 12th Street, NW, Room 309
Washington, DC 20024
202-863-2458

Institute on Black Chemical Abuse
2616 Nicollet Avenue, South
Minneapolis, Minnesota 55408
612-871-7878

March of Dimes
1275 Mamaroneck Avenue
White Plains, New York 10605
914-428-7100

Methadone Anonymous
410-837-4292

Mothers Against Drunk Driving (MADD)
511 East John Carpenter Freeway,
  Suite 700
Irving, Texas 75062
214-744-6233
1-800-GET-MADD

Nar-Anon Family Group
213-547-5800

Nar-Anon Hotline
1-800-780-3951

Narcotics Anonymous
818-780-3951

National Asian Pacific American Families Against Substance Abuse (NAPAFASA)
420 East Third Street, Suite 909
1147 South Alvarado
Los Angeles, California 90013-1647
213-617-8277

National Association for Children of Alcoholics
11426 Rockville Pike
Rockville, Maryland 20852
301-468-0985

National Association for Native American Children of Alcoholics
Post Office Box 18736
Seattle, Washington 98118
206-322-5601

National Association of Lesbian and Gay Alcoholism Professionals
1147 South Alvarado
Los Angeles, California 90006
213-381-8524

National Association of Perinatal Addiction Research Education (NAPARE)
11 East Hubbard, Suite 200
Chicago, Illinois 60611
312-541-1272 (publications)
1-800-638-BABY (telephone
  counseling)

National Black Alcoholism Council, Inc.
1629 K Street, NW, Suite 802
Washington, DC 20006
202-296-2696

National Clearing House for Alcohol and Drug Information
Post Office Box 2345
Rockville, Maryland 20847
301-468-2600
1-800-729-6686

National Coalition of Hispanic Health Services Organization (COSSMHO)
1501 16th Street, NW
Washington, DC 20036
202-387-5000

National Council on Alcoholism and Drug Dependence, Inc.
12 West 21st Street
New York, New York 10010
212-206-6770
1-800-NCA-CALL

National Organization on Adolescent Pregnancy and Parenting Programs
4421-A East West Highway
Bethesda, Maryland 20814
301-913-0378

Network of Colleges and Universities Committed to the Elimination of Drug and Alcohol Abuse
Office of Educational Research and Improvement
U.S. Department of Education
555 New Jersey Avenue, SW
Washington, DC 20208-5644
202-357-6265

Office for Substance Abuse Prevention (OSAP)
Rockwall II, 4th Floor
5600 Fishers Lane
Rockville, Maryland 20857
301-443-0377

Office on Smoking and Health
3005 Rhodes Building (Koger Center)
Chamblee, Georgia 30341
404-488-5705

Rational Recovery Systems
Post Office Box 800
Lotus, California 95651
916-621-2667

Women for Sobriety
Post Office Box 618
Quakertown, Pennsylvania 18951
1-800-333-1606

~ E ~

The 12 Steps of Recovery

1. We admitted we were powerless over alcohol and that our lives had become unmanageable.
2. We came to believe that a Power greater than ourselves could restore us to sanity.
3. We made a decision to turn our will and our lives over to the care of God *as we understood Him.*
4. We made a searching and fearless moral inventory of ourselves.
5. We admitted to God, ourselves, and to another human being the exact nature of our wrongs.
6. We were entirely ready to have God remove all these defects of character.
7. We humbly asked Him to remove our shortcomings.
8. We made a list of all people we had harmed and became willing to make amends to them all.
9. We made direct amends to such people wherever possible, except when to do so would injure them or others.

These are the 12 Steps developed and used by Alcoholics Anonymous. They can be found in Alcoholics Anonymous. (1976). *Third edition of the big book* (pp. 59–60). New York: AA World Services, Inc. The 12 Steps are reprinted with permission of Alcoholics Anonymous World Services, Inc. Permission to reprint the 12 Steps does not mean that AA has reviewed or approved the contents of this publication, nor that AA agrees with the views expressed herein. AA is a program of recovery from alcoholism *only*—use of the 12 Steps in connection with programs and activities which are patterned after AA, but which address other problems, or in any other non-AA context, does not imply otherwise.

10. We continued to take personal inventory and, when we were wrong, promptly admitted it.
11. We sought through prayer and meditation to improve our conscious contact with God, *as we understand Him,* praying only for our knowledge of His will for us and the power to carry that out.
12. Having had a spiritual awakening as the result of these steps, we tried to carry this message to alcoholics and practice these principles in all our affairs.

Twelve-Step recovery programs modeled after AA substitute the appropriate words for "alcoholism" and "alcoholics." As an example, Narcotics Anonymous (NA) substitutes the words "addiction" and "addicts"; otherwise, the steps remain exactly the same (Narcotics Anonymous, 1988).

⁓ References ⁓

Alcoholics Anonymous. (1976). *Third edition of the big book* (pp. 59–60). New York: AA World Services, Inc.

Narcotics Anonymous. (1988). *Fifth edition* (p. 17). Van Nuys, CA: NA World Services, Inc.

Index

Page numbers followed by a "*t*" indicate tables; those followed by an "*f*" indicate figures.

DATE DUE

~~DEC 7 1997~~	OCT 1 8 2001
DEC 3 0 2005	NOV 1 8 2001
~~MAR 1 5 1999~~	APR 2 0 2002
NOV 1 6 1999	MAY 1 8 2002
APR 14 2000	AUG 0 2 2002
	DEC 1 7 2007
DEC 0 1 1999	
FEB 2 6 2000	NOV 0 4 2003
MAR 2 1 2000	MAR 0 9 2004
	FEB 2 8 2006
MAY 1 6 2001	